# Theory and Praxis

## Women's and Gender Studies at Community Colleges

edited by
Genevieve Carminati and Heather Rellihan

Gival Press

Arlington, Virginia

Published by Gival Press, an imprint of Gival Press, LLC.

For information please write:

Gival Press, LLC

P. O. Box 3812

Arlington, VA 22203

www.givalpress.com


First edition

ISBN: 978-1-940724-22-5

eISBN: 978-1-940724-23-2

Library of Congress Control Number: 2019948115


Cover art: © Ninanaina | Dreamstime.com

Photo of Chara Andrews by Chara Andrews © 2019.

Photo of Hannah Bairo by Hannah Bairo © 2019.

Photo of Ibiene Minah by Ibiene Minah © 2019.

Photo of Jimmy Lynch by Jimmy Lynch © 2019.

Photo of Kayla Calvin by Kayla Calvin © 2019.

Photo of Jozette Belmont by Jozette Belmont © 2019.

Photo of Kayla Miskell by Kayla Miskell © 2019.

Photo of Prnaya Green by Prnaya Green © 2019.

Design by Ken Schellenberg.

# Contents

# Introduction

## Heather Rellihan in collaboration with Genevieve Carminati

Women's and gender studies (WGS)[1] at community colleges are vibrant academic spaces that cultivate critical thinking and civic engagement. Courses in WGS nurture students' critical consciousness by developing an awareness of power and privilege, giving them the tools to analyze the world around them and the skills to make the changes they want to see. Because community colleges draw students from less privileged groups, WGS spaces are critical assets for community colleges in that they give students the tools for understanding and articulating the ways in which their lives have been affected by systems of privilege, structured inequality, and discrimination. The opportunity for students to position their personal experiences in the context of larger structures stimulates critical thinking skills, promotes empathy, and inspires the self-understanding and self-growth conducive to student success. WGS also gives students the ability to be change-makers in their communities, encouraging more thoughtful participation in civic processes and inspiring activism. To see the value of these courses and programs, you need only talk to WGS students themselves. As part of our research for this book, we surveyed students taking WGS courses at community colleges around the country asking them to assess their experiences.

Many students noted their women's and gender studies classes were different from other courses they'd taken because of the focus on drawing connections between the course materials and their own lived experiences. This

---

1    For consistency, we will use women's and gender studies or WGS to include programs/departments that are named women's studies, women's and gender studies, gender and women's studies, gender and sexuality studies, or other related variations. See Rellihan and Stoehr's essay, "The Status of Women's and Gender Studies at Community Colleges" (included in this anthology) for more information on the variety in naming conventions across the field.

helped them process the course materials on a different level and promoted self-discovery and personal growth while encouraging them to develop important skills like active listening and empathy. Gillian Sobocinski, a student at Nassau Community College in New York, said of her Introduction to Women's Studies course, "This was the first class that I had ever taken in which I felt like I and the other students had the freedom to talk about issues that were highly relevant and important to our lives…. Women's studies prepares students to be more knowledgeable, proactive, and empathetic citizens in the world. We need people like that in every career field." Jazmine Yambo, a student in Introduction to Women's Studies at Montgomery College in Maryland said,

> This course has allowed me to become more aware of how I, and others, contribute to gender stereotypes…. After speaking with people in my class about things we have been through, I feel like it is my responsibility to let others know that their words affect people…. I see that I am not the only one who has dealt with uncomfortable situations about gender, which makes me feel like I'm not alone.

When talking about their WGS courses, students emphasized the value of the community they built through discussions with their classmates and the value of hearing their classmates' stories and opinions. Dowu Abaku, a fellow Introduction to Women's Studies student at Montgomery, captured a sentiment that surfaced in many responses: "It is a class that has discussions that mean something…. I have had the best conversations in this class." This sense of community is increased when WGS programs and departments consciously create events and activities that bring students together with others across the institution (see Carminati's "Personal Narratives in WGS at Community Colleges: Rewards," included in this essay, for an example).

Because they had a different relationship to the course materials, and because the course materials helped them see themselves differently, many students emphasized themes of empowerment and self-knowledge when they discussed their experiences in a WGS classroom. Alyssa Brown, a student in an Introduction to Women's and Gender Studies course at Chandler-Gilbert Community College in Arizona, said, "I have learned how to better stick up for what I want to achieve both in my personal and my professional life." Dalayna Jimenez, also a student at Chandler-Gilbert, shared a similar sentiment saying, "I just learned to be more open and to not be afraid of who I am and what I want." Veronica Barrios and Ariana Martinez, fellow students at Chandler-Gilbert, remind us that WGS classes often help correct internalized stereotypes and limiting narratives about what it means to be female. Barrios said,

> The course has helped me realize that being a girl is not a bad thing.... It is interesting to see that I was actually ashamed of being a girl, but I did not let it stop me. The weird thing is that it was stopping me. Subconsciously I was limiting myself because I did not want to come off as too masculine.... I now know ... that being strong and outgoing is not a bad thing, and that I should be proud to be a girl. I can stop beating myself up for being a girl.

Martinez echoed Barrios's comments, explaining, "[S]ometimes us women/girls aren't aware of our fullest potential due to what society says and this course reminds us who we are [and] what we can achieve." Casey Fegley, a student who earned a Certificate in gender and sexuality studies (GSS) at Anne Arundel Community College in Maryland, articulated a similar point about the value of her GSS coursework in cultivating self-knowledge and empowerment. As a student in her late thirties, she realized how valuable some of her coursework would have been for her in her early twenties—the age of many of her classmates. "Back then," she said, "when I was their age, I didn't know who I was or what I wanted, I only thought I did. And those thoughts about myself and what my goals should be weren't formed by me, they were given to me." Andi Torres, an Introduction to Women's Studies student at Nassau Community College, articulated a sentiment expressed by many students: "My life is forever changed because of women's studies. It made me reflect on myself and see myself through a new lens."

Part of seeing themselves through a new lens also involved new skill sets: the students explained that they learned active listening and critical thinking skills. Linda Ngoue-Onana, a student at Montgomery College, said her WGS course "is different than other courses because it requires me to think on a deeper and more personal level…. This course forces me to have an open mind compared to most of my classes which are memorization based." Ibiene Minah, a student in Introduction to Women's Studies at Nassau Community College, noted how she learned to be aware of her own privilege and use that awareness to become a more reflective listener. As a person with a marginalized identity, Ibiene said it was important to her that her teacher emphasized privilege because it made space for her experiences to be heard, but she said she also realized that she had to be attentive to her own privileges. Emphasizing the value of intersectional theory, she said, "[T]here are still privileges I hold that create blind spots for some experiences, and I need to make sure that whenever someone is relaying something from their point of experience I am holding space for that to be validated and acknowledged even though it's not a personal experience of mine."

A final theme that emerged in the students' responses was the connection between coursework and activism. Students consistently noted how their coursework inspired them and gave them the tools to help make progressive social change around the issues that are important to them. Jimmy Lynch, who earned a Certificate in women's and gender studies at Jefferson Community and Technical College in Kentucky, said, "What I liked most about my Introduction to Women's and Gender Studies course was my introduction to the area of male engagement. I had long felt ineffective in confronting issues of gender-based violence and through this course I was exposed to opportunities to become involved in prevention of gender-based violence." Mo Mitchell, a student who took both Introduction to Women's Studies and Gender and Mass Media in the U.S. at Anne Arundel Community College, also made connections between her studies and the work she wants to do in the world. She noted that her experiences in WGS courses made her see the importance of voting and that she will encourage people to vote to make changes "in the direction we want to see our country go." In her future career she would like to do work that helps empower women, encouraging "more mothers to build better communities for each other." Emily Dean, a student in Women and Films at Chandler-Gilbert, also discussed how what she learned in class helped her see the importance of activism. She said, "I think it's important because … we are the people who can change these stereotypes and inequality so that our kids don't have to deal with it one day." Making the connection between the personal and the political, Casey Fegley from Anne Arundel Community College said, "As far as parenting, I definitely learned things that I took home to my daughters, and I feel like they benefited from my education in that way, too."

WGS spaces and the liberatory feminist pedagogies that these spaces promote are critical to community college students, particularly because of the demographics served by those institutions. As scholars like Stanley Aronowitz argue, the fact that community colleges provide *access* to higher education for working-class and other marginalized groups is not enough. Indeed, Aronowitz challenges the access narrative that "class deficits can be overcome by equalizing access to school opportunities without questioning what those opportunities have to do with genuine education" (108). He says, "The structure of schooling already embodies the class system of society, and, for this reason, the access debate misfires" (108). Pointing to the post-World War II period of expanding access to education, he says that now

> working-class students are able, even encouraged, to enter universities and colleges at the bottom of the academic hierarchy—community colleges but also public four-year colleges—thus fulfilling the formal pledge of equal opportunity for class mobility even as most of these institutions suppress the intellectual content that would fulfill the mobility promise. (110)

While Aronowitz focuses on working-class students, his argument can be extended to other marginalized groups that community colleges disproportionately serve. For education to be liberatory for these groups, access alone is insufficient. This is why it is important that the WGS classrooms at community colleges offer transformational educational spaces, spaces whereby the students that Aronowitz calls "timeservers"—working-class students disconnected from an alienating education and motivated only to earn a credential because they've been told they need one for the marketplace—can become what Paulo Freire calls "co-investigators in dialogue with the teacher" (81). Because community colleges disproportionately serve less privileged students, the role of WGS classrooms on community college campuses is significant. With its focus on connecting the personal and political, exposing the constructedness of knowledge, centering the experiences of the oppressed, and emphasizing a liberatory praxis that connects knowledge and activism, the WGS classroom can provide what Freire calls education "as the practice of freedom" (80).

• • • • • • • • • • • • • • • • • • • • • • • • • • • • • • • • • • • • • • • • • • • • • • • • • • • • • • • • • • • • • • •

*Personal Narratives in WGS at Community Colleges: Rewards*

Genevieve Carminati

At Montgomery College, our scholarship program has been beneficial to growing and showcasing our Women's and Gender Studies Program. Not only has it brought us more students—as the applicants are required to have completed at least one of our courses, but it has also involved our college community in meaningful ways that have connected many of its members with our program. The benefits to the students go beyond tangible effects. Scholarship award winner Lakeya J. McCoy wrote, "No one succeeds by their self. It's help like these scholarships that makes it possible for us to go to college and earn a degree."* Sharmilee Rahman, another award winner, observed further, "The mistreatment and challenges we face in our patriarchal society should not discourage the kinds of ambitions and achievements women can have if they are given a chance to show off their best skills. Being ambitious as a female is never a bad thing." Additionally, Philaisha Carter explained how far-reaching she felt the influence of her award would be: "Winning this scholarship I hope that my daughter will be proud of me and know that she too could win a scholarship because of her own intelligence."

Since 1987, when our awards were more modest, we have grown our annual scholarships to amounts of $500 to $1,000. We select students in our program who excel academically, exhibit leadership, participate in service, and demonstrate commitment to issues having to do with women and gender; we also consider need. Our scholarship winners come from almost every department and program in the college. As award winner and STEM student Shayna Berman reminded us in her application, the scholarship can encourage students in many disciplines that are demanding of them. She noted, "In fact, only 18% of engineering students are women. This award will help inspire me to push through some of the challenges that may come with that. It would remind me what I stand for and who has my back."

The funds for our scholarships are provided by endowments from members of both the local and college communities, as well as by donations and funds raised at our annual Women's and Gender Studies Program Scholarship Reception. Even in what is considered a fairly affluent county, our community college students are often living day-to-day financially. Students have told us that the scholarship has helped them afford everything from a much-needed pair of shoes or winter coat, to a new computer or a summer class, and more. As winner Ragini R. Chabra observed, "Women's Studies has taught me that if you help a woman, you help a family." Margaret K. Courtney was quite succinct about the impact of the award on her education, when she averred, "Winning the Women's and Gender Studies Scholarship will allow me to continue my studies."

Largely, of course, these funds pay for classes and books and contribute to success and completion. Past winners have gone on to graduate school and to study medicine and law. They proudly include their scholarship awards on their CVs. However, just as important, these awards give students a sense of confidence, a sense that the work they are doing and endeavor to do matters. They recognize themselves as scholars in the discipline, and we are encouraged by the range and promise of their research. Christopher D. Williamson, a scholarship winner, noted, "I recently wrote a paper in my Women's Studies class highlighting Shirin Neshat, an Iranian visual artist who focuses her work on women's and gender issues in Iran and the Islamic world ... I hope my paper encourages people to use their creative lens to advocate for women's health and reproductive rights, gender equality, and LGBT issues." Also, recipient Elisia George acknowledged the value of academic study to our understanding of our own time and culture. "As a Study Travel participant, my research paper was, 'The Cherokee People, A Matrilineal Society'.... The awareness that there is a group of men who do believe that women can be effective leaders gives me hope for the future, that someday sooner rather than later a woman will be the leader of this great nation we live in."

Many of our award winners are international students who are not eligible for other kinds of financial aid. These students have reported that they might have left school if not for these awards. Many also have indicated in their application essays that gender discrimination had restricted their access to opportunities in the past. "Growing up in Vietnam, a society where Confucius' teachings are embedded within our culture, limited me from realizing how oppressed I was," award winner My Phan asserted. She added, "To break that chain of oppression, women, themselves, must understand that they are worth much more." Scholarship winner Savita Bansi expressed a similar observation of her native culture. "In India I had experienced many challenges as an impoverished woman. I yearned for an education; however, it was my brother who was considered a worthy candidate." Scholarship winner Djatougbe Nadine Dogbe, an international student from Togo who came to the United States alone on a Diversity Visa, explained the demands of her circumstances: "My father sold his most precious wealth for me to come to the U.S.; therefore, I want to at least help provide my family with daily food."

Additionally, because we weigh the impact of need in our holistic considerations of applicants, there are students who qualify for our awards who would not be in contention for other scholarships. We recognize that especially women students often have family responsibilities or health or reproductive considerations that interrupt their educations, affect their income, and make focus on studies difficult. "I am a married mother of four, working two jobs and fully registered in school. I have been unable to secure any financial assistance because my household income is slightly above the required threshold. I am forced to borrow and work round the clock to make ends meet," award winner Akwen Bayong told us. Additionally, students struggling with gender identity issues could find these concerns overwhelming other aspects of their lives, including their studies. As scholarship winner Anjenee Cannon rightfully pointed out, "It is important that all students feel safe on campus and that all faculty members take into consideration that not every person in their class is necessarily what you call 'straight' or 'heterosexual.'" We weigh these personal issues in examining academic records.

Lastly, the students who attend our awards reception are inspired by the award winners' accomplishments and commitment to service. It is an opportunity for students to learn from the leaders and thinkers among their peers, and to become aware of what's also possible for them. As scholarship recipient Julian Phillips powerfully expounded, "Women's and gender studies are important to me academically because I feel there is always more research and work to be done to assert the existence and importance of those excluded by the patriarchal rule over academia. My goals in the art field are interlocked with the lack of women's and gender-variant space in the art world at large." Namrah Batool Ashraf echoes that need for societal transformation. This award winner wrote, "I want to change the way women are perceived and treated in our society. It is a horrifying feeling leaving the house every day in fear because I am a woman. As Mahatma Gandhi once said, 'Be the change you want to see in this world.'"

Our scholarship program is unique in that it involves and reaches out to the whole college. The scholarship applications are read and reviewed by a diverse committee of faculty and staff. People from all over the college—and some from the local community—donate and shop at our fundraising silent auction. Many think about items to donate when they travel or shop at sales. Faculty members recommend students from a variety of disciplines and from all three of our campuses. We are proud that we reach such an array of students and involve such a wide spread of faculty members. Volunteers for our program also come to us from throughout the college, giving as much time and assistance as they are able. An example of a fairly recent volunteer activity we've initiated is to ask those who'd like to contribute to bring a potted flowering plant to our awards reception. It's a small gesture that can make a big impact when the whole auditorium is full of bright flowers. It's a means of greeting student award winners with a message of support and congratulations.

Our program can be a model for others in that it shows that most people would like to help community college students, especially women and LGBTQ+ students, be successful. They just need to be given an opportunity to be involved, even in what some might think is a minor way. As for our student scholarship winners, they don't see anything about the award's impact as minor. "I greatly enjoyed the Women's Studies Honors project of interviewing a woman working in the public sphere, and writing an essay about her," scholarship winner Claire E. Lapina reported. "She left me with a few words of great advice, 'Define what you want to be, and then be it.' I know that I want to be educated and go on and make a difference in this world and that this scholarship will help me do it."

* Quoted excerpts were all written by Montgomery College Women's and Gender Studies Program Scholarship winners and have been extracted, with permission, from their scholarship applications.

••••••••••••••••••••••••••••••••••••••••••••••••••••••••••••••

## The Challenges

While the work of teaching women's and gender studies at community colleges is important and rewarding as is evidenced by the student narratives above, it also comes with significant challenges. Professors of WGS at community colleges and four-year colleges and universities alike often struggle with teaching what at times can be difficult subject matter, topics that might intersect with students' personal experiences in ways that require more emotional labor on the part of the instructor, and topics which incite resistance and sometimes anger. For example, teaching about the #metoo movement, or helping students unpack and analyze the testimony of Christine Blasey Ford and the Brett Kavanaugh hearing, requires careful classroom management skills: providing opportunities for questions and personal stories, but also holding space for anger and fear. The ways in which subjects like this intersect with students' personal experiences—whether it be their own experiences of sexual violence, comments they've heard made by family members, or conversations they've had with friends—make teaching these classes fraught in ways that other academic subjects are not. But it's not just the work that goes into teaching these topics in the classroom. It's also the need for the emotional labor that these topics necessitate *outside* the classroom. As teachers of WGS courses, we know that any discussion related to sexual assault—or sexual harassment, or discrimination in the workplace, or inequality in the home, or any one of a number of issues that are part of a WGS curriculum—will prompt students to share their personal stories with us. They need us to listen and help them process these experiences. They need us to direct them to resources and help them negotiate the ways in which these experiences have affected, and continue to affect, their lives. This emotional labor is important and necessary, but it is *work*, and because it is often invisible to our supervisors and our institutions it is under-recognized and undervalued.

WGS programs and departments at both community colleges and four-year schools also face challenges in response to larger conversations around the values of college education. WGS professors struggle to articulate and defend the value of our field in the face of neoliberal ideology that undervalues the liberal arts, the humanities, interdisciplinary departments, and other fields that don't translate neatly into particular occupations that meet "market needs." The neoliberal "reform" of higher education, with its market principles, and corporate accounting culture, has had profound effects on the vision of education and its connection to the public good. The neoliberal philosophy violates some of the core beliefs of WGS as a field and so it is not an overstatement to say that in the current academic climate many WGS programs feel like they are fighting for their lives. In his book, *Neoliberalism's War on Higher Education*, Henry Giroux explains what's at stake:

> [N]eoliberalism as a form of economic Darwinism attempts to undermine all forms of solidarity capable of challenging market-driven values and social relations, promoting the virtues of an unbridled individualism almost pathological in its disdain for community, social responsibility, public values, and the public good.... it thrives on a kind of social amnesia that erases critical thought, historical analysis, and any understanding of broader systemic relations. In this regard, it does the opposite of critical memory work by eliminating those public spheres where people learn to translate private troubles into public issues. (2)

In neoliberal academia, feminist pedagogy—the very ways of learning and knowing that undergird the WGS classroom—is more than devalued; it's viewed as dangerous: "Critical learning has been replaced with mastering test-taking, memorizing facts, and learning how *not* to question knowledge or authority. Pedagogies that unsettle common sense, make power accountable, and connect classroom knowledge to larger civic issues have become dangerous at all levels of schooling" (6). And so the work that we do as WGS educators places us under increased surveillance, necessitating that we spend more and more of our time defending our programs and our pedagogy.

In some ways this precariousness is nothing new. Women's and gender studies programs first emerged as part of a critique of traditional models of knowledge production and academic culture, and have continually had to manage a delicate balance between questioning academia and protecting their position within the academy: "a tricky position to be in," as Alice Ginsberg describes it in her essay "Triumphs, Controversies, and Change: Women's Studies 1970s to the Twenty-First Century" (15). She says, "Women's studies was, and is, a central part of the academy at the same time that it continues to challenge and critique it" (14-15). The work of teaching, providing emotional support to students, managing our programs and departments in what sometimes feels like a hostile environment, and continuing to voice our concerns about the project of academia is part of teaching women's and gender studies across the country. However, for those who teach WGS at community colleges there are often additional factors that make the work more challenging—and increasingly so in the current neoliberal environment.

Because community colleges are marginalized within academia, many of us teaching women's and gender studies at community colleges have to contend with additional burdens that our colleagues at four-years schools don't face, or face to a lesser degree. The current neoliberal focus on defining college education as the acquisition of job skills to meet market needs affects all WGS programs (and other fields as well). However, because community colleges are *already* precarious within higher education, and because community college students disproportionately come from marginalized groups—groups whose exploitation has historically been the foundation for capitalist gain—neoliberal ideology has successfully pushed its way into the administration of community colleges and has been hard to fight. Community college WGS programs and departments are small. Very few programs have full-time faculty lines in WGS and oftentimes there is little in the way of compensation for the administrative work that keeps these programs going. Many who teach WGS at community colleges are housed in other departments where their WGS work may seem peripheral and may not be valued for the purposes of tenure, promotion, and annual reviews. In many schools, WGS courses fall under the structural umbrella of another department or exist in the abstract as a combination of cross-listed courses, each of which has its own "home" department. In some community colleges there are only one or two people who teach WGS courses, and in some places, WGS courses are taught mostly by adjuncts who face the additional isolation that goes along with the exploitative positioning of adjuncts in today's academic system. Without full-time faculty lines or dedicated compensation for administration of the program, and with the instability of personnel that often comes with the use of adjunct professors, many WGS programs at community colleges are sustained through small groups of people who are motivated to do the work because of their passion for the field, but with little in the way of remuneration. It's true that many of these factors that describe the experience of teaching WGS at community colleges can be found at some four-year schools—particularly at small liberal arts colleges, for example—but it is a question of degree.

Because of the conditions described above, the National Women's Studies Association (NWSA), a professional organization for teachers, scholars, and activists in WGS, can seem like a beacon in the night for WGS folks at both two-year and four-year schools. With a mission of support and advocacy for women's and gender studies, NWSA defines the work of the body and its members as a series of interventions into the production, dissemination, and use of knowledge in ways that subvert "ideologies, systems of privilege or structures that oppress or exploit some for the advantage of others" ("About"). NWSA pledges to "illuminate the ways in which women's studies are vital to education; to demonstrate the contributions of feminist scholarship that is comparative, global, intersectional and interdisciplinary to understandings of the arts, humanities, social sciences and sciences; and to promote synergistic relationships between scholarship, teaching and civic engagement in understandings of culture and society" ("About"). The annual NWSA conference is important for many WGS educators because it is a respite from questions about the value of the field. Many attendees see this conference as an exercise in self-care: a place where they can go and be welcomed and accepted and valued.

However, despite the organization's attention to inequality and its mission to subvert systems of privilege, there are still hierarchies within the organization. Understanding this, NWSA offers space for members who are "underrepresented within society or NWSA" to form caucuses ("Constituency Groups"). One such caucus is the Community College Caucus, a constituency group focused on supporting and advancing the project of women's and gender studies at two-year institutions. For decades, the Community College Caucus has been an important advocacy group for women's and gender studies at community colleges, a place for its members to commune with fellow community college WGS educators and focus on issues that are particular to the academic spaces they navigate.

Each year, the Community College Caucus meets as part of NWSA's annual conference. These yearly gatherings are wonderfully rich and supportive spaces, particularly for many of us who run very small programs. The caucus meeting is a space where we can share ideas, ask questions, and feel kinship with a larger community. However, as nurturing as these meetings always are, comparing notes and sharing stories brings with it the stinging reminder of our doubly marginalized position within the academy. At our home institutions, among other community college folks, many of us feel like outsiders because we are in women's and gender studies. We face the familiar devaluing of women's and gender studies as a field ("What are you going to do with a degree in women's studies?" as the misguided script goes), and this has only intensified with the current skills-training and vocational focus that has taken hold at community colleges across the country. Unfortunately, at NWSA, where we have a welcome reprieve from questions about the field, we feel devalued as *community college* professors. In both obvious and subtle ways, we are reminded that academia still sees community colleges as lesser approximations of "real" college (see Rellihan's "Personal Narratives in WGS at Community Colleges: Challenges," included in this essay, for examples). Sharing our stories with each other is cathartic, but it's also hurtful—particularly when we recount experiences with our WGS colleagues at four-year institutions. We understand the stereotypes surrounding community colleges, but we expect better from WGS folks who are ostensibly committed to dismantling hierarchy, and yet sometimes seem oblivious to the ways in which their rendering of community college sustains hierarchies of race, class, and gender. In recent years, as academic feminism has swelled to more largely define NWSA, insurgent activisms have been replaced with bureaucratic policies, and the space at the borders—the places that WGS at community colleges occupy—has shrunk to accommodate the performance of academic status: elite scholars, prestigious institutions, and doctoral programs. These changes further marginalize feminist projects outside the academic mainstream, including community colleges folks, but also including women's centers and activists inhabiting spaces outside academia. Consequently, the only space where many of us who teach WGS at community colleges feel fully recognized is in the Community College Caucus.

It should come as no surprise then, that the idea for this book emerged during a meeting of that caucus. After our familiar laments about the invisibility of community colleges at NWSA, we discussed what we felt was an underlying hypocrisy: WGS is committed to an intersectional analysis of hierarchy, oppression, and social justice—and indeed the field of WGS emerged in part as a protest against the ways in which traditional academia furthered inequality through the mechanisms of education—but WGS simultaneously reifies hierarchies that diminish community colleges. In our Community College Caucus meetings, we questioned whether the field of WGS was falling prey to the very cultural practices and structural inequalities that it used to rail against.

••••••••••••••••••••••••••••••••••••••••••••••••••••••••••••••••••••••••

*Personal Narratives in WGS at Community Colleges: Challenges*

Heather Rellihan

In March of 2013, about five years after I completed my PhD, a representative from the College of Arts and Humanities (ARHU) at my alma mater contacted me to ask if I would speak to current graduate students on a panel about "professional pathways after graduate school."* Initially I was happy to receive the invitation. During my time as a graduate student, the idea of teaching at a community college had never been mentioned by any of my mentors, any professors I took classes with, or any of my fellow students. Therefore, it never entered my mind as an option until one day when I happened upon a job advertisement for a local community college. When I saw the advertisement for the position (which happily I ended up getting hired for, and is the position I currently hold), I considered applying, but I didn't know anything about community colleges, and I had questions. I went to my mentors and asked them things like: Is there tenure at community colleges? Will there be time to write and encouragement to publish at community colleges? Do community college professors make the same amount of money as professors at four-year schools? No one knew the answers, which further otherized community colleges in my mind. So years later, when I received an invitation asking me, a community college professor, to come and speak to graduate students I was pleased. I thought it was great that the school was making an effort to provide more information and encouragement for graduate students to consider community colleges among their career options. However, my response to the invitation changed as I read the email more closely.

The email explained that the event was designed to give current graduate students "an opportunity to hear from ARHU alums about their career paths and tips and resources for finding jobs 'outside academia.'" The invitation went on to explain that there had been a "similar event in the fall for students interested in learning more about pursuing tenure and tenure-track careers in academia" and that the panel discussion I was being asked to speak at would be divided into "four different professional pathways: Government, NGOs & Think Tanks; Museums & Archives; Community College & Non-Higher Ed Teaching; [and] Academic Administration & Arts Organizations."

I was confused. It seemed that there were two events: one the previous semester that focused on "real" academic jobs, and another event for the current semester that was focused on jobs "outside academia." I was a tenured professor at a college, but I was being asked to speak on a panel about jobs "outside academia." At first, I thought that the problem was that the email writer simply didn't know what job I held. After all, I didn't know her. Apparently, my department had forwarded my name to the dean's office and so things might have just gotten confused in the process. But then I realized that community college teaching was specifically mentioned as one of the four "professional pathways" that structured the event. So clearly, whoever designed the event consciously framed community college teaching as "outside academia." I decided to play dumb. I wrote back saying that there must have been a mix-up and that they must have intended to invite me to the previous semester's panel, the one on academic jobs. The event coordinator emailed back explaining that no, they knew I worked at a community college, they still wanted me to come speak, and that they were using the term "outside academia" "very broadly." What followed was a back and forth that eventually moved from the event coordinator to an associate dean. The associate dean said that while the fall panel had been focused on "the academic job search," they wanted the spring event to be "a more interactive forum for grad students to have exposure to, and real conversation with, a range of professionals who have graduated with an arts and humanities PhD, both within and beyond the academy." In her framing, the fall and spring panels were not mutually exclusive or opposites, but the spring event was just more inclusive. She went on to explain that she hoped I would come and speak so that I could offer the graduate student attendees insights "about how community college teaching may be *unique* compared to what they have experienced at UMD" (emphasis mine). I declined to speak on the panel but noted that if the university decided to offer a new panel, in an upcoming semester, where community college teaching was not separated from other college-level teaching, I would be happy to participate. I was snarky, and my best self might have sent a more carefully worded email, but in the moment I felt justified. Community college students continually receive messages that they are not real college students, as I told the associate dean, and I would not participate in that narrative.

Was I overreacting? On the one hand, I don't think anyone was intentionally trying to offend me, or for that matter to say that they thought community colleges are not a part of academia. I've planned discussion panels like this before and the truth is that events often evolve and change over the duration of the planning process and, especially if a number of people are involved in the planning, different perspectives can be added to the event in ways that are inconsistent. Maybe one planner thought that graduate students should learn about community college teaching and another planner wanted to expose students to opportunities with NGOs and both got added to the same event, a separate event from the one about teaching at four-year schools, through a series of edits that were more a result of happenstance than a unified vision.

The associate dean didn't take me up on my offer to speak at a future campus-wide event, but several years later I was reminded of the event because I was contacted again by the university, but this time from my home department. I was asked to speak to graduate students in the program I had graduated from, something I had done once before. The first time I spoke to the graduate students from my program I was on a panel with others from my graduate school cohort and we all spoke about our experience in the program and our paths after completing our PhDs. The second time, I was again asked to talk about my "professional career path post PhD," but this time the panel was framed a bit differently: the heading for the panel was "Non Academia & NGO Positions." I went through the same back and forth I had done with the previous panel. This time I ended up going to speak. I'm not sure why. Maybe because I had relationships with people in my department I was more hesitant about taking a stand. As before, I didn't feel like the person was trying to be offensive. I did feel hurt, though. Maybe because it confirmed for me what I had suspected: that my department didn't view me as one of them. Maybe because I hold women's studies to a higher standard: I believe that because the field is committed to understanding social hierarchies and advocating for the marginalized that they should be better able to see the ways in which the othering of community colleges hurts the marginalized students that disproportionately attend these schools. I see myself as a college professor and I see my students as college students. However, my interactions around this panel and the previous event, combined with many other experiences I've had since I've started working at a community college, seem to indicate that other people don't view me as a "real" college professor and don't view my students as "real" college students.

I went back in forth in my mind about whether I should share these stories. On the one hand, I think it's wonderful that my alma mater has been trying to present community college teaching as a career pathway for its graduate students. I wish that option had been presented to me when I was a graduate student. Furthermore, I don't think that the slights that I perceived were intentional, and, on some level, I can understand why professors and administrators at a research university view community college teaching as something quite different from what they do. However, I think it's important to talk about these stories because they reflect stereotypes about community colleges that are widespread throughout the culture, and they reveal the othering that community college professors often feel when interacting with our peers at four-year schools. I've shared these stories from my vantage point, talking about how they've affected me, but one of the questions we might ask is how this othering of community colleges affects community college students. How does it affect a student's sense of self when they get the message that they are not legitimate college students? Does it affect how they view their potential? Does it affect what they think they can achieve? Does it affect their ability to persist and succeed? And on a larger scale, how do these stereotypes affect how funding is allocated to community colleges? How does it affect the ways in which outside stakeholders define and restrict what a community college education can be? My point is that these stereotypes about community colleges have consequences, and for this reason I thought it was valuable to share my story.

*The email discussions referenced in this narrative occurred in March 2013 and February 2017. I have chosen not to include any names.

• • • • • • • • • • • • • • • • • • • • • • • • • • • • • • • • • • • • • • • • • • • • • • • • • • • • • •

Community colleges cater to historically underserved and marginalized communities. Perhaps the most significant difference between community colleges and four-year colleges and universities relates to socioeconomic status (SES). Students in community colleges disproportionately come from low-income households. In "Our Economically Polarized College System: Separate and Unequal," Anthony Carnevale and Jeff Strohl explain:

The bottom half of the bifurcated college system includes more than 1,000 community colleges, along with 299 less-prestigious four-year colleges.... Nearly 80 percent of the lowest-income students go to colleges in the bottom half of the postsecondary system. Compared to less- or non-competitive, somewhat competitive, or highly competitive 4-year schools, community colleges are the *only* category that has more students from the bottom socioeconomic quartile than from the top quartile. (Carnevale and Strohl, "Our Economically")

Hierarchies of race and class are both reflected and perpetuated by the bifurcation of higher education: "This polarization of the postsecondary system is doubly concerning, because it mirrors the parallel concentration of white students and students from affluent families at the top and a concentration of African Americans, Hispanics, and students from low-SES families at the bottom" (Carnevale and Strohl, "How Increasing" 78). Community colleges enroll 41% of all undergraduates, but disproportionately serve students of color with 56% of all Native American undergraduates, 52% of all Hispanic undergraduates, and 43% of black undergraduates ("Fast Facts"). Thirty-six percent of community college students have parents with no college experience compared to the 29% average for all undergraduate institutions (Ma and Baum 9). Community colleges are also female (and feminized) spaces: 56% of community college students are female ("Fast Facts"); 57% of management, 73% of business and financial operations, 81% of office and administrative support, 53% of instructional staff, and 65% of student academic affairs and other education services positions are held by women ("DataPoints: Female Campus Administrators"); and community colleges employ a larger percentage of full-time female professors (51%) than doctorate-awarding universities (31%) or bachelor's and master's degree-granting colleges and universities (42%) (West and Curtis 7). About 20% of community college students report having a disability, compared to 17% at public four-year institutions ("DataPoints: Students with Disabilities"). In short, community colleges disproportionately serve disadvantaged groups in our society—the very groups that WGS endeavors to support. So why isn't there more of a focus on community colleges at NWSA or within the broader WGS culture?

Part of the reason is that because the field of WGS is itself often placed at the boundaries of academia; it is always already vulnerable. One of the ways the field has dealt with this vulnerability has been to use the "master's tools": adopting the rituals of academic performance and value has helped solidify women's and gender studies within the academy. There is some value to this strategy. After all, without the larger field of women's and gender studies, community colleges wouldn't be able to offer WGS courses, and without four-year WGS programs and departments for our students to transfer to, it would be harder to make the case for the existence of WGS at community colleges. But this strategy comes at a cost. With more support from NWSA and the larger field of women's and gender studies, community college WGS programs could better serve their students.

And so, emerging from the discussions of the Community College Caucus the goals for this book are threefold. First, we want to honor the work of women's and gender studies at community colleges—to name the important work that WGS faculty, staff, and students do in these locations and to recognize the value of this work to the larger communities that two-year colleges serve, the field of women's and gender studies, and national and international bodies of informed activists and citizens. The presence of WGS at community colleges is woefully under-researched. There are only a handful of published articles on WGS at community colleges, and this is the first book to focus on the topic. *Theory and Praxis: Women's and Gender Studies at Community Colleges* aims to raise awareness around the WGS work being done at community colleges by bringing together articles that look at this work from various angles. A key feature of the book is the inclusion of student narratives. In addition to the collection of academic essays, we highlight individual WGS students at community colleges in our "Student Voices" sections. These featured sections throughout the book focus on student experiences of WGS—including students who are majoring in WGS and those who have completed WGS courses as part of their work towards a degree in a different field—and showcase the ways in which WGS has contributed to students' career aspirations, activist work, personal growth, and sense of self.

The second goal of this anthology is to share best practices within the community of WGS at community colleges. Because of the often-isolating nature of teaching in small programs, this book is meant to bring together different voices to create conversation about feminist pedagogy, navigating institutional dynamics, and explaining the importance of our work within the larger narratives around higher education.

The final goal of the book is to inspire a call to action. For all those who believe in the transformative potential of WGS, and who believe that WGS programs are important components of academia, we ask for your help in strengthening WGS programs at community colleges. As Sara Hosey argues in her essay in this collection:

> It must be part of the larger feminist agenda to more fully support the work that goes on in community colleges. Ignoring community college students, faculty, and work reflects a larger surrender to a neoliberal postfeminist severing of the personal and the political. That is, if you don't see and struggle with and for students in community colleges, you become one of the voices telling these individuals, you are not real students, you are on your own, your voices, stories, and needs are not important.

In the current neoliberal academy, WGS programs are more important than ever. When higher education is defined by "job training, quantitative measurements, and the development of curricula to prepare students for particular occupations" students "are no longer educated for democratic citizenship. On the contrary, they are being trained to fulfill the need for human capital" (Giroux, *Neoliberalism's War* 33-4). As students historically underserved by higher education, and from social classes historically exploited through capitalism, community college students have the most to gain from resisting this narrative, and the most to lose if they don't. WGS classrooms are important spaces on community college campuses where students engage in a resistant pedagogy that teaches "the knowledge and skills necessary to allow them to think critically and hold power and authority accountable" (34).

## Theory and Praxis

*Theory and Praxis: Women's and Gender Studies at Community Colleges* centers around a philosophy of education in line with the emancipatory principles of critical pedagogy, principles that see a symbiotic relationship between educational theory and classroom practice, and which root pedagogy in the process of progressive social change. We see critical pedagogy as foundational to the field of WGS and particularly essential in the community college classroom. It is through critical pedagogy that the theories undergirding our field are made manifest in the everyday work we do with our students. However, as Amanda Loos notes in her essay in this collection, "Pedagogical theory cannot *simply* be applied across all educational environments without recognition of the particular character and dynamics of those communities.... We must name community college classrooms as uniquely vulnerable, volatile, vibrant, radical, inspiring and sacred educational spaces, rendered invisible by hierarchical thinking in academia." Therefore, *Theory and Praxis: Women's and Gender Studies at Community Colleges* takes as its focus the call and response of educational theory, social justice, and women's and gender studies specifically within the community college classroom. As Loos explains, "It is precisely because community colleges often operate as borderland spaces that they are most in need of, and most conducive to, vibrantly exciting pedagogical practices."

Critical pedagogy, a way of teaching that consciously connects learning with democracy and social justice, emerged and developed during the 20th century influenced by the work of scholars like John Dewey, W.E.B. DuBois, Carter G. Woodson, Myles and Zilphia Horton, Herbert Kohl, Jonathan Kozol, Maxine Greene, Samuel Bowles and Herbert Gintis, Martin Carnoy, Michael Apple, and Ivan Illich (Darder et al. 3-5). Paulo Freire became a central figure to this movement with his 1968 book *Pedagogy of the Oppressed* which articulates a progressive view of education that grounds learning in political agency and social justice and criticizes "the banking concept of education," the common pedagogical practice emphasizing rote memorization and through which students become "'receptacles' to be 'filled' by the teacher" (72). Within the banking concept "[e]ducation thus becomes an act of depositing, in which the students are the depositories and the teacher is the depositor. Instead of communicating, the teacher issues communiqués and makes deposits which the students patiently receive, memorize, and repeat" (72). Freire sees the banking concept of education as a dehumanizing process of maintaining inequality: "The capability of banking education to minimize or annul the students' creative power and to stimulate their credulity serves the interests of the oppressors, who care neither to have the world revealed not to see it transformed" (73). Freire's career was dedicated to challenging the banking concept of education and advocating for an emancipatory pedagogy of the oppressed,

> a pedagogy which must be forged *with*, not *for*, the oppressed (whether individuals or peoples) in the incessant struggle to regain their humanity. This pedagogy makes oppression and its causes objects of reflection by the oppressed, and from that reflection will come their necessary engagement in the struggle for their liberation. And in the struggle this pedagogy will be made and remade.

Henry Giroux has been a prolific advocate for Freire's vision by criticizing contemporary neoliberal "reforms" of education as inherently antidemocratic and a return to the banking concept of education. Giroux argues that neoliberalism has discouraged critical education while increasing conceptual and cultural illiteracy. He claims that "[e]ducation within the last three decades has been removed from its utopian possibilities of educating young people to be reflective, critical, and socially engaged agents" because education is being redefined "in purely instrumental and anti-intellectual terms" (*Neoliberalism's War*, 31, 32). He condemns the neoliberal view of education as job training, the obsessive focus on quantitative measurements and the phenomenon of teaching to the test that comes with it, and the framing of education as a private commodity rather than a public good. Advocating instead for Freire's vision of education, Giroux says, "Pedagogy is a mode of critical intervention, one that endows teachers with a responsibility to prepare students not merely for jobs but for being in the world in ways that allow them to influence the larger political, ideological, and economic forces that bear down on their lives" (37).

Critical pedagogy is an intentionally decentralized and fluid set of principles and practices that resists a contained definition. However, this body of pedagogical practices is unified by intent and there are, therefore, particular features that characterize critical pedagogy. The first is a commitment to social justice: "Critical pedagogy is fundamentally committed to the development and enactment of a culture of schooling that supports the empowerment of culturally marginalized and economically disenfranchised students" and "seeks to help transform those classroom structures and practices that perpetuate undemocratic life" (Darder et al. 9). Freire says,

> One of the greatest obstacles to the achievement of liberation is that oppressive reality absorbs those within it and thereby acts to submerge human beings' consciousness. Functionally, oppression is domesticating. To no longer be prey to its force, one must emerge from it and turn upon it. This can be done only by means of the praxis: reflection and action upon the world in order to transform it. (51)

The goal of critical pedagogy is to address social inequality by making its processes visible, providing students the space and language to understand power and privilege, and using pedagogical practices that allow learners to draw connections between the course materials and their own lives: learning must be a reflective practice increasing understanding of the self and the relationship between the individual and the society. As Giroux explains, "Critical pedagogy takes as one of its central projects an attempt to be discerning and attentive to those places and practices in which social agency has been denied and produced" ("Critical Pedagogy" 3).

Critical pedagogy is also defined by its insistence that knowledge must be contextualized, and that the production of knowledge must be unmasked in order to demonstrate the ways in which knowledge is connected to larger power struggles in the culture. For critical pedagogy, knowledge is a contested site of struggle. As Peter McLaren explains, "Knowledge acquired in school—or anywhere, for that matter—is never neutral or objective but is ordered and structured in particular ways; its emphases and exclusions partake of a silent logic. Knowledge is a *social construction* deeply rooted in a nexus of power relations" (63). Because "some forms of knowledge have more power and legitimacy than others," it's important for students to learn to ask "how and why knowledge gets constructed the way that it does, and how and why some constructions of reality are legitimated and celebrated by the dominant culture while others clearly are not" (63).

Finally, critical pedagogy is marked by its efforts to create counter-hegemonic educational spaces and practices: "The term counter-hegemony is used within critical pedagogy to refer to those intellectual and social spaces where power relationships are reconstructed to make central the voices and experiences of those who have historically existed at the margins of public institutions" (Darder et al. 12). The classroom must encourage students to see themselves as agents of social change and give them the tools to challenge power while instilling in them a sense of social and civic responsibility. The counter-hegemonic classroom gives students hope by giving them the tools to be political agents and encouraging a belief in their political efficacy.

Women's and gender studies classrooms are important counter-hegemonic spaces in higher education, and these spaces are particularly necessary at community colleges. Because community colleges are open-access institutions, students come with a range of preparedness. One of the ways in which community colleges differ from many of their four-year counterparts is that community colleges are more likely to serve students who struggled in their educational journey. Many community college students are adequately prepared for college and have academic records similar to their peers at four-year schools, but because of the open-access mission, community colleges also serve students who have underperformed in K-12. Part of the mission of critical pedagogy is to reconsider academic underperformance—situating individual problems in context and in conversation with larger structural problems like failing schools; education "reforms"; budget cuts; and race, class, and gender privilege. Critical pedagogy offers an emancipatory perspective for both teacher and student in the conversations around academic struggle because it is grounded in "the assumption that all people have the capacity and ability to produce knowledge and to resist domination" coupled with the recognition that "how they choose to resist is clearly influenced and limited by the social and material conditions in which they have been forced to survive and the ideological formations that have been internalized in the process" (Darder et al. 12). Through critical pedagogy, teachers and students are encouraged to understand academic behaviors within the larger educational framework that privileges and normalizes particular lived experiences while silencing and marginalizing others. An analysis that places academic performance in conversation with larger ideological formations and their effects on the reproduction of inequality gives students and teachers "the basis for understanding not only how the seeds of domination are produced, but also how they can be challenged and overcome through resistance, critique and social action" (Darder et al. 12). Critical understanding of knowledge formations coupled with an emphasis on the students' role as knowledge producers is an emancipatory pedagogy that is needed to both encourage marginalized students to succeed within the present system and to give them tools to imagine a more democratic future. In this way the focus on contextualizing knowledge and making transparent the role of power and privilege in knowledge formation gives students the tools to understand their own experiences in the education system and helps create a counter-hegemonic classroom.

In *Teaching to Transgress* bell hooks reminds us of the importance of education as a counter-hegemonic act. Her own experience explains what's at stake, particularly for subordinate groups. She describes her experience as a black student moving between a segregated school where learning was framed as part of antiracist struggle, to an integrated school where "[k]nowledge was suddenly about information only. It had no relation to how one lived, behaved. It was no longer connected to antiracist struggle" (2-3). This contrast revealed to her the ways in which learning can be used for liberation or control: "Bussed to white schools, we soon learned that obedience, and not a zealous will to learn, was what was expected of us. Too much eagerness to learn could easily be seen as a threat to white authority" (3).

As you read the essays in this collection, our hope is that you will keep this contrast in mind: when education teaches students to be political actors and critical thinkers it can be liberatory, a place of pleasure, a "practice of freedom" (3-4); however, learning can also be a tool of control, a way to reinforce hierarchy and oppression, a method for encouraging citizens to submit to authority (4). hooks says that her experience in classrooms "that were about domination and the unjust exercise of power" taught her "a lot about the kind of teacher [she] did not want to become" (5). The commitment to the field of women's and gender studies is a commitment to education as liberation, but this commitment necessitates vigilant self-analysis and introspection. We must continually examine and re-examine our curriculum and pedagogy. This commitment also requires that we become politically engaged in the public discourse on the role of education. As the neoliberal paradigm becomes more entrenched in academia and politics, resistance becomes more risky, but also more necessary. There is a lot at stake for our field, our students, our careers, and our communities. We hope that this book strengthens your belief in critical pedagogy and provides you sustenance for feminist movement.

## The Essays

In their essay, "The Status of Women's and Gender Studies at Community Colleges," Heather Rellihan and Alissa Stoehr provide an overview of WGS offerings on community college campuses. They note a significant range, from colleges that provide only one or two WGS courses housed in other departments (usually including the foundational Introduction to Women's Studies course) to stand-alone programs and departments that offer associate degrees and other academic credentials in WGS. Two essays provide a historical foundation for understanding WGS at community colleges in the present moment. In her essay, "Curriculum Transformation in Community Colleges: Twenty Years Later," Genevieve Carminati revisits a 1996 special issue of *Women's Studies Quarterly* that focused on curriculum transformation at community colleges, explaining how the essays in this issue can be instructive for thinking about the challenges that we face in WGS at community colleges today. She urges us to take strength from the long tradition of inspiring and often radical scholarship and pedagogy that has come before us—and which the journal chronicles—and to use this history to inform our current efforts to develop and reinvigorate courses, and to maintain and grow our programs. Judith M. Roy's essay, "A Community College President of NWSA: A Personal Narrative," also provides a historical framework. She recounts her experiences serving as the president of the National Women's Studies Association—the only community college faculty to ever do so. Her personal narrative helps provide a sense of how the organization has changed, and what these changes mean for WGS at community colleges.

Several of the essays in the collection examine the position of community colleges within the hierarchy of academia and position community colleges as innately activist spaces. Building on Gloria Anzaldúa's theory in *Borderlands/ La Frontera: The New Mestiza*, Amanda Loos positions community colleges as borderlands in her essay, "Hunger for Justice in the Borderlands: Re-Framing Antiracist Feminist Pedagogies for an Urban Community College." Focusing on the women's and gender studies classroom, she says that "[t]ransformative pedagogies used effectively at these borderland spaces could serve ... as a vibrant model for intersectional feminist praxis and as a source for productive alliance toward justice in education." However, to keep these spaces transformative, Loos cautions that we must resist the call to merely "teach to transfer." She says, "If we are only 'preparing' our students for transfer without teaching for justice and transformation, we simultaneously silence our students and continue to render their communities invisible." In her essay, "The Community College as an Enabling Institution: Women's Studies Programs Resisting the Neoliberal Severing of the Personal and Political," Sara Hosey positions WGS programs at community colleges as important spaces for contesting the severing of personal and political that is part of neoliberal and postfeminist ideologies. Grounding her analysis in feminist and disability studies, Hosey interrogates the messaging around community colleges looking at, for example, the current renderings of "non-traditional" students. She says that when "traditional students"—"individuals who are white, able-bodied, middle and upper class and 18-21 years old"—are used as the default to mark others as "non-traditional," the personal challenges of the "non-traditional" student are framed as "personal, rather than political." However, she argues that "if we use feminist and disability studies perspectives in order to remember the political in the personal and the personal in the political" we can "forge enabling institutions" that move away from a model where the focus is on "fixing" the student to a model that tries to analyze and fix the environment.

In her essay, "Our Stories to Tell: Situating Activism in the Intersections of Class, Women's/Gender Studies, and Community Colleges," Jill Adams positions women's and gender studies at community colleges as inherently activist spaces but explains that the work being done at two-year schools is often invisible in national narratives about college activism. She traces the history of community colleges, noting that from their inception they were focused on an activist mission—making college education accessible to people from less privileged and underserved backgrounds. However, she argues that because narratives about college activism are based around a four-year model, activism on community college campuses isn't seen for what it is. She asks how our definition of college activism might shift if the experiences and activities of community college students were centered. Esther Schwartz-McKinzie's essay, "Keep 'Doing Good': Women's and Gender Studies Programs and VAWA Education Initiatives against the Tide," discusses a specific activist project at Montgomery College: the development of SpeakUpMC, a climate survey that provides insight into their students' understanding of, and experiences with, sexual violence. Though initially prompted by updated requirements of the Violence Against Women Act, Schwartz-McKinzie explains the intrinsic value of this work to community colleges. Citing statistics from the survey results, she emphasizes the need for community colleges to comprehensively address issues of sexual violence, even in absence of a federal mandate.

One of the manifestations of the neoliberal shift within academia is the focus on learning outcomes assessment. While the underlying philosophy of having students be able to demonstrate what they've learned is not new, the specific conventions and practices that have become formalized in the institution of Learning Outcomes Assessment (LOA) are often positioned in tension with feminist pedagogical practices. However, in their essay, "Assessing Student Learning in Gender, Sexuality, and Women's Studies: Curricular and Faculty Development in the Two-Year College," Jessica Van Slooten, Amy Reddinger, Holly Hassel, and Ann Mattis provide alternative framing for assessment. They recount the history of assessment within the Gender, Sexuality, and Women's Studies Program at the University of Wisconsin Colleges and demonstrate how by focusing on "threshold concepts" they were able to create assessment projects that helped strengthen their program, better serve their students, and create community across the University of Wisconsin Colleges. With an emphasis on a collaborative approach focused on improving student success, they position assessment as "a transformative feminist pedagogical practice."

Several of the essays in the collection talk about strategies for growing and energizing WGS programs. In "Petticoats, Pumps, and Pantyhose: Creating Student Success through a Women's Studies Learning Community,"

Donna Thompson and Paquita Garatea discuss their success with learning communities. They argue that the stronger social relationships that learning communities encourage can increase student success rates, particularly for marginalized students. They also point to learning communities as a way to strengthen and grow WGS programs noting that, "The successful implementation of gender-focused learning communities demonstrated the viability of women's studies courses" and that this success allowed them to grow their program.

Two essays talk about developing and teaching courses that reflect the evolution of the field of women's and gender studies. In her essay, "Introduction to LGBTQ Studies: Designing the Course," Grace Sikorski explains the development of the Introduction to Lesbian, Gay, Bisexual, and Transgender Studies course at Anne Arundel Community College. Sikorski uses her experience developing the course, going through her college's curriculum oversight process, and finally teaching it, to offer specific advice for programs seeking to add a course on LGBTQ studies to a WGS curriculum, with particular attention paid to the community college institutional environment. She offers strategies for explaining the value of the course in the context of the college's statements on diversity, equity, and inclusion, and the regional accrediting organization's definition of general education coursework. In his essay, "Chiseling Away at the Foundations of the Patriarchy: On Teaching Masculinity Studies at an American Community College," Richard Otten discusses his experience teaching Introduction to Masculinity Studies at a two-year school. The Introduction to Masculinity Studies course reflects new trends within the field of WGS that offer important space for analysis of how the construction of gender affects men, with an emphasis on the analysis of privilege. Because of the less privileged communities that two-year colleges draw from, student experiences with male privilege look different than they would at a more elite institution, providing useful material for intersectional analyses.

We conclude the book with an essay from Red Washburn entitled, "Endangered Studies, Women's, Gender, and Sexuality Studies and Community Colleges in #MeToo Times: A Case Study of Kingsborough Community College as a Microcosm of Neoliberal Education." Washburn recounts the recent challenges for the WGS program at her institution, using the specifics of these experiences to explore how the neoliberal paradigm in academia and the current political environment endanger WGS at community colleges. While she notes that "Kingsborough is just one example," she says that "it provides a critical case study for community colleges across the nation struggling with administrations restructuring and eliminating programs, as well as for understanding how the politics and practices of solidarity are essential to keeping women's, gender, and sexuality studies intellectually alive." Indeed, she argues that "[t]he future of the field depends on strategies of risk and defense connected to the politics of solidarity" and part of the value of her essay, and one of the reasons why we wanted to use it at the conclusion of the book, is that it leaves the reader with a wealth of strategies for engendering and cultivating solidarity within and across institutions.

## A Call to Action

In the introduction to her anthology, *Women's Studies on Its Own*, Robyn Wiegman explains the focus of her project: "[t]o trace, in a positive political grammar, the difference that the present makes for thinking about Women's Studies as a knowledge formation, academic institution, agency of the state, and pedagogical insurgency" (4). In our volume, we'd like to shift the focus of her question. When we center our analysis of the field of women's and gender studies on *community colleges* how does our understanding of the field change? Can this reframing change our view of women's and gender studies as a knowledge formation, an academic institution, an agency of the state, and a pedagogical insurgency? In our view, an increased focus on community college students and programs is a much-needed counter to academic feminism's embrace of the elite. Shifting energy and resources to support WGS programs at community colleges in order to support the least advantaged students is consistent with the ethic of our field in that it seeks to empower the marginalized and dismantle social hierarchy. With 40% of all college students studying at community colleges, it's also in the self-interest of four-year schools. Community college programs can help bachelor's programs grow by sending them well-equipped junior-level students.

In her 2008 essay, "Women's Studies—The Early Years: When Sisterhood Was Powerful," Paula Rothenberg recounts the utopian vision of the field's founding: "Early Women's Studies was rife with possibilities that seemed to hold out the opportunity for real and lasting change.... the early years that brought with them unimaginable opportunities and excitement, the promise that nothing would ever be the same" (67-8). She acknowledges, though, that perhaps inevitably, women's studies "was transformed both by the academy as it was institutionalized and professionalized and by corporate culture as it was trivialized" (67-8). She says,

> In order to qualify as an academic enterprise, many of us have had to prove ourselves by learning to look, act, and talk like "academics" even as we tried to transform the meaning of what it meant to be one.... For some, the challenge was how to succeed in academia without compromising their values too much, while others were more than happy to do whatever was necessary to become "legitimate" and move up the career ladder. To this day, some Women's Studies programs and departments are as radical and independent as they were at the start while others seem to have forgotten the meaning of sisterhood. (83)

Despite these acknowledgements, Rothenberg's narrative can be read as hopeful. By emphasizing the promise of the early days of women's studies "when sisterhood was powerful," and pointing to examples where the field had evolved, she seems to hold out hope that powerful sisterhood isn't limited to the past (85). She says, "One step backward, two steps forward, and then we go back again" (68).

We think that we are at a place where the field needs to self-correct: we've moved backward (again) and we need to move forward (again). While women's and gender studies has made tremendous contributions to the study and advancement of women, the LGBTQ community, people of color, and other marginalized groups, this work has been uneven. Students at community colleges are marginalized because their institutions—institutions that cater to those with less economic, political, and cultural power—remain at the borders of academia. These students need more help from the field of women's and gender studies, and this necessitates a re-envisioning of the work we do and where we put our energies. The rise of institutional feminism, with its adherence to the performance of academia, may have caused us to lose focus on what brought feminism into the academy in the first place: to make change in the ways in which knowledge formation and academic practice reflect and perpetuate social hierarchy. Antonia Darder, Marta Baltodano, and Rodolfo Torres remind us that hegemony is a process that involves continual maintenance: "[E]ach time a radical form threatens the integrity of the status quo, generally this element is appropriated, stripped of its transformative intent, and reified into a palatable form. This process serves to preserve intact the existing power relations" (9). Supporting women's and gender studies at community colleges is a specific way that the field can self-correct, to ensure that the radicalness of our foundation as a field is not being appropriated, stripped of its transformational possibilities, or hollowed out to a less threatening likeness.

Our WGS colleagues at four-year schools can reach out to local community colleges and help them streamline transfers and build relationships that help share resources. WGS journals can intentionally focus on WGS at community colleges, helping to stimulate research around this important feminist work. Individual scholars at more prestigious institutions can reach out to their colleagues at two-year schools, developing relationships and inviting them to work on cooperative projects. NWSA can ensure that folks from community colleges serve important and visible roles within the organization. NWSA could also sponsor travel funding to enable more professors from community colleges to attend its national conference. The Community College Caucus also has work to do. We need to address the lack of racial and ethnic diversity in our group. The Community College Caucus is comprised of faculty who teach WGS at community colleges around the country, and though the disproportionate amount of white faculty at community colleges is a national issue, and though we might not be able to change hiring practices on this level, we can work on this issue on at least two fronts: First, we can work to ensure that faculty of color who teach WGS at community colleges feel welcomed and valued in the Community College Caucus. We can also reach out to WGS faculty at community colleges who don't attend NWSA and find ways to create community outside of, and in addition to, the annual NWSA conference. Second, we must work both at our own institutions and within our caucus to discuss and address barriers to the recruitment, hiring, and promotion of faculty of color in our field and at our respective institutions. Finally, all of us—those of us at community colleges and at four-year schools, those of us in academia and those of us working across other parts of our society—can be more thoughtful about the stereotypes we perpetuate about community colleges and their students, and understand how marginalizing practices that hurt community college students help entrench hierarchies of race, class, and gender. We can do the kind of critical cultural work that our field is known for by unpacking these stereotypes and challenging the practices that create and maintain hierarchies within academia. We must engage in a politics of solidarity, remembering that "Freire's understanding of solidarity challenges critical educators to break with alienating practices of competition, internalized notions of superiority, tendencies to demonize difference, and our 'colonized' dependence and yearning to be recognized or legitimated by those who hold official power" (Darder et al. 19). By devoting as much support to women's and gender studies at community colleges as we do to elite schools and PhD programs, women's and gender studies can reinvigorate the ideals that were part of the movement's founding identity.

Gillian Sobocinski, an Introduction to Women's Studies student at Nassau Community College, sums up the need for WGS at community colleges. She says, "I really love and believe in the power of WGS. I think that this subject can change the world. Education is powerful, and if more students can learn about this integral subject, I think that in the future we will see immense positive change in our world. And we certainly need that right now." The editors and essayists in this book share Sobocinski's belief in the power of women's and gender studies. We believe it has the power to change the lives of the students in our classes, to guide them to be better critical thinkers, more reflective and introspective learners, and more engaged members of their community. We think the focus on critical pedagogy—with its emphasis on theory and praxis—gives WGS students a different, more empowering relationship to knowledge, and that their new relationship with academic learning leads to student success. As each WGS student goes out into the world better prepared to listen to marginalized voices, stand up against inequality and oppression, and fight for their communities, we think these classes have the power to change the world. As you read the essays in this collection, we ask that you work in whatever capacity you can to support women's and gender studies at community colleges. Help us continue this important liberatory work.

# Works Cited

"About." National Women's Studies Association, www.nwsa.org.

Aronowitz, Stanley. "Against Schooling: Education and Social Class."
*The Critical Pedagogy Reader*, edited by Antonia Darder, Marta P.
Baltodano, and Rodolfo D. Torres, Routledge, 2009, pp. 106-212.

Carnevale, Anthony P., and Jeff Strohl. "How Increasing College Access
Is Increasing Inequality and What to Do about It." *Rewarding Strivers:
Helping Low-Income Students Succeed in College*, edited by Richard D.
Kahlenberg, Century Foundation Press, 2010.

————. "Our Economically Polarized College System: Separate and
Unequal." *The Chronicle of Higher Education*, 25 Sept. 2011, www.
chronicle.com/article/Our-Economically-Polarized/129094/.

"Constituency Groups." National Women's Studies Association, www.nswa.
org.

Darder, Antonia, et al. "Critical Pedagogy: An Introduction." *The Critical
Pedagogy Reader*, edited by Antonia Darder, Marta P. Baltodano, and
Rodolfo D. Torres, Routledge, 2009, pp. 1-20.

"DataPoints: Female Campus Administrators." *American Association
of Community Colleges*, vol.4, iss. 5, March 2016, www.aacc.nche.
edu/2016/03/18/datapoints-female-campus-administrators/.

"DataPoints: Students with Disabilities." *American Association of
Community Colleges*, vol. 6, iss. 13, September 2018, www.aacc.nche.
edu/2018/09/26/datapoints-students-with-disabilities/.

"Fast Facts." *American Association of Community Colleges*, 2018, www.aacc. nche.edu/research-trends/fast-facts/.

Freire, Paulo. *Pedagogy of the Oppressed*. Continuum, 2003.

Ginsberg, Alice E. "Triumphs, Controversies, and Changes: Women's Studies 1970s to the Twenty-First Century." *The Evolution of American Women's Studies: Reflections on Triumphs, Controversies, and Change*, edited by Alice E. Ginsberg, Palgrave Macmillan, 2012, 9-37.

Giroux, Henry A. *Neoliberalism's War on Higher Education*. Haymarket Books, 2014.

———. "Critical Pedagogy in Dark Times." *On Critical Pedagogy*. Bloomsbury Academic, 2011.

hooks, bell. *Teaching to Transgress: Education as the Practice of Freedom*. Routledge, 1994.

Ma, Jennifer, and Sandy Baum. "Trends in Community Colleges: Enrollment, Prices, Student Debt, and Completion." *College Board Research*, 2016, trends.collegeboard.org/sites/default/files/trends-in-community-colleges-research-brief.pdf.

McLaren, Peter. "Critical Pedagogy: A Look at the Major Concepts." *The Critical Pedagogy Reader*, edited by Antonia Darder, Marta P. Baltodano, and Rodolfo D. Torres, Routledge, 2009, pp. 61-83.

Rothenberg, Paula. "Women's Studies—The Early Years: When Sisterhood Was Powerful." *The Evolution of American Women's Studies: Reflections on Triumphs, Controversies, and Change*, edited by Alice E. Ginsberg, Palgrave Macmillan, 2012, 67-86.

West, Martha S., and John W. Curtis. *AAUP Faculty Gender Equity Indicators, 2006*, American Association of University Professors, 2006, www.aaup.org.

# The Status of Women's and Gender Studies at Community Colleges

Heather Rellihan and Alissa Stoehr

Community colleges are going through a period of significant change. Revisions to organizational structures, cuts in funding, new government-initiated "reforms," onerous reporting mechanisms, increased standardization, the diminishing role and power of faculty, the rise of big data and its accompanying value system, and new metrics for measuring the worth of education have come together to create massive shifts in the mission, philosophy, and operation of community colleges. In his book, *Nontraditional Students and Community Colleges: The Conflict of Justice and Neoliberalism*, John Levin explains the role of the neoliberal paradigm in inspiring these changes, and the costs for community college students. He says, "Neoliberalism is an ideological commitment to competition, in the form of social Darwinism, to state reduction of social programs and to state support for players, especially corporations, in international markets. Neoliberalism is a political project aimed at institutional change, and education is one of those institutions where the norms are undergoing severe pressure to change"[2] (50).

While neoliberal ideology is affecting all of academia, its effect is particularly significant for community colleges because of the student demographics at these institutions, institutions Levin refers to as the "have-nots" of higher education. He says, "the 'have-nots' or low salient institutions and programs include those colleges without wealth, prestige, and social and economic impact and those programs that are undervalued.... Compared to prominent

---

2    See also John Campbell and Ove Pedersen's *The Rise of Neoliberalism and Institutional Analysis*.

4-year colleges and universities, community colleges can be viewed as 'have-not' institutions, and all of their students, subject to negative judgments, are viewed as on the periphery of middle-class status" (2). As the pressure from neoliberalism builds within colleges and universities, and particularly at two-year schools, market demands and the needs of corporations more largely define the work of higher education, minimizing the value of other outcomes that have traditionally been a focus of schooling, and mitigating the ability of community colleges to achieve their social justice mission: to increase access to higher education for students from historically underserved populations.

The ideology that undergirds the field of women's and gender studies (WGS[3]) is consistent with the social justice mission of community colleges, and so it is not surprising that WGS has a long and valuable history at community colleges around the country. The shifts in community college education— changes accompanying the neoliberal turn in academia—place WGS in an increasingly precarious position while at the same time making the project of WGS even more crucial at two-year schools. WGS curriculum and pedagogy emphasize skills, values, and philosophies that are a necessary counter to the neoliberal focus on market needs, competition, and the primacy of economic valuings. The world of community college education needs what WGS brings to academia: an increased focus on civic engagement, the cultivation of students' belief in their political efficacy, a critical awareness of the workings of power and privilege in society, and concerted efforts to dismantle systems of structural inequality.

The goal of this essay is to survey the presence of WGS at community colleges, and to situate the work of WGS within this larger context of the valuing and value systems of higher education. This essay will provide an overview of WGS courses and programs at community colleges and illustrate the significance of WGS to students, their institutions, and the larger community. The first section provides information on schools throughout the country, detailing the contributions of WGS courses, programs, and faculty to the academics and culture of their institutions. The second section looks at the motivations

---

3    Because of the variety in naming (see below), we will use WGS to collectively refer to the courses and programs/departments within the field referred to variously as women's studies, women's and gender studies, gender studies, etc.

and experiences of the people who create and maintain WGS at community colleges. Using interviews with WGS faculty, we explore the social justice ideals that fuel this work and the importance that it has for students. It is our hope that sharing this information will underscore the significance of WGS at two-year schools and demonstrate the interrelatedness between WGS and the social justice mission of community colleges. We hope that the essay will encourage information sharing among institutions and create a stronger community of WGS educators at two-year schools throughout the country.

## I. WGS at Community Colleges: The Database[4]

This section provides a detailed look at the presence of WGS at community colleges. The information provided comes from a database five years in the making and which is a synthesis of two separate research projects: each of the authors of this chapter separately researched WGS at two-year schools (Stoehr, as part of her dissertation research and Rellihan, as a project that emerged from her experience as the coordinator of a WGS program and her desire to create greater communication between WGS at different community colleges). This database is the first of its kind. Prior to our work, no master list of schools offering WGS courses and credentials at community colleges existed. There are larger lists of WGS programs and departments at colleges and universities that include some community colleges, but these lists do not disaggregate in order to allow a focus on only two-year schools. Additionally, there have been state-based listings of WGS at community colleges—for example, as part of her 2008 master's degree project, Lindsy Gollihar compiled a list of 16 community colleges in California that offered women's studies. There have also been conference presentations that provided information on the development of WGS programs at two-year schools in the United States, but these presentations were not published and in most cases were limited to programs/ departments that provided credentials in WGS. Therefore, the information presented below is an important addition to our understanding of WGS at community colleges in that it records more variables and provides more depth

---

4    To view the database go to http://tinyurl.com/yy9p9g7e.

(including schools that offer credentials in WGS, but also schools with other types of WGS presence), and because of our intent to make this information widely available as a tool for research sharing. Because WGS programs at community colleges are small and often isolated (in some cases they are the only school in their state to offer WGS), this database can help create community, facilitate the sharing of information, and create conversations around best practices. Particularly in neoliberal academia with its undervaluing of WGS, and with its increased surveillance and reporting demands and continued budget cuts, it is important for WGS programs/departments at community colleges to be able to share information and strategies. It is our hope that this database will enable more information sharing and a greater sense of community within WGS at two-year schools.

All of the information in the database has been reviewed at least twice, but in most cases many additional times over the five-year period between 2013 and 2018. Therefore, while we feel confident in a high degree of accuracy, we offer the following information with a few caveats. One concern we have is that we are undercounting. Our research focused primarily on college websites, including college catalogs for multiple years, program/department/ division websites, and schedules of classes or course search functions within a school's website. In many cases, supplementary or confirming information was acquired through surveys, email correspondence, phone calls, and direct interviews. However, because our research was predominantly web-based, schools that had no web presence for their WGS courses/program/department were unlikely to have been counted. Because schools that offer a credential in WGS are more likely to have a web presence on their school's website (most schools' sites include a list of available credentials), there is a greater likelihood that schools within that classification (Category A, see below) are captured in our research. However, for schools that offer only a few WGS courses, and those that might not have any unifying structure (no formal WGS program or department), it is more likely that they could have been missed. For these reasons, our numbers likely undercount the total number of schools that have some WGS presence, though to the extent that there is undercounting we think it is more likely in Categories B and C (see below).

We wanted our database to record the presence of WGS at community colleges, allowing for a range in terms of what that presence looks like. Therefore, we use three categories to measure this presence ranging from schools that offer a few WGS courses to schools that offer formal credentialing opportunities in WGS. We discuss the specifics of these groupings and their criteria below, but first we want to explain the motivation for this categorization. We thought it was important to recognize the importance of WGS at community colleges in various forms. While offering a credential like an Associate of Arts degree in WGS might mark a more developed WGS presence, it is important not to establish that as the gold standard. Depending on the size of the school, the politics of the region, the educational philosophy of the institution, and the opportunities for WGS transfer at regional four-year institutions, offering a WGS credential might not be viable or desirable for a particular community college. And, as anyone who has taught a course like Introduction to Women's Studies knows, providing the opportunity for students to take even one WGS course can be transformational. We also know that many schools that do not offer credentials in WGS nevertheless have a significant presence on their campus—sponsoring extracurricular and co-curricular activities, encouraging student activism, and working to develop a welcoming climate for students. Therefore, we wanted to honor various manifestations of WGS at community colleges and the value this presence brings to the students, the institution, and the larger community.

However, in order to provide a reasonable scope for our research, we had to create some boundaries around what would be included. We want to acknowledge the constructedness of these boundaries, though: What is included in our database is based on specific criteria that we defined as marking a "WGS presence," but it is certainly possible to make the case for different criteria. There are many schools that were not included in our database because they did not meet our specific requirements for inclusion in any of our three categories but where someone could reasonably argue that the school *does* have a WGS presence and should be included. For example, LaGuardia Community College in New York is not in our database because they did not meet the criteria for any of our three categories, but they have an active Women's Center that offers a number of gender-related services and sponsors valuable programming like the Greatness Results After Choosing Excellence (GRACE) leadership program which aims to "provide confidence and a sense of empowerment that will translate beyond the classroom" ("Women's Center"). In fall of 2018, the

GRACE program offered workshops on topics like negotiating salaries and "the role of popular culture and its influence on the perception of women, business practices and self-reflection" ("Women's Center"). Similarly, we did not include Napa Valley College in California. They don't offer a credential in WGS, but they do offer a Certificate in LGBT studies, and professional trainings including Basic Safe Space for Educators and LGBT Awareness for Law Enforcement. We point out these examples to note that our decisions about what was and was not included were judgment calls that other researchers might have made differently, resulting in different numbers.

A number of factors made research on the presence of WGS at community colleges difficult. Reviewing these challenges is instructive because the difficulties we encountered as researchers are, in many respects, the same difficulties students will encounter when they look for information. We offer the following discussion of the challenges we faced doing our research in the hopes that it may prompt individual WGS programs and departments to think about their web presence and how students find information about WGS at their institution.

One of the most significant difficulties in searching for information about WGS has to do with naming. Debates around naming have taken place in individual institutions and within the field as a whole for two decades. Many schools have debated whether to use the name women's studies—the name historically used with the founding of most programs and departments and the name used by the national professional organization, the National Women's Studies Association—or to use what some see as a more inclusive name like gender studies. Some schools have opted for a combination using the name women's and gender studies or gender and women's studies. In recent years, some schools have added a third term—sexuality—to reflect important scholarship on the LGBTQ community and the development of queer studies as a body of theory within the field. These debates have produced variety in the naming conventions within the field, resulting in inconsistencies that can be confusing: there is no single name that a student can search for in order to determine if a school offers WGS courses or credentials.

As researchers familiar with the field, we knew to search for multiple name variations. Indeed, we found that community colleges in the United States used many variations including "women's studies," "women's and gender studies," "women and gender studies," "gender studies," "gender and women's studies," "gender and women studies," "women, gender, and sexuality studies," and "gender and sexuality studies." Adding to the confusion, we found that some search engines, particularly the search functions within some online college catalogs, cannot handle the apostrophe after "women." Therefore, searching for "women's" would return no results, while searching for "women" would. This is something that a researcher repeating a search on a hundred different college catalogs would eventually learn, but perhaps not something a student looking at one catalog would figure out.

## Naming of WGS Programs at Community Colleges[5]

- Schools Using the Name *Women's Studies*

   Anoka-Ramsey Community College, Bergen Community College, Berkeley City College, Bucks County Community College, Cabrillo College, Central Lakes College, Chandler-Gilbert Community College, Chemeketa Community College, City College of San Francisco, Clark Community College, Clatsop Community College, College of Southern Maryland, College of Southern Nevada, Community College of Allegheny County, Community College of Baltimore County, Community College of Philadelphia, Cosumnes River College, Cuyahoga Community College, De Anza Community College, Doña Ana Community College, Eastern Shore Community College, El Camino College, Folsom Lake College, Foothill College, Fresno City College, Front Range Community College, Gateway Community College, Gulf Coast Community College, Harold Washington College, Hawkeye Community College, Howard Community College, Hudson County Community College, Kansas City Kansas Community College, Lane Community College, Las Positas College, Mesa Community College, Minneapolis Community and Technical College, Normandale Community College, Northern Virginia Community College, Norwalk Community College,

---

5    In this list we included only schools that fall into one of our three categories, see below.

Onondaga Community College, Paradise Valley Community College, Parkland College, Prince George's Community College, San Diego Mesa College, Santa Ana College, Santa Monica College, Southwestern College, Suffolk County Community College, Three Rivers Community College, Tidewater Community College, Walters State Community College, Waubonsee Community College
Total: 53

- Schools Using the Name *Women('s) and Gender Studies or Gender and Women('s) Studies*
  Bluegrass Community and Technical College, Brookdale Community College, Borough of Manhattan Community College, Casper College, Central Arizona College, Cerritos College, Evergreen Valley College, Greenfield Community College, Hostos Community College, Inver Hills Community College, Jefferson Community and Technical College, Kingsborough Community College, Mercer County Community College, Montgomery College, Monterey Peninsula College, Nassau Community College, Northampton County Area Community College, North Seattle College, Oakton Community College, Ohlone College, Pima Community College, Portland Community College, Raritan Valley Community College, Richard J. Daley College, Sacramento City College, Seattle Central College, Shoreline Community College, Sierra College, South Mountain Community College, Tompkins Cortland Community College, Triton College, Walla Walla Community College, West Valley College
  Total: 33

- Schools Using the Name *Gender Studies*
  Big Bend Community College, Century College, Grand Rapids Community College, Herkimer County Community College, Rose State College
  Total: 5

- Schools Using the Name *Gender and Sexuality Studies*
  Anne Arundel Community College, College of Lake County, Monroe Community College, Saddleback College
  Total: 4

- **Schools Using Other Names**
  University of Wisconsin Colleges (Gender, Sexuality and Women's Studies),
  Pasadena City College (Gender, Ethnicity, and Multicultural Studies), Wilber
  Wright College (Women's, Gender, and Sexuality Studies)
  Total: 3

In addition to the use of different names at different institutions, we found that in many cases there was a history of different names *within* an institution. Through the course of our research it became clear that a number of schools had changed their program/department name in the previous decade, which can obviously create confusion—particularly if students are getting information from advisors or other staff that may not be familiar with WGS or naming conventions within the field. We found that name changes at individual institutions—changing the name of a program from women's studies to women's and gender studies, for example—were made to reflect the evolution of scholarship within the field, and often with the intention of increasing enrollment or course offerings. For example, in 2009 Anne Arundel Community College (AACC) in Maryland changed the name of its program from women's studies to gender and sexuality studies. The motivation at AACC was twofold: changing the name would hopefully encourage more males to take the courses and allow a wider range of course offerings. Under the original name, AACC's curriculum oversight committee resisted the inclusion of new courses like Introduction to LGBT Studies and Introduction to Masculinity Studies. For those knowledgeable in the field, it makes complete sense that these two courses are part of women's studies, but to many, offering a course on masculinity under women's studies seemed counter-intuitive. At AACC changing their name to the Gender and Sexuality Studies Program was meant to prevent that confusion and avoid bureaucratic hurdles.

While changing program and department names makes sense for these and other reasons, it made our research difficult—particularly when the change was recent, and particularly when all of the markers of a program's identity were not consistently changed—and we imagine this must make it difficult for students too. We found many examples where naming was inconsistent within one institution. For example, a program that currently uses the name gender and women's studies might still label courses in the catalog with the prefixes WST or WOM, relics of the program's previous iteration as women's studies. Similarly, we found places where different names were used in different places on a school's website. For example, at Bluegrass Community and Technical College (BCTC) in Kentucky the program is called the Women's & Gender Studies Program, but the description of options students can select within their Associate of Arts degree uses another name: the AA with Women's Studies Focus Area ("Women's & Gender Studies"). Like BCTC, two different names were used at Bergen Community College in New Jersey. The title for the WGS page on Bergen's website is the Women and Gender Studies Program, but the text on that same page uses the name women's studies as does the linked brochure ("Women and Gender Studies Program"). The credential offered at Bergen also uses the name women's studies: the AA in Liberal Arts, Women's Studies Option. Similarly, at North Seattle College in Washington the program is called Gender and Women's Studies (sometimes Gender & Women's Studies), their introductory course is Introduction to Gender Studies and their course prefix is WMN ("Gender & Women's Studies"). Some might dismiss minor differences in naming as inconsequential, but these details should be considered in light of recent changes in how students acquire information about their academic options. Students now get more of their information from school websites, many institutions are moving away from paper to searchable digital catalogs, and school websites increasingly rely on search engines for navigation rather than URLs, which magnifies the problems with naming inconsistencies.

We should note that in some cases inconsistencies in naming within an institution were intentional—the use of different names was based on enrollment strategies, pedagogical perspectives, or views of the field. For example, when AACC changed its program name from women's studies to gender and sexuality studies they did not change the name of their courses, so the foundational course in the program remained Introduction to Women's Studies. This was done intentionally because, rather than reformatting the foundational course to incorporate gender studies and sexuality studies, AACC chose to add two additional introductory courses: Introduction to Masculinity Studies and Introduction to LGBT Studies. Here the inconsistency in naming was the product of a well-reasoned strategy related to enrollment and course offerings. Nevertheless, inconsistency in naming across institutions, within one institution over time, and within one institution at one time, created confusion for us as researchers, and likely creates ongoing confusion for students.

## Categories Used in the Database

Our database includes schools that have a WGS presence at their institution with a range reflected by three categories. Category A includes schools that offer a credential in WGS. The credential takes different forms depending on the number of required credits and the degree conventions at the institution and includes schools that offer one or more of the following: 1. an associate's degree in WGS (for example, Cabrillo College in California has an AA degree in women's studies and Monterey Peninsula College, also in California, offers an AA degree in gender and women's studies); 2. a focus area for WGS within a broader associate's degree (for example, Brookdale Community College in New Jersey offers a Women's and Gender Studies Option within their AA in humanities, and Northampton Community College in Pennsylvania offers a Women's and Gender Studies Concentration within their AA in liberal arts); 3. a stand-alone credential other than an associate's degree including certificates or letters of recognition in WGS (the following examples demonstrate the range in terms of naming and required credit hours: Anne Arundel Community College in Maryland offers both a 9-credit Letter of Recognition and a 15-credit Certificate in gender and sexuality studies, Ohlone College in California offers a 12-credit Certificate of Accomplishment in gender and women's studies, San Diego Mesa College in California offers a 15-credit Certificate of Performance in women's studies, and Three Rivers Community College in Connecticut offers a 21-credit Certificate in women's studies).

Category B includes schools where there are multiple WGS courses under some cohesive organizational structure, but no credentialing opportunity in WGS specifically—though there may be credentialing options in a related field. For example, Anoka-Ramsey Community College in Minnesota has a program designator, women's studies; separate course prefix, WOST; and offers a variety of WGS courses including Introduction to Women's and Gender Studies, Biology of Women, Gender in Society, Psychology of Women, Women in American Culture, Women in a Global Perspective, and History of Women in Modern America. Anoka-Ramsey does not offer a credential in WGS, but in fall of 2018 they launched a new Certificate in diversity studies, which includes coursework in WGS. Nassau Community College in New York, also in Category B, has the Women and Gender Studies Project described as a "multidisciplinary project emphasizing diversity" that "serves hundreds of students each academic year" with "[s]ponsoring departments [that] include Art, Communications, Economics, English, History, Health/PED, Library, and Sociology" ("Interdisciplinary Studies"). Nassau does not offer a credential in WGS, but it has a program coordinator and a strong campus presence that includes a course prefix, WST, and the following WGS course offerings: Introduction to Women's Studies, Gender in Popular Culture, The Goddess in World Religions, Women's Issues in Global Context, and Philosophy of Sex and Gender.

Category C includes schools that offer Introduction to Women's Studies (or Introduction to Gender Studies, etc.) and at least one other gender-focused course, but do not have a WGS structure or credentialing option in WGS. For example, Tidewater Community College (TCC) in Virginia offers three WGS courses including Introduction to Women's Studies, Women's Health, and Sociology of Gender. However, there is no unifying structure for WGS—these three classes are offered under different departments. TCC also has a Women's Center. Established in 1993, it "offers comprehensive, specialized services to educate, empower, enhance and engage women so they can define, pursue and achieve their academic and personal goals" ("The Women's Center - Student Support Services"). These services include the Women Inspiring Self-Empowerment (W.I.S.E.) program which "[p]repares students for leadership and civic engagement with mentorship and service projects." The Women's Center also organizes events for Women's History Month and "develops special programming for Intimate Partner Violence in October, campaigns for Sexual Assault Awareness Month in April and hosts the annual Women's Leadership Breakfast each spring" ("The Women's Center - Student Support Services"). Big Bend Community College in Washington does not have a unifying WGS structure. As with other schools in Category C, it offers WGS courses housed in different departments, including: Gender Studies (under humanities), Women's Literature (under English), Women in American History (under history), and Gender and Power (under sociology). Kansas City Kansas Community College also offers WGS courses housed in different departments: Introduction to Women's Studies, Men and Masculinities, and Women in Religion are all offered under humanities; Women in Literature is offered under English. Certainly, a lot of schools that now are now in Category A and Category B— institutions that offer WGS credentials and/or have a WGS program or structure—started out by offering one or two WGS courses in various disciplines on campus. Schools in Category C that want to develop their WGS presence could benefit from a sharing of strategies and information from schools in Categories A and B. The process that other schools have used to develop and articulate a more robust WGS presence, and the explanation of how a WGS program and/or credentialing option benefits students, the institution, and the larger community many help those schools in Category C build on what they already have.

## Community Colleges with a WGS Presence

- Schools in Category A

    Anne Arundel Community College, Bergen Community College, Bluegrass Community and Technical College, Brookdale Community College, Borough of Manhattan Community College, Cabrillo College, Casper College, Central Lakes College, Century College, Cerritos College, Chandler-Gilbert Community College, City College of San Francisco, Clark Community College, College of Lake County, College of Southern Nevada, Community College of Baltimore County, Cosumnes River College, Cuyahoga Community College, De Anza Community College, Evergreen Valley College, Folsom Lake College, Foothill College, Fresno City College, Greenfield Community College, Gulf Coast Community College, Harold Washington College, Hostos Community College, Howard Community College, Hudson County Community College, Inver Hills Community College, Jefferson Community and Technical College, Kingsborough Community College, Mesa Community College, Minneapolis Community and Technical College, Monroe Community College, Monterey Peninsula College, Montgomery College, Normandale Community College, Northampton County Area Community College, Norwalk Community College, Oakton Community College, Ohlone College, Onondaga Community College, Paradise Valley Community College, Parkland College, Pasadena City College, Pima

Community College, Portland Community College, Raritan Valley Community College, Rose State College, Sacramento City College, Saddleback College, San Diego Mesa College, Santa Ana College, Santa Monica College, Shoreline Community College, Sierra College, Southwestern College, Suffolk County Community College, Three Rivers Community College, Tompkins Cortland Community College, Triton College, University of Wisconsin Colleges, Walters State Community College, West Valley College, Wilbur Wright College
Total: 66

- ## Schools in Category B
  Anoka-Ramsey Community College, Berkeley City College, Bucks County Community College, Central Arizona College, Chemeketa Community College, Clatsop Community College, Community College of Allegheny County, Doña Ana Community College, Front Range Community College, Gateway Community College, Grand Rapids Community College, Hawkeye Community College, Lane Community College, Las Positas College, Mercer County Community College, Nassau Community College, North Seattle College, Prince George's Community College, Seattle Central College, South Mountain Community College, Walla Walla Community College
  Total: 21

- ## Schools in Category C
  Big Bend Community College, College of Southern Maryland, Community College of Philadelphia, Eastern Shore Community College, El Camino College, Herkimer County Community College, Kansas City Kansas Community College, Northern Virginia Community College, Richard J. Daley College, Tidewater Community College, Waubonsee Community College
  Total: 11

## Region[6]

| Region | Schools | Number of Schools |
|--------|---------|-------------------|
| Northeast | New England (Connecticut, Maine, Massachusetts, New Hampshire, Rhode Island, and Vermont) | 3 |
| | Mid Atlantic (New Jersey, New York, and Pennsylvania) | 18 |
| | Total for Northeast | 21 |
| Midwest | East North Central (Illinois, Indiana, Michigan, Ohio, and Wisconsin) | 11 |
| | West North Central (Iowa, Kansas, Minnesota, Missouri, Nebraska, North Dakota, and South Dakota) | 8 |
| | Total for Midwest | 19 |
| South | South Atlantic (Delaware, Florida, Georgia, Maryland, North Carolina, South Carolina, Virginia, District of Columbia, and West Virginia) | 11 |
| | East South Central (Alabama, Kentucky, Mississippi, and Tennessee) | 3 |
| | West South Central (Arkansas, Louisiana, Oklahoma, and Texas) | 1 |
| | Total for South Region | 15 |
| West | Mountain (Arizona, Colorado, Idaho, Montana, Nevada, New Mexico, Utah, and Wyoming) | 10 |
| | Pacific (Alaska, California, Hawaii, Oregon, and Washington) | 33 |
| | Total for West | 43 |

## Making Connections: Extracurricular and Co-Curricular Programming in WGS

In addition to tracking which community colleges offered WGS credentials and WGS courses, our research included an analysis of the extracurricular and co-curricular events that contribute to the presence of WGS on campus. We found that WGS programs and departments were often a cen-

---

6    We used regions and divisions as defined by the US Census Bureau.

ter of diversity, equity, and inclusion work on their campus. It is clear that most schools view the work of WGS as extending outside the classroom to activities and events that involve the campus and wider community. We found evidence of various different types of extracurricular and co-curricular programming that included WGS-focused academic conferences, panel presentations, discussions, film showings, and workshops. These events and activities demonstrated an attention to the key debates and theories within the field and often focused on bringing national conversations into a local discussion. Many schools offered workshops designed to empower students by creating support networks and addressing structures of power and privilege. We found WGS to be thriving spaces of public pedagogy where events and activities provided both WGS students and the larger community space to discuss and analyze issues related to gender and sexuality through understandings of structured inequality, social hierarchy, privilege, and intersectionality.

Several of the schools in our database organize WGS-related conferences giving students opportunities to attend and participate in academic presentations and providing space for the sharing of ideas. For example, the Women's and Gender Studies Program at Oakton Community College in Illinois sponsors a biennial Women's and Gender Studies Conference that features a keynote speaker and "scholarly and creative work by feminist activists, writers, scientists, visual and performing artists, and scholars" ("Women's and Gender Studies Conference"). Presenters include faculty as well as undergraduate and graduate students. The focus of their spring 2019 conference, *Intersect This!: Poverty and Privilege Through the Lens of Gender and Sexuality*, was "the effects of poverty and privilege as they are experienced through intersecting systems of racism, sexism, classism, transphobia, homophobia and other forms of oppression within the current political and cultural climate" ("Women's and Gender Studies Conference"). The Women's and Gender Studies Conference at Oakton provides community college students important opportunities: student presenters gain experience in writing a proposal, applying to a call for papers, and presenting at an academic conference—rare opportunities for community college students. The larger Oakton community also benefits because the conferences allows space to share ideas, create conversations, and develop and contribute to scholarship within the field.

A number of community colleges have women's centers and at many schools these spaces serve as the center of programming around women's and gender-related topics and provide services that help their students succeed. For example, Northern Virginia Community College's (NOVA) Women's Center was established in 2008 through the work of faculty, staff, and students: "The focus groups, co-facilitated by student leaders, surveyed international students, parents, nontraditional aged students and student leaders on campus [and] determined there was a need for co-op childcare opportunities, workshops on various topics related to health and well-being, and space designated for conversations among women or for quiet reflection between classes" ("History"). The center was renamed The Jean Braden Center for Women, Gender and Social Equity, in 2017, to better reflect the inclusive mission: "This change both honors the original commitments and concerns of the founders of the Center while also reflecting the dynamic cultural changes within the field of gender studies and the needs of our student and community populations" ("History"). The center has an internal governing board made up of faculty, staff, and students as well as an external advisory council comprised of representatives from outside organizations. The center provides programming, resources, and referrals. An example of its programing is an annual mentoring event they co-sponsor called Women Helping Women that focuses on empowering students to achieve their goals. A 2017 student participant explained how the event builds community and support structures: "I thought I was alone in my struggles but looking around this room I see that I am surrounded by others just like me" ("7th Annual"). The 2018 Women Helping Women event, *Together! Finding Your Passion, Power and Place*, included ninety-one attendees and featured a session where former students "shared stories about how they overcame personal struggles and persisted in graduating and continuing on their academic and career paths" and explained "how they used NOVA resources such as the Women's Mentoring program ... faculty, staff and most importantly each other for support" ("Women Helping").

Lane Community College in Oregon offers a number of events and services through their Gender Equity Center. They define their mission using the language of WGS, focusing on themes of inclusion, intersectionality, and dialogue:

The Lane Community College Gender Equity Center exists for students, staff, and faculty and is focused on supporting an inclusive campus environment where all genders and sexual identities are valued and supported. We promote the exploration of the social construction of gender and how gender intersects with race, ethnicity, class, sex, sexual orientation, ability, age, nationality, and belief systems. The Gender Equity Center operates from a foundation of Brave dialogue where all ideas rooted in inquiry and learning are welcome. ("Gender Equity Center")

Among their services they provide LGBTQ support and advocacy, resources and workshops on healthy masculinity, and gender inclusive bathrooms. They also make referrals to campus services and local service organizations. One of their primary initiatives is the Women in Transition program whose mission is to empower "women to become economically self-sufficient and improve their lives through access to education" and which offers two courses: Life Transitions and Career and Life Planning ("Women in Transition"). In 2016, they celebrated the 30th anniversary of the Women in Transition program.

Many of the WGS programs and departments in our database participate in national events and initiatives that create co-curricular activities for WGS students and help raise awareness on campus around topics like feminist activism, domestic violence, and women's bodies and sexuality. For example, Clatsop Community College in Oregon has sponsored events including The Vagina Monologues, The Clothesline Project, and One Billion Rising. At many schools—like Kingsborough Community College in New York, Jefferson Community and Technical College in Kentucky, and Montgomery College in Maryland—WGS programs help their institutions mark Women's History Month. For example, in 2018 San Diego Mesa College in California hosted its 7th annual Gracia Molina de Pick Feminist Lecture Series, an event that brings together members of the college community to remember Molina de Pick's feminist legacy. In 2018, the event featured historian and author Maria Garcia who discussed the history and contributions of Chicanas in San Diego communities. We also found that a number of WGS programs and departments organize film series. For example, in 2018 the Women's and Gender Studies Department at Cerritos College in California marked its 31st annual celebration of Women's History Month with events including a film festival entitled *Feminists' World: Celebrating Transnational Feminisms through Fearless Females in Film* ("Women's History Month").

Many schools sponsor events that give students the opportunity to participate in larger national conversations and draw connections between course materials and the world outside the classroom. For example, in fall 2017 Greenfield Community College (GCC) in Massachusetts created a student group called Collective Voices, Common Ground. The group provides "a forum for discussing current social issues and bringing together students interested in activism on campus" (Copeland). Two students from the group, Sequoia Lebreux and Lu Vincent, created a #MeToo board on campus, using a physical space to create dialogue, share stories, and provide information about sexual assault and harassment. Vincent explained the motivation for creating space on campus to discuss the #MeToo movement saying, "This is a national, if not global thing that is alive right now, so we thought, let's see what's happening on our campus, how we can help represent this here" (qtd. in Copeland). Lebreux says the board allows for people to participate in whatever way is useful for them: "… we'd seen a lot of #MeToo campaigns where there were very personal statements. People are certainly welcome to do that, but this is a place where you don't have to do that … if you want to leave your mark, that's a great first step in bridging that gap between never talking about something, to moving into a space … Maybe we won't talk about it today, but we're getting there!" (qtd. in Copeland). Later that year, the school organized an academic discussion entitled *The #MeToo Movement: A Panel Discussion*.

The events and activities we detailed above are just some of the many examples we found in our research of WGS at two-year schools. Indeed, a significant part of the presence of WGS on community college campuses is the use of programming as public pedagogy: the events and activities encourage discussion, debate, and dissent and promote civic engagement and community through the cultivation of empathy and understanding. Extracurricular and co-curricular events sponsored by WGS help engage students, allowing them to make connections between their coursework and their lives outside of the classroom, but this programming has a wider reach. These events enrich the campus and the larger community and are an important marker of the value of WGS programs to their respective institutions.

## II. Personal Stories in WGS at Community Colleges

The information we have included in our database is useful in identifying trends and giving a sense of similarities and differences in WGS programs across the country. However, our research indicates that the heart of these programs and departments is *people*. Researching WGS programs at community colleges in the United States, we came across a similar story over and over again: the presence of WGS at community colleges was usually the result of a small group of passionate people who believed in the value of WGS and whose dedication to these programs was what kept them alive and thriving. It is the dedication of these individuals—who are usually working with limited resources, going above and beyond what their job requires of them, and doing work that is often undervalued or under-recognized—that's fueling WGS at community colleges.

We want to honor this work and recognize the dedication of the faculty and staff at two-year schools who have created and maintained the WGS courses, credentials, programs, and events that we discussed above by concluding our essay with the words of few of these individuals. To include these voices, we turn to the dissertation of one of the co-authors. Stoehr completed her dissertation, *The Present Status of Women's and Gender Studies Programs at Community Colleges,* in 2016. As part of the research for her dissertation, she interviewed eight professors who teach WGS courses at community colleges in the United States.[7] These professors' stories demonstrate a broad range of experiences in teaching WGS at two-year schools. Some came from institutions with well-developed WGS programs or departments while others'

---

7    To maintain anonymity as part of Stoehr's research design, participants used pseudonyms and the schools were not named. For more information on the data collection and findings, see Chapter 3 in her dissertation.

schools only offered a few WGS courses. We include excerpts from these interviews below in order to provide a different vantage point from which to assess the status of WGS at community colleges and to paint a richer picture of the feminist commitment to social justice that undergirds so much of this work.

## Why Do Faculty Teach WGS at Community Colleges?

The participants in Stoehr's dissertation research discussed the reasons why they teach women's and gender studies at community colleges. For Lisa, an instructor and former chair of the WGS program at her school on the West Coast, teaching WGS became an expression of her feminist ethic. Lisa's school was among the first community colleges to establish a women's studies department—in 1975—and the first to offer an AA degree in women's studies. Lisa talks about how her work teaching WGS brought together various strains of activism in her life. She says, "I started doing 'Third world liberation poetry' in the mid-1950s, and my feminist consciousness deepened as I became a mother.... I then started teaching a violence against women course and doing rape prevention work at my institution's Medical Center" (62). She describes her teaching in activist language saying, "It is a political commitment, and a devotion to social justice issues. I also have a working-class consciousness, so I love working with these types of students. I feel a real devotion to feminism" (62).

Susan, an instructor and chair of her WGS program at a school on the West Coast, also talks about teaching WGS at a community college as an expression of a political consciousness and as a deliberate decision to engage in social justice work through education. She says,

> I am definitely at the community college level because of being able to work with a broader base of students, specifically those students from under-represented groups. After I graduated with my Bachelor of Arts degree in Feminist Studies, my goal was to be involved in education for critical consciousness. That was my version of changing the world—looking at the role of education in

not only producing workers, but also community education. It is
also about labeling what I teach "women's studies." (75-76)

For many faculty in WGS at two-year schools, providing the benefits of feminist analysis to community college students, students who disproportionately
come from historically marginalized groups, fuels the motivation for their
work.

Angela, professor and chair of her WGS program at a school on the West
Coast, also emphasized the connection to social justice work. She explains,
"I get to teach students how to think critically about structural inequalities,
whether it be class, race, sexuality, ability, or gender. Students start to recognize that they are not alone in their life experiences. This is social justice work.
I teach women's studies at a community college because that is the choice that
I have made, not because I am not qualified to teach anywhere else" (125).
Elizabeth, an assistant professor who teaches WGS at a school in the Midwest, echoes this sentiment, explaining that she feels like her work makes a
real difference in the lives of the students. The WGS program at Elizabeth's
school was established in 1998 and offers an AA degree with a concentration
in women's and gender studies. Elizabeth says, "I love teaching. I love working with students and getting that 'aha' moment" (76). She explains, "I feel
like my work is a work of empowerment. I can actually support students before they give up hope that they can actually make a difference as well. Here
are the tools you need, and you can do whatever you want to do" (76). Dana,
who is an associate professor and chair of the WGS program at her school in
the Midwest, says "I feel that I have a real-life impact on my students. This is
education changing people's lives. I feel the work I do is social justice work"
(76). Her school's WGS program, established in 1985, offers two options for
credentials in WGS: women's studies can be selected as an emphasis within
the AA in liberal arts, or students can earn a Certificate in women's studies.

The connections between teaching and social justice work evidenced in
these responses exemplify the sentiments that we hear repeatedly in our informal conversations with WGS faculty at community colleges. We also found
this theme evidenced in the documents, syllabi, and events highlighted on the
websites we analyzed during our research. Jane, an associate professor who
is the coordinator of the WGS program at her community college, captures

a theme we found consistently throughout our work. She says, "Teaching is activism" (76). WGS professors at community colleges view what they do as social justice work both because the subject matter of the field focuses on issues of social hierarchy and oppression, but also because they have chosen to work with community college students, a demographic that historically has had less access to higher education.

## Why Do Students Take WGS Courses at Community Colleges, and What Do They Get from These Courses? What Are the Benefits to the Institution?

Dee, a WGS instructor from a school in the Midwest, notes that many students are drawn to WGS courses because of their interest in social justice work. The WGS department at her school—established in 1973—offers a Certificate in women's studies. Dee says: "I think that students enroll in women's and gender courses at my institution because of their strong interest in social activism, anti-oppression work, and personal growth" (60); "Women's studies is often the destination for students wanting to study anti-racism work, queer studies, poverty, classism, and social justice movements" (72).

Stoehr's participants emphasized the value of WGS coursework for personal growth and self-understanding. Dana says, "A lot of the students find the material in women's studies courses to be compelling and new, and really helpful for understanding their own lives" (65). Susan also emphasizes this transformative potential for WGS students. She says,

> This is all about transformative pedagogy, and education for liberation. That is how students are reflecting in our classes. Women's studies transforms a sense of possibility for students and for their world so that they can be involved in their communities. We see that students, particularly in other representative groups of higher education, have higher GPAs and increased levels of academic success at our college than students who have not taken a women's studies course before. I think that women's studies have taught students to be more engaged in their own education. (66)

Sometimes the transformational potential comes from creating space for dialogue and understanding. Elizabeth explains,

> Some students come in with no knowledge of the actual terms and/or a certain level of bias. The goal for me at that point is to say that I am not trying to change your view but am just trying to have you be open to the possibility that other people have different views, and to respect those differences. I can hold my view, and also listen to a number of different views without feeling like I need to change you. I just need to understand and respect your difference just as you can learn to understand and respect mine. There is less need from students to push back when taking this approach. You try and get them to simply have an intellectual understanding of the issues and people's perspectives and see that both views are valid on some level. Students can see that there are more nuances than maybe they thought there were. (86)

Susan and Elizabeth emphasize a theme that we hear consistently in our conversations with WGS professors and that we see reflected in the learning objectives for many of the programs: education should connect the personal and political. WGS classrooms allow a space for students to make connections between their own lives and the course materials. The students' lived experiences—and the opinions and beliefs that those lived experiences generate—should be considered and analyzed as part of the content of the course.

Many of the participants pointed to the effect of WGS courses on the campus culture and climate. Jane explains the importance of providing space to talk about gender and inequality. She says, "Students have never thought about these issues before" (62), and "Students are finding words for what they are experiencing, like discrimination" (71). Jane also points to effects outside of the individual WGS classroom. The WGS program at her school, which offers a Certificate in women's and gender studies, was created about a decade ago. Since that time, she thinks the WGS program has affected the larger campus community: "Conversations on our campus are now happening differently. Faculty are talking more, and senior faculty are also introducing activism projects into their courses.... Students are finding their voice."

(62). She explains that "the moment that students find the language they need, and affirm their experiences is so important" (62). Dee points out how giving students the opportunity to develop that language can benefit the institution and the community. She says, "Our students tend to be active in naming issues they see on campus supported by the work in our courses, so issues are challenged and we tend to bring in events and programming that involve students and employees in learning more, raising awareness, and partnering with community agencies" (88). Angela has also observed the ripple effects of WGS courses at her institution. She says: "The faculty that teach the women's studies courses and the courses themselves increase the number of safe spaces for lots of different kinds of students. I have seen a huge shift in our students over the last 15 years in terms of their attitudes with things like LGBT issues. We are having larger campus discussions about inclusivity, sexual orientation, and disabilities" (63).

WGS programs and departments at community colleges are often the center of diversity, equity, and social justice work at the school. The academic expertise of the WGS faculty and the enthusiasm of WGS students are rich sources for anti-oppression and consciousness-raising work, and this work can help the institution address equity gaps, cultivate a more welcoming campus climate for all students, and position the college as a leader for social justice advocacy in the larger community. WGS programs at community colleges benefit the students who take the courses, and they benefit the larger community through the focused training and expertise that prepare WGS students to graduate as more engaged citizens and contributors to their career fields. However, WGS programs also have a benefit outside of the classroom in helping make their institutions and communities more just, welcoming, and equitable. These intangible benefits of WGS programs and departments cannot be quantified like course success rates or numbers of conferred degrees, but the benefits are nevertheless significant and meaningful to the students, the institution, and the community.

## III. Conclusion: The Future of WGS at Community Colleges

The transformational potential of the WGS classroom, and the value to students—and particularly community college students—was a key message voiced by the interviewees in Stoehr's dissertation, and a message that we found consistently throughout our research. Susan articulated the sentiments of so many who teach WGS at community colleges. She says,

> Women's studies is transformative and has the potential to genuinely transform people's lived experiences, their lives, and their sense of possibility for themselves and the world.... We help our students take ownership of their lives and their decisions. This interdisciplinary discipline allows us to address the full experience of people's lives. For us to be able to do that in our work as educators is profound. (72)

For WGS professors the classroom is full of potential and promise—both inspiring and energizing. However, many WGS professors at community colleges contrast their experience working with students with the difficulties of navigating the administrative elements of their jobs. Many WGS communities at two-year schools are chronically precarious. In the "Preface to the 2016 Edition" of her book, *Not for Profit: Why Democracy Needs the Humanities*, Martha Nussbaum explains the larger context, and while her argument focuses on the humanities, the spirit of her comments captures the struggle for many who teach WGS at two-year schools:

> The humanities have been threatened since their very beginning. Socratic questioning is unsettling, and people in power often prefer docile followers to independent citizens able to think for themselves. Furthermore, a lively imagination, alert to the situations, desires, and sufferings of others is a taxing achievement; moral obtuseness is so much easier.... The battle for responsible democracy and alert citizenship is always difficult and uncertain. But it is both urgent and winnable, and the humanities are a large part of winning it. (xxiii)

This precariousness of WGS at community colleges is evident in the places like Prince George's Community College in Maryland, Herkimer County Community College in New York, and Front Range Community College in Colorado where a credential in WGS had previously been offered, but where the AA or Certificate has since been deactivated, and it is evident in our informal conversations with WGS professors, many of whom recount the ever-present threat of having their programs cut and/or losing funding in the face of new models of community college education that value instrumental and vocational skills training over courses that emphasize critical thinking, civic engagement, and personal growth.

However, the precariousness we found in some places should not overshadow the excitement and growth we have found at other schools. We found that many existing programs are expanding, and new programs are being created. For example, in 2017 Borough of Manhattan Community College (BMCC) began offering an AA in gender and women's studies. Brianne Waychoff, one of the coordinators of the program said, "At BMCC, students have responded enthusiastically to women's studies courses, and now they can focus their interest in a more organized course of study, one that supports their higher education and career goals" ("BMCC Offers"). Wilbur Wright College in Chicago presents another encouraging example. In fall 2017, they began offering Introduction to Women's and Gender Studies, and in spring 2018 they began offering a credentialing option for students to demonstrate specific training in women's, gender, and sexuality studies (WGSS): students who take Introduction to Women's and Gender Studies and three additional WGSS-related courses receive a designation in women's, gender, and sexuality studies on their transcript. In some cases, schools whose WGS programs had been cut have been able to rebound. In 2015, Cabrillo College received a $166,000 grant from the Baskin Foundation to revive its women's studies program (Guzman). The grant was part of a larger effort by the Baskin Foundation to support women's studies at community colleges and helped Cabrillo rebuild after budget cuts had reduced their course offerings by half in 2010 (Guzman). The executive director of the foundation explained the reason for their support for WGS programs at community colleges: "I really want to send that message that women's educational equality has to include feminist analytical thought as a legitimate category of academics in order for us to progress as a society" (qtd. in Guzman).

WGS at community colleges and the feminist analytical thought it cultivates provide important transformational potential for its students, and as such, it functions as a significant space of resistance within higher education. The curriculum and pedagogy of WGS can be an important part of efforts to remind community colleges of their social justice mandate. Levin argues that the neoliberal paradigm that has swept over community college administrations is "antithetical to justice for disadvantaged populations," and, he emphasizes, there is a lot at stake: "For the community college, the economic and competitive orientation over the past twenty-five years has skewed the access mission and compromised quality by treating students as economic commodities while the institution increasingly served markets in favor of communities" (193). The students at community colleges are often students who have had fewer advantages in their education. Consequently, they are the ones that need a feminist classroom the most. For this reason, it is important to recognize the value of WGS at community colleges, to strengthen and bolster these courses and programs, and to create community across two-year schools to help this important work grow and spread.

# Works Cited

"BMCC Offers Gender and Women's Studies Major." *BMCC | About BMCC,* www.bmcc.cuny.edu/news/news.jsp?id=13577.

Copeland, Christine. "Collective Voices, Common Ground." *Greenfield Community College,* 9 Mar. 2018, www.gcc.mass.edu/marketing/2018/02/09/collective-voices-common-ground/.

"Gender & Women Studies." *North Seattle College,* northseattle.edu/programs/gender-women-studies.

"Gender Equity Center." *Lane Community College,* www.lanecc.edu/gec.

Gollihar, Lindsy A. *Hyperlinked Scholarship: Exploring the New Existence of www.ccwsw.org, the Community College Women's Studies Web.* 2008, San Francisco State University, Master of Arts Creative Work Project Narrative.

Guzman, Kara Meyberg. "Baskin Foundation Grant Revives Cabrillo's Women's Studies." *Santa Cruz Sentinel,* 4 Feb. 2015, www.santacruzsentinel.com/2015/02/04/baskin-foundation-grant-revives-cabrillos-womens-studies/.

"History." *Northern Virginia Community College,* www.nvcc.edu/alexandria/women/history.html.

"Interdisciplinary Studies." *Nassau Community College,* https://collegecatalog.ncc.edu/current/programs/interdisciplinary_studies/index.html

Levin, John S. *Nontraditional Students and Community Colleges: The Conflict of Justice and Neoliberalism*. Palgrave Macmillan, 2007.

Nussbaum, Martha. *Not for Profit: Why Democracy Needs the Humanities*. Princeton UP, 2010.

"The 7th Annual Gracia Molina de Pick Feminist Lecture Series Featured Renowned Author Maria Garcia." *Latest News*, 16 March 2018, http://www.sdmesa.edu/_resources/newsroom/posts/gracia_molina_lecture_series.php

"7th Annual Women Helping Women." *Intercom*, 24 Apr. 2017, blogs.nvcc.edu/intercom/2017/04/17/7th-annual-women-helping-women/.

Stoehr, Alissa. *The Present Status of Women's and Gender Studies at Community Colleges*. Diss. Iowa State University, 2016. Web. 21 Dec. 2018.

"Women and Gender Studies Conference: *Intersect This! Poverty and Privilege Through the Lens of Gender and Sexuality*: Call for Proposals." https://crgw.wiscweb.wisc.edu/wp-content/uploads/sites/378/2018/12/CALL-FOR-PROPOSALS-2019-.pdf

"Women and Gender Studies Program." *Bergen Community College*, bergen.edu/academics/academic-divisions-departments/interdisciplinary/ws/.

"Women Helping Women 2018." *NOVAinsider*, insider.nvcc.edu/2018/04/23/women-helping-women-2018/.

"Women's & Gender Studies." *Bluegrass Community and Technical College*, bluegrass.kctcs.edu/education-training/programs/womens-studies/index.aspx.

"Women's Center." *LaGuardia Community College, New York*, `www.laguardia.edu/womencenter/.

"The Women's Center - Student Support Services." *Tidewater Community College*, www.tcc.edu/student-services/personal-support/womens-center.

"Women's History Month Film Festival." *Cerritos College*. http://cms.cerritos.edu/ws/_includes/docs/whm_2018_film04.pdf

# Student Voices: Prnaya Green, Anne Arundel Community College

Arnold, Maryland

Prnaya Green is a gender and sexuality studies major at Anne Arundel Community College (AACC). Once she graduates from AACC she plans to transfer to a WGS program at a four-year school. Prnaya is involved in her community in various ways. She is fiercely passionate about pushing back against inequality as it relates to race, gender, sexuality, and socio-economic status. Currently, she is focused on improving the relationship between law enforcement and policed communities and has completed several ride-alongs with Anne Arundel County police. She is working on ways to share these experiences with people who haven't had this opportunity for various reasons. Prnaya also views her childcare business as community service and uses her interactions with children to encourage acceptance, to model resistant discourses, and to provide support for families. Her work is fueled by her belief that the personal is political.

*How did your WGS course(s) help you in your private life (interpersonal relationships, parenting, self-esteem, self-love, etc.)?*

"[Introduction to Women's Studies] brought the strength of my voice to a new level. Before I took the course, I had a lot of anger to yell at the world about, but after the course I wasn't just angry and yelling about my pain. I was a passionate Black woman armed with experience, statistics, and credible sources to reinforce everything that she wanted to share. It enabled me to heal, learn, teach, and change the space I take up in my community."

*Would you recommend the course(s) to other students? If so, why?*

"I would TOTALLY recommend this course to other students. Women need to know that the idealized images that they see of themselves are present because they are profitable, not because they are perfect. People of color need to know that their absence in textbooks and the media has nothing to do with an inadequacy within themselves. Lastly, everyone needs to be challenged and held accountable for the roles we play in racism, sexism, heterosexism, able-ism, etc."

*Why did you decide to major in WGS?*

"I decided to major in WGS because I was beyond tired of men touching me without my permission. I was determined to figure out why they were so comfortable and allowed to exercise autonomy over MY body. I needed a powerful way to fight back without physically fighting each man who violated me. Also, as I adjusted to adulthood, I began feeling uncomfortable with the roles assigned to my gender (e.g. submission and silence)."

*What are your career and/or activist plans?*

"At this point in my life, my goal is to educate my community in traditional classrooms and in homes. I continually see how gaps within our societal institutions cause and perpetuate oppression, so my work is centered around filling that gap with unbiased information. In fact, I have created a workshop that focuses on racial injustice in America and teaches participants how to realize and combat their own biases."

# Curriculum Transformation in Community Colleges: Twenty Years Later

Genevieve Carminati

The *Women's Studies Quarterly* (*WSQ*) 1996 fall/winter double-issue would likely surprise many in the discipline today, with its special spotlight on *Curriculum Transformation in Community Colleges: Focus on Introductory Courses* (Fiol-Matta). It might seem unexpected to those in both current two-year and four-year women's and gender studies (WGS) programs that a respected journal of the field would turn over all its pages to such scholarship at community colleges, but it is to our benefit that they did. The history it tells shows the rigorous and extensive work undertaken in the 1980s and 1990s to transform courses in community colleges to include women and what was then termed "minorities." The text is a reminder to us now of how much we might lose if such work is curtailed or not supported, as many WGS programs continue to be reduced and threatened, especially at community colleges, because of economics and politics.

I was fortunate to discover this text a few years back on the shelf of our Montgomery College (MC) WGS program's Reading Room. (The journal can now be accessed electronically through JStor, the digital library.) Our Reading Room is not as grand as it sounds, as it is a small conference room that we are now made to share with others at the college. However, in the early days of our program, then called just Women's Studies, the space was exclusively ours, used for office hours, small meetings and discussions, student clubs and, well, reading, as its name suggests, feminists and gender texts. The period discussed in the *Quarterly* was a time of great hopefulness for the Women's Studies Reading Room at Montgomery College. Change to curriculum was being made that was essential and important. I can readily relate the glorious start of our WGS program at MC to the essays in this special edition of *WSQ* because Montgomery was one of the community college programs that participated in two curriculum transformation projects discussed in its pages: the Fund for Improvement of Post-Secondary Education (FIPSE) funded Maryland Community College Project in 1989, and the 1993 Ford Foundation Curriculum Mainstreaming and Teaching Initiative (CMTI) (Fiol-Matta "Editorial" 11-12).

As mentioned above, many WGS programs at community colleges are under threat or have been curtailed or eliminated. This past year, our own MC certificate program was reviewed for viability and is still in need of proving itself. Although I was told that retaining the program did not cost the college any money, there is concern about keeping a certificate curriculum on the books that wasn't producing sufficient graduates. Obviously, we want to enroll and graduate more students, and we gladly accept the challenge of growing our program, as that is our goal as well. However, the threat of the elimination of our certificate is as daunting and real for us as it is for other programs. At the same time, though, new WGS community college programs are continuing to be developed throughout the country. At a 2018 panel presentation of the Program Administration and Development (PAD) pre-conference at the National Women's Studies Association conference, some community college presenters reported only recently initiating programs and courses. One stated purpose for the PAD panel was to "compare our experiences and identify strategies for making our labor visible while navigating institutional red-tape that demands GWSS [Gender, Women's, and Sexuality Studies] remain palatable and often keeps us invisible" ("Becoming Visible"). Clearly, these newly created community college programs face real challenges and need the backing of those of us who have worked to keep WGS pertinent and vital at our colleges over the past years.

For long-standing programs like my own that are looking to inject some fresh breath into their curriculums, as well as those trying to defend their continued existence, or the just-developed or developing programs that could use some support and guidance, I highly recommend this *WSQ* double-issue. What does the text have to offer? At the very least, through the many examples it details, it can help in developing programs and courses; it can provide historic background that may seem amazingly current to our efforts today; and it can help in training faculty in feminist pedagogy and in diversifying course materials. (Unfortunately, the text does not seem to understand that gender and sexuality studies were fundamental to their work. The writers address "male minorities" and very occasionally "sexual preference," but the discipline in 1996 was still emergent, a definite shortcoming in making use of this text today.)

The text is divided into seven sections; their titles demonstrate its scholarly, visionary, and interdisciplinary approach: "Overview of Faculty Development Projects: What Happens, What Works"; "Consciousness, Experience, Pedagogy, and the Curriculum"; "In the Classroom: English, Speech, Dance"; "In the Classroom: Social Science and History"; "In the Classroom: Mathematics, Physics and Computers"; "Resources: Course Syllabi"; and "Resources: Bibliographies." I list all the section titles because although for the purposes of this essay I will focus on mostly the first two, readers might have interest in readings beyond those. Each section comprises from three to six essays, making for quite an extensive volume. Although never stated as a goal, these writings are blueprints for creating programs that future community college women's and gender studies faculty could follow. What some today might see as timid or even shortsighted, the writings of this text and its full impact as a whole should be read as a revolutionary recognition that nothing short of a full re-vision of community college academe was necessary if there were to be women's and gender studies programs. Of course, I am especially invested in learning the history of the work described, since Montgomery College is one of the colleges that the issue discusses.

As Betty Schmitz, recognized expert and consultant for the FIPSE project (Goldenberg and Parry 25), writes in the *Encyclopedia of Diversity in Education*:

> Curriculum transformation is the process of creating new course and curricula in all disciplines based on critical examination of knowledge about race, class, gender, disability, religion, class [sic], sexual orientation, gender expression, and nationality. Emerging as a systemic educational change strategy in the late 1960s, curriculum transformation addresses both content integration and classroom pedagogy and contributes to diversity initiatives aimed

at institutional transformation. Curriculum transformation also calls for the development of inclusive perspectives within inter-disciplinary fields, such as women's studies, U.S. ethnic stud-ies, queer studies, and disability studies. Teaching these studies across the curriculum ensures that all students graduate with comprehensive knowledge of diversity, complementing diversity requirements with focused study of difference in various fields. (589)

In Schmitz's definition, the correlation between the goals of curriculum transformation and the missions of WGS is made clear, especially at commu-nity colleges where our populations often reflect the diversity being promoted and recognized in this work. In "Editorial, The Community College in the United States: A Profile in Innovation and Change," Lisa Fiol-Matta, editor of this special *WSQ* double-issue, echoes the importance of this intersection of purposes. "Recognizing the role that community colleges play in the over-all education schema of the United States is important for women's studies professionals and others engaged in curriculum transformation," she asserts (10). She supports her argument by reasoning that "the majority of community college students" and "over half of community college faculty" are women (10). Additionally, she avers that women faculty are more likely than their male colleagues to retain currency in their fields and participate in professional de-velopment, conferences, and research, all essential to successful curriculum transformation. Of course, today we recognize that not all women and not only women promote and support women's and feminist studies. Still, Fiol-Matta makes a strong point when she notes that courses that can result from curricu-lum transformation projects will more readily reflect the diverse populations of community colleges, which she supports through statistical demographics of the time (11). Contrasting these figures with current numbers shows a clear decrease in the percentage of white student enrollment, from 81.1% noted by Fiol-Matta to 49% in 2016 (Ma and Baum), for a more ethnically and racially diverse student population. Women continue to outnumber men at community colleges, remaining a fairly steady proportion, from 58.4% in 1994 (Fiol-Matta 5) to 56% in 2018 (AACC Fast Facts). Such statistics demonstrate that the need for transformed curriculum in community colleges might now be even stronger than it was at the time of the publication of this text. Yet, Fiol-Matta reminds us that reforming the curriculum in the community college was not/ is not merely an attempt to better reflect the diversity of our student bodies, "while it is a compelling argument" ("Editorial" 6) for such work. Instead, "[n]o matter what the demographics," she asserts that "courses need to be balanced so as to include the complexity of subject matter, including dissenting voices, critiques of the disciplinary approaches, and gaps in the traditional knowledge base" (6). Here, she advises, is the means by which we can endeavor to support an honest "and complete learning process for all students" (6). Fiol-Matta makes apparent the shared goals of these projects with those of women's and gender studies:

> The task of transforming the curriculum should involve all who are interested in educating for truth and justice.... All levels of the educational system ... will be strengthened if we can embrace as a common goal equitable treatment of all and critical inquiry into the nature of knowledge and learning. (13)

Shirley Parry has shown that the emergence of women's studies as a discipline and early work on curriculum transformation projects were interconnected. Parry, professor emerita of English and women's studies at Anne Arundel Community College (AACC), was the AACC campus coordinator for the Towson-Maryland Community Colleges FIPSE Curriculum Integration Grant and designed and administered Anne Arundel's summer faculty curriculum integration seminars on gender and race for many years. She also authored and co-authored two essential articles for this WSQ special double-issue. In explaining the parallel and interrelated timelines, she made clear, "Curriculum Integration/Transformation Projects really couldn't happen until a) women's studies scholarship was sufficiently developed ... and b) until women's studies was recognized as a 'legitimate discipline'" (Parry, "Interview"). She clarifies that once women's studies had gained credence in the academy, advantage could be taken of the work that had been done to transform the curriculum by bringing the study of women and gender into course design. Her account is echoed by Elaine Hedges, who notes that the transformation projects of the 1970s and 1980s emerged out of research and teaching on women. Thus, she writes in "Curriculum Transformation: A Brief Overview," they focused "increasingly on issues of diversity and on the interrelationships among gender, race, class, ethnicity and other forms of difference. Rethinking both what and how we teach has become more complex and more challenging, and the experience of successful projects is therefore more valuable" (21). Hedges sees the goals of women's studies and those of curriculum transformation overlapping and complimentary, especially in their benefits to students: awareness and familiarity with new intellectual content; linking intellectual learning with the experiential; developing a voice and a feeling of empowerment; forming critical viewpoints; and "recognizing difference and diversity" (20). Additionally, Parry shows that community colleges were always involved in both scholarship on women and related curriculum transformation projects. She reports that as early 1976, *College English* published an article entitled "Women's Studies in Community Colleges," with a second publication by the same title appearing in 1980 in the *Women's Studies Monograph Series*, printed by the National Institute of Education ("Interview"). A forerunner to the *Women's Studies Quarterly* double issue was first published in 1990 and then again in 1994. This anthology was titled *The Community College Guide to Curriculum Transformation*, edited by Elaine Hedges, Myrna Goldenberg, and Sara Coulter. It contained eight essays that later were included in the *WSQ* publication discussed here (Parry, "Interview"). As noted above, this is a vast collection of essays; for the purposes and limitations of this essay, I can only explore a few. The discussion that follows focuses on the benefits of two of these essays to community college WGS programs today, as well as some history that might be edifying for current programs and faculty.

In "Faculty Development: A Consortial Model," by Myrna Goldenberg and Shirley C. Parry, the authors outline their methodology for a massive curriculum transformation project involving five community colleges in Maryland, including my own, Montgomery College, as well as Anne Arundel Community College, Prince George's Community College, Community College of Baltimore, and Essex Community College, all working in alliance with

Towson State University.[8] The two-year project was subsidized by FIPSE, beginning in the summer of 1988. The essay is both instructive and inspirational about such collaborative, intensive curricular reform and professional development. I recognize that 1988 is very much in the past, and the funding for speakers and released time available then for this work is not so readily offered now. What the essay reports as "modest amounts of released time," I am sure many of us would covet for our program curriculum and faculty development projects: "Four of the five colleges supported at least five faculty participants … with a minimum of three hours of released time for three consecutive semesters" (28). Also, while I appreciate that those in that era often struggled to convince administrators and colleagues of its importance (Schmitz and Williams 560-561), I admit that it might be more difficult to make the case for the continued need to bring women's and gender studies into current curricula. Our success in the past could limit our growth and progress now, as curriculum transformation might be seen as already having achieved its goals. Still, as our WGS colleagues report, such work continues to be needed in community colleges, with programs still being founded and courses still being created ("Becoming Visible"). "Faculty Development" presents a framework that could be adapted to reach our program goals effectively now.

So, what is useful for current WGS programs in the model presented in Goldenberg and Parry's essay? If we concede that faculty development is an ongoing, necessary process for program vitality and currency, we can find what they've written as edifying. Their project emphasized an interdisciplinary, collaborative approach: "The coordinators' focus on the new scholarship in their disciplines, along with their enthusiasm, encouraged the project participants to study the new materials and to consider their applications to the classroom" (24). The project consisted of both planning and implementation stages. In the planning stage, the participants met for retreats, studied feminist and transformation theory, as well as other foundational materials, and designed objectives and sample syllabi for the courses they were updating (25). The implementation stage, sustained over three semesters, involved readings

---

8   Today Community College of Baltimore is known as Baltimore City Community College, Essex Community College is part of the Community College of Baltimore County, and Towson State University is known as Towson University.

and discussions, guest speakers, more specific course revisions and implementation, a summer institute, consultation with home departments/disciplines, and presentations at conferences and workshops. Consultants in various fields gave lectures pertinent to the work and met with other interested faculty—those not participating in the project—who would like to integrate similar scholarship in their courses, obviously to extend the reach of the work (26-27). Goldenberg and Parry emphasize the need for revision, evaluation, reportage, and feedback. They especially note that faculty journals of their experiences were essential to the process: "[In] the long run the journals proved to be an effective stimuli for coming to terms with the course revision, for approaching course revision systematically and analytically, and for evaluating the effect of revisions as they occurred" (27).

Further, Goldenberg and Parry tell us in "Faculty Development" that when community college faculty have the opportunity to focus on new pedagogical approaches, they become energized "about relearning the content of their fields" (28). The authors emphasize creating projects that work against isolation, that encourage exploring new perspectives, that promote diversity, support reflection, and share scholarship (28-29). The authors conclude in hopes that they have shared a model that others can employ in their own programs:

> Genuine curriculum change is a long-term process. Curriculum transformation projects can establish the foundation and goals for change as faculty continue to explore new materials and methods in subsequent semesters. To be successful, the projects must respond to the needs of the institutions and faculty they are serving. (29)

"Writing Everybody In," by Myrna Goldenberg and Barbara Stout, presents an overview of the Towson/Maryland Community Colleges Project, a two-year project beginning in 1989 "to bring recent scholarship on women and minorities into the curriculum" (31). Their project involved six institutions, of which five were community colleges, including my own. Goldenberg and Stout make the case that college course offerings and curricula have continuously changed and see their project as participating in that three-century pattern.

However, they recognize the challenges as well as the need for that change. "The expansion of the curriculum has always paralleled and continues to parallel the democratization of both the student population and the system of higher education," they explain (31). The authors note that goals of their project were particularly important to community colleges. These included that the course work reflects the student body; that the circumstances of teaching in a community college be recognized; and that the importance of language and writing be a major focus. For this project, courses in ten disciplines underwent curriculum transformation: the arts; biology; business; composition; criminal justice; history; American literature and world literature; nursing; psychology; and sociology. For each, Goldenberg and Stout outline specific ways course content was changed; many of these changes can remind us even today to be alert to our own biases and lapses. One example under composition notes, "two concerns about teaching argument: lack of emphasis in textbooks on reaching consensus; students' unwillingness to challenge or take a stand" (37). Another in nursing suggests having students consider the right of nurses to be heard in policymaking and whether their voices can influence policies (39).

Seven principles were employed to reach the objectives of their endeavor (33-34). A review of the list shows standards important to all community college curriculum projects, especially those in our discipline. The authors remind us that this work begins with scholarship and research. "Community college students have as much right to academic currency as university students," they assert. However, they recognize the strictures on community college faculty because of workload. Here, they are encouraging institutional support for curriculum projects that afford faculty time and space for such endeavors. They declare that "community colleges are teaching institutions," and that the goals of feminist pedagogy relate well to the community college mission, including "active learning," "collaboration," and students' involvement and commitment to their own learning (34). This they call, "a pedagogy of empowerment" (34), certainly a term whose meaning transcends the years. Third, the focus of their transformation project was on introductory courses, a focal point we can recognize currently, as many of these courses now make up the offerings in our degrees and certificates. At some point, those who preceded almost all of us took on this work, strove to remake the community college curriculum using a gender lens. As Goldenberg and Stout assert of their project, "students need to have the full view of a subject provided by the multiple vision that comes from scholarship which does not ignore gender, race, class, sexual preference, and ethnicity" (34). (Of course, we would not say "sexual preference" today, but still we can at least understand their version of inclusion.) Additionally, the authors discuss that curriculum transformation requires commitment on the part of faculty, but also of the college. They insist that colleges must make resources available for this work, both in terms of budget and support (35). The budgetary concerns many of us now face in community college programs might make this principle seem impossible to achieve and perhaps shortsighted. Yet, our struggles to transform or build curriculum certainly are made much less problematic and operate more smoothly when we can obtain support, even in a small part. Their fifth principle reminds us to value a variety of input because it is people who create knowledge and "the reformulation of knowledge is constant and continual" (34). Moreover, Goldenberg and Stout write, reforming curriculum should be ongoing. Faculty should share reports on course modifications and their effectiveness with others, and they should have opportunities to continue to revise courses and disseminate their results for feedback (33-34).

The seventh and final principle the writers explain, in "Writing Everybody In," is the importance of using stage theory for curriculum reformation projects. Application of this theory requires three stages: integration, transformation, and reconceptualization (35). Throughout these stages, they advised faculty participants in their project to consider these questions as they examined components of their courses: "Where are the women and minority men? Why are they missing? What are the effects of exclusion? How would this course change if it reflected scholarship on women and minority men? How can the language be more accurate? How can I teach more effectively?" (35). As its name suggests, the first stage of integration requires adding materials that bring more diverse pedagogy and resources to the class. The course changes to include these additions, "but the broad outlines and boundaries of the course remain the same" (35). However, in the transformation stage, the course accommodates new additions by eliminating some topics and substance that kept the course narrow in focus. "They change the course topics to reflect the fullness of the subject," Goldenberg and Stout explain. As I have noted throughout this essay, the goals of curriculum transformation and the mission of community colleges, as well as that of women's and gender studies, all embrace the notion that what is taught should better reflect the needs and identities of the students; in the transformation stage, this awareness guides the work. Reconceptualization, the third and final stage, seems to be one we can always be working toward, striving continually to be aware as we create new curricula and as we teach: "[T]he instructor gives the course new shape and vision, challenges the assumptions: language, content, organization of knowledge, the politics and power structures of the discipline" (36). As a result of their project, Goldenberg and Stout and their faculty participants became aware of the great need that existed to make what was taught better reflect and confirm the identities and experiences of community college students. To achieve this, student involvement is required; active learning is the unquestionable result. "The primary goal is to move from 'received' to 'connected' and finally to 'constructed' knowledge and passionate knowing," they encouragingly claim (40).

The conclusion offered by Goldenberg and Stout seems to look ahead and speak to us now. It could even serve as a call to action. They assert:

> The student body will continue to grow in number and diversity, and the curriculum will need reform, just as it always has. For the near future, it seems important for community college faculty and students to have the opportunity to update in the areas on which this essay has focused. The special mission of the community college, which is to empower its students by moving them from passive to active learning, verifies the need for more transformation projects. (43)

Although published over twenty years ago, *Women's Studies Quarterly, Curriculum Transformation in Community Colleges: Focus on Introductory Courses* can be a valuable resource for all WGS programs at community colleges today. Whether we are creating and developing new curricula and programs, defending the ones that we already have, or focusing on faculty development, we will find significance in its pages. The work that precedes us reminds us that we are vulnerable, that our discipline is still rather new and often considered controversial and maybe unnecessary, but also that we continue a long tradition of scholarship and pedagogy. This essay has barely reported on the richness contained in this collection of writings and the many ways it can inspire and remind us of the most basic intentions and aims of women's and gender studies in community colleges. As the writings it contains come from community college scholars across the country from multiple and often surprising disciplines, most of us will find, as I have, much that is valuable for our work today in women's and gender studies.

In her "Editorial" that introduces the *WSQ* collection, Fiol-Matta is prescient and inspiring when she writes: "Because they will leave the community college classroom for the workplace in a world increasingly affected by global economic trends and transnational migrations, all students, including those from dominant groups, will benefit from challenging assumptions derived from the experiences of privileged groups" (6-7). Our own time is one of strict budgetary oversight, obsessive enrollment counting, reports required to justify our existence, and increasingly influential conservative and neoliberal political agendas in higher education. Corporate models more and more dominate and influence college functioning and structures. However, as Fiol-Matta shows, our responsibility to our students is great, and growing greater. Although they do not foresee the multiple ways in which our discipline would widen intersectionally and expand more inclusively, especially in the field of sexuality, these writings remind us of our origins and the seriousness of purpose and commitment that made—and continues to make—women's and gender studies at community colleges meaningful and essential for our students.

# Works Cited

AACC Fast Facts 2018. American Association of Community Colleges. https://www.aacc.nche.edu/wp-content/uploads/2018/04/2018-Fast-Facts.pdf

"Becoming Visible: The Collaborative Administration and Development of GWSS Programs at Community Colleges." Just Imagine, Imagining Justice: Feminist Visions of Freedom, Dreammaking and the Radical Politics of Futures, Pre-Conference: Program Administration and Development, National Women's Studies Association Conference, 8-11 November 2018, Hilton Atlanta, Atlanta, GA. Conference Presentation.

Fiol-Matta, Lisa. "Editorial: The Community College in the United States: A Profile of Innovation and Change." Fiol-Matta, pp. 3-15.

———., editor. *Women's Studies Quarterly: Curriculum Transformation in Community Colleges, Focus on Introductory Courses.* The Feminist Press, 1996.

Goldenberg, Myrna, and Shirley Parry. "Faculty Development: A Consortial Model." Fiol-Matta, pp. 23-30.

———., and Barbara Stout. "Writing Everybody In." Fiol-Matta, pp. 31-44.

Hedges, Elaine. "Curriculum Transformation: A Brief Overview." Fiol-Matta, pp. 16-22.

Ma, Jennifer, and Sandy Baum. "Trends in Community Colleges: Enrollment, Prices, Student Debt and Completion." *Research Brief.* College Board Research, April 2016.

Parry, Shirley. Personal Interview. 12 January 2017.

Schmitz, Betty. "Curriculum Transformation, Higher Education.
    *Encyclopedia of Diversity in Education*, edited by James A. Banks, vol.1,
    SAGE Reference, 2012, pp. 589-593.

————., and Anne S. Williams. "Seeking Equity Through Curricular
    Reform: Faculty Perception of an Experimental Project." *The Journal of
    Higher Education*, Vol. 54, No. 5 (Sep-Oct 1983), pp. 556-565.

# Student Voices: Jozette Belmont, Kingsborough Community College

Brooklyn, New York

Jozette Belmont started her education at Kingsborough Community College, where she earned an AA in liberal arts with a concentration in women's and gender studies. Following this she transferred to Brooklyn College, where she earned a dual BA in psychology and women's and gender studies. Most recently she began pursuing an MA in women's and gender studies at The Graduate Center, CUNY, where her research focuses on the impact of sex education on queer women. This experience as a student provided her with an interdisciplinary foundation that predicates on issues of marginalization, and the impact of structural forces on oppressed groups. Currently, she utilizes these skills as a development assistant at Peer Health Exchange, a nonprofit organization that recruits college students to teach sex education to New York

City public high schools. Her goal is for her work to be the basis for positive social change, specifically within the fields of women's health and education. Looking into the future, she hopes graduate school will give her the tools to claim her education, and help future students do the same. She plans to continue in the field of WGS, but eventually pursue a PhD so she can research and teach at community colleges to give back to the same communities she was once part of.

*What did you like about your WGS course(s)?*

"My favorite part of WGS courses is the open and in-depth discussions. Many other classes prioritize lectures and offer less room for student voices. WGS courses allow everyone to learn about varying identities, positionalities, and social locations in a safe space."

*How did your WGS course(s) contribute to your career goals? How did the course(s) prepare you for the workforce?*

"WGS courses directly impact my research, academic, and professional goals. I continue to use the information I learned in WGS courses in my everyday life, especially in my current position. Concentrating in WGS during my time at Kingsborough gave me the courage to transfer to a senior college and apply to graduate school. Without the incredible work and effort put forth by educators in the WGS department at Kingsborough, I would not be where I am today."

*Why do you think it's important for college students to take women's and gender studies courses?*

"I think every college student should take WGS courses regardless of their major. Interdisciplinary disciplines such as WGS offer a necessary critique of structural forces and systems of marginalization.... Everything we learn has relevance and importance in our everyday lives. Any person can utilize feminist frameworks to apply to their own fields or personal lives."

*How was/were your women's and gender studies course(s) different from the other courses you took in college?*

"The WGS courses I took were open, communicative, and forced us to look at the world with a critical lens.... WGS courses focused on respecting the opinions of others while discussing marginalization and discrimination in a concrete manner, while non-WGS courses often avoided difficult conversations."

# Hunger for Justice in the Borderlands: Re-Framing Antiracist Feminist Pedagogies for an Urban Community College[9]

Amanda Loos

> Love can bridge the sense of otherness. It takes practice to be vigilant, to beam that love out. It takes work. (bell hooks, *Teaching Community: A Pedagogy of Hope*)

> The struggle is inner: Chicano, *indio*, American Indian, *mojado*, *mexicano*, immigrant Latino, Anglo in power, working class Anglo, Black, Asian—our psyches resemble the bordertowns and are populated by the same people. The struggle has always been inner, and is played out in the outer terrains. Awareness of our situation must come before inner changes, which in turn come before changes in society. Nothing happens in the "real" world unless it first happens in the images in our heads. (Gloria Anzaldúa, *Borderlands/La Frontera: The New Mestiza*)

Community college educators operate at the slippery boundaries between center and margin, domination and liberation, trauma and healing. As community college faculty, staff, and students, we are so often devalued, dismissed, or rendered invisible within the hierarchies to which "higher" education clings so fiercely. Yet, we create the educational spaces of approximately forty-one percent of all college students in the United States including an overrepresen-

---

9    I wish to extend my gratitude to Dr. Ann Russo, at DePaul University, who mentored me through the original project that led to this essay. Ann's commitment to teaching, writing, living, parenting, and working transformatively continues to be a tremendous inspiration. Her support has been invaluable in my own journey to refresh my feminist practice.

tation of low-income and minority students ("Community College Fast Facts," "Higher Education Leaders"). At the City Colleges of Chicago, where I have been a faculty member in arts, humanities, and women's and gender studies since 2002, students come to our work together across *all* the many borders of the city's intense segregation and disparity. Then, they experience additional layers of marginalization by elitist conceptions of "real" academia, narratives that serve to devalue their education at the "community college *level*" despite our parallel course offerings with four-year schools and our immensely transformative classrooms. Furthermore, given our demographics and the history of using community colleges to supply a "workforce" in our capitalist system, we are particularly vulnerable to corporatizing.[10]

As such, community colleges often create microcosms of the power structures of the larger society, crystallizing the embodied experiences of interlocking oppressions. Our students' engagement with "theory" is not abstract; they live and breathe the many traumas, joys, and resistances of intersectional feminisms. The majority of my students are themselves the women described by M. Jacqui Alexander in *Pedagogies of Crossing*. Alexander theorizes the "critical geography" of global capitalism, which relies on the exploited labor of women. She says:

> In a fundamental sense, the pervasiveness and persistence of low-wage work—for women in export processing and free-trade zones; in the *maquilas*; in the "informal" economy; in the gaps left wide-open by the state; in flexible part-time work at McDonald's, Sears, Wal-Mart and J.C. Penny; or multiple food chains; in home work, not only in the North and South, but in Hong Kong and Korea, in Dublin and Gujarat, in Lagos and Dakar, in Eastern Europe, and in Kuwait and Jordan—is itself a consequence of asymmetrical gendering.... Since women constitute the bulk of the workforce, they experience the daily force of these myths

---

10   For more on the painful corporatizing of Chicago City Colleges in recent years, see my article "Invisible Battlefields: A Call to Stand with Community Colleges on the Frontlines of Resistance" in *Praxis: Journal of the Arcus Center for Social Justice Leadership*, March 2, 2016. http://www.kzoo.edu/praxis/invisible-battlefields/. We are now an institution in recovery from a series of ill-advised policy changes.

in gendered and classed terms. Their supervisors are most often men; and they least often experience a high degree of upward mobility. These are the very experiences that inform women's organizing strategies, enabling them to theorize exploitation—the gap between the value they produce and the remuneration they receive in contrast to the owners and managers of capital. These experiences constitute the pedagogies through which women yearn for justice, through which they collectively come to know "tenemos hambre de justicia." (104)

I have repeatedly stood witness to this hunger for justice among my students in our work together, as they so often come to the classroom already activated around issues of justice in their own lives.

In course development, advising, and assessment, however, community college educators are trained to prepare students for transfer and to see ourselves as the "keys" to our students' entrance into academic, professional, economic, and "cultural" opportunity. As I work to "check" my own privilege (as a white-raced, middle-class, cisgendered woman, in a heterosexual marriage, who studied at elite institutions), I have become more and more troubled by this assumed power. Considering the role of community colleges within what bell hooks calls "dominator culture," teaching to assimilate into mainstream higher education can be painfully silencing. As hooks describes:

Black folks coming from poor, underclass communities, who enter universities or privileged cultural settings unwilling to surrender every vestige of who we were before we were there, all "sign" of our class and cultural "difference," who are unwilling to play the role of "exotic Other," must create spaces within that culture of domination if we are to survive whole, our souls intact. Our very presence is a disruption. ("Choosing the Margins" 155)

Community colleges are not "privileged cultural settings" as universities are, but my students' experience in our classroom is often their first entrance into academic life and status, often the first in their family.

In this sense, community colleges often operate as a borderland,[11] as Gloria Anzaldúa theorized in her beautifully transformative feminist text, *Borderlands/La Frontera: The New Mestiza*. So many community college students—certainly mine—claim their family origins in the actual borderland between the United States and Mexico, *"una herida abierta*, where the Third World grates against the first and bleeds. And before a scab forms it hemorrhages again, the lifeblood of two worlds merging to form a third country—a border culture" (Anzaldúa 25).[12] Community colleges also form a borderland as a convergence of cultures and identities, and, by extension, multiple perceptions of gender and feminism: "Borders are set up to define the places that are safe and unsafe, to distinguish *us* from *them*. A border is a dividing line, a narrow strip along a steep edge. A borderland is a vague and undetermined place created by the emotional residue of an unnatural boundary. It is in a constant state of transition. The prohibited and forbidden are its inhabitants" (25-26).

Women's and gender studies classrooms at community colleges operate at these borders in vital ways. In my context, they often speak across the lines between urban communities of color and mainstream academic feminism at four-year institutions. Personally, surviving Chicago's intersecting oppressions equips my students to observe, give voice to, and erode systemic injustice, putting social justice theories more immediately to work. In turn, their voices should penetrate and inform academic feminism, yet they study against the "unnatural boundary" where community colleges and universities bleed.

Recognizing the value of my students' personal experiences, I work to resist the many pressures merely to "teach to transfer," and I urge academic feminism to resist the many pressures to dismiss community colleges as lesser copies of a university. Transformative pedagogies used effectively at these bor-

---

11   Seeing community colleges as a borderland originates from my colleague Ana Arredondo, of Daley College and DePaul University's WGS program, and is rooted in our ongoing collaboration. We presented it during a roundtable entitled "Heartbroken in the Borderlands" at DePaul during spring 2016 (along with Kelsey Schultz) and during faculty and professional development events.

12   Many of these same students are DACA recipients, their status and future hanging in the balance of government shutdown.

derland spaces could serve instead as a vibrant model for intersectional feminist praxis and as a source for productive alliance toward justice in education.

## Intimate Others: Transformative Pedagogy as Accountability in the Community College Borderlands

White supremacy makes it painfully easy to reduplicate oppressive power structures and escape accountability, particularly in a system that rewards students and faculty for completion of "degrees of economic value." Corporate interests masked as federal policy have lead community college administrators to pressure-cook completion rates, railroading students into career "Pathways" that often entirely erase liberal arts, much less WGS courses. Full-time faculty who are overtaxed by teaching loads, top-down mandated initiatives, and lane advancement hurdles, and part-time faculty whose labor is increasingly exploited below a living wage, might be more likely to fall back on many of our own privileges from the larger social systems, more comfortable than *una herida abierta* of an activated community college classroom. In this sense, even in our courses with WGS or other social justice content, it might be the path of least resistance to teach to transfer, thinking about our classrooms as mini-versions of a university, and our learning objectives aligned with a student's projected WGS path into mainstream academia. This is, in fact, a primary mission of our job and isn't altogether without value; however, if we stop there, we are more likely to recreate the already solidified hierarchies of race, class, gender, and sexuality that antiracist feminisms work so tirelessly to unlearn in the predominantly white and privileged spaces of "higher" education. If we are only "preparing" our students for transfer without teaching for justice and transformation, we simultaneously silence our students and continue to render their communities invisible.

Therefore, as feminist educators in the community college borderlands, we have an urgent imperative to conscientiously practice antiracist feminist pedagogies, celebrating rather than resisting intersectionality. We must be vigilant to self-reflect and be accountable. Rather than shrink from the challenge, we must continue to be activated by the tremendous potential for our classrooms and college communities to gather "individuals who actually occupy different locations within structures, sharing ideas with one another, mapping out terrains of commonality, connection, and shared concern" (hooks, *Teaching to Transgress* 130).

In this way, we should aim to transform one another with interconnectedness and love, overcoming our resistances and celebrating with our students when we "bridge the sense of otherness" (hooks, *Teaching Community* 162). hooks writes:

> Though the politically progressive clamor is for "diversity," there is little realistic understanding of the ways feminist scholars must change ways of seeing, talking, and thinking if we are to speak to the various audiences, the "different" subjects who may be present in one location. How many feminist scholars can respond effectively when faced with a racially and ethnically diverse audience who may not share similar class backgrounds, language, levels of understanding, communication skills, and concerns? (*Teaching to Transgress* 112)

Being accountable in our teaching practice at community colleges requires that we recognize both our students and ourselves in hooks's question and be diligent in actively responding to this imperative, even when we feel ill-equipped or under-supported. My career as an educator in an urban community college has taught me that passionate teaching—with actively transformative, antiracist, feminist pedagogies—is a necessity, not a luxury.

My resistance to traditional academic teaching is not born from an inability to be successful at it; I am the product of humanities programs in privileged college and graduate school environments.[13] My own experience as a community college student was in a dual-enrollment program in high school, a sign of being academically "advanced," not marginalized (though the school and community were).[14] Neither my undergraduate college nor graduate university

---

13   I attended New College of Florida and the University of Chicago, respectively.

14   Fortunately, I inherited a profound respect for community colleges early in my life when my mother restarted her education at a community college as a nontraditional student, transferring to complete her bachelor's and master's degrees.

embraced what Paulo Freire has famously coined the "banking system of education"; however, although academically rigorous and in some cases radical, they were predominantly white institutions that most valued preparing students for success in academia. With just a handful of very meaningful exceptions, I was shown that teaching academically meant leaving the students' and faculty's "feelings" and personal stories at the door. We may have *read* and *discussed* feminist and social justice theory. However, our classrooms typically did not *model* how to be together in a feminist community across racial, class, and gender differences, much less intersections of ages, abilities, ethnicities, citizenship status, and all of the many other interlocking oppressions commonly experienced among students at community colleges.

I started to unlearn how I was taught to teach with the naïve but important awareness that community colleges were inherently radical places in providing access to "higher education" for everyone from everywhere. Earlier in my career, I thought that including women's studies, black studies, LGBTQ studies, etc. into our general education curriculum marked our success as a progressive institution, and that by then adding a few active learning or feminist techniques we were really destabilizing an already decentered learning environment.

Now mid-career, after learning from my students and developing a greater critical consciousness about systemic oppression, I realize that these actions were only the first steps.[15] The real work comes in *how* we teach. Personal, collective, and political transformation occurs in building community, forming intimacy across power lines, practicing deep listening and accountability, healing from collective traumas, naming and challenging the interlocking oppressions of white supremacist capitalist heteropatriarchy, using joy and love as radical methods, nurturing our students' (often) already-intersectional feminisms, remembering to self-care to care for our students, and teaching and learning with our whole spirits: all the "too emotional" stuff of "women's work." I am inspired by bell hooks's call to teach with our hearts and our spirits. She says:

---

15  This consciousness further awakened during my sabbatical/graduate work at DePaul University's particularly justice-oriented Women's and Gender Studies Program, where I experienced transformative justice classrooms, especially with Dr. Ann Russo and Dr. Laila Farah.

To be guided by love is to live in community with all life. However, a culture of domination, like ours, does not strive to teach us how to live in community. As a consequence, learning to live in community must be a core practice for all of us who desire spirituality in education.

All too often we think of community in terms of being with folks like ourselves: the same class, same race, same ethnicity, same social standing and the like. All of us evoke vague notions of community and compassion, yet how many of us compassionately went out to find an intimate other, to bring them with us today? (*Teaching Community* 163)

Urban community colleges, especially, allow us to find "an intimate other" sitting right next to us. We therefore have a profound opportunity, and an imperative, to teach for real and far-reaching transformation, with feminist pedagogies that are *also* anti-racist and intersectional. We still maintain and reinforce dominator structures if we are not transforming *both* our curricula *and* our active teaching methods, to build relationships across power lines to *model* the important work of community-building in our community college classrooms.

We must continue observing, analyzing, reading, writing, thinking, discussing, learning—teaching skills students will need to navigate the rest of their paths in higher education, while we wait for higher education to become more socially just. I feel deeply that, while all academic spaces would benefit from transformative pedagogies, community colleges cry out for them. Our students find connections with one another through/despite societal, collective, and personal obstacles and their stories of success reveal tremendous wisdom and political power, with far-reaching and profound effects in communities, families, economies, and cultural production. The academic work we do together to name systemic oppressions should also seek to hold higher education accountable for the ways in which it has systemically silenced and devalued almost half of all its students.

## Naming Our Spaces, Claiming Our Inspirations: The Invisibility of Community Colleges in Feminist Pedagogical Theory

In *Pedagogies of Crossing* M. Jacqui Alexander defines pedagogy as "the imperative of making the world in which we live intelligible to ourselves and to each other," especially against white supremacist heteropatriarchy (6). "*Pedagogies*," she continues, "is intended to intervene in the multiple spaces where knowledge is produced…. Because within the archaeologies of dominance resides the will to divide and separate, *Pedagogies* points to the reciprocal investments we must make to cross over into a metaphysics of interdependence" (6). For foundation and continued nourishment, I have turned to a selection of such powerful antiracist and intersectional feminist pedagogies. These have helped me to consider how to practice accountability, while also further understanding the place my students and I co-occupy at the margins of higher education.

Tellingly, although community colleges bear the brunt of the "will to divide and separate" in the dominant educational system, in my readings of these transformative writings, I have not discovered a direct address to educators in community colleges, nor a recognition of the unique spaces that my students both occupy and cross. Most feminist writings on pedagogy assume the reader to be concerned with teaching for justice in four-year colleges and universities or to be outside of academic spaces altogether.[16]

As borderland spaces, however, community colleges require an additional layer of theory-making. Pedagogical theory cannot *simply* be applied across all educational environments without recognition of the particular character and dynamics of those communities. This requires a re-framing of these theoretical writings with consideration for urban community colleges as borderlands—publicly funded, increasingly corporatized, and historically colonized/colonizing. We must name community college classrooms as uniquely vulnerable, volatile, vibrant, radical, inspiring and sacred educational spaces, rendered invisible by hierarchical thinking in academia. How should community college students' inherently intersectional feminisms re-inform pedagogical theory-

---

16   bell hooks and AnaLouise Keating are partial exceptions in that they taught at open-enrollment schools and invite us to translate their work to our own teaching environments, whatever those might be.

making? They have been unrecognized as the students in pedagogical texts, but their experiences are recognizable as the topics of study.

For instance, Alexander interrogates an important misassumption: that those at the margins do not have the time to theorize or organize. She says:

> ... in spite of the histories of working-class and poor people's movements in the United States, a false opposition continues to circulate between the needs of survival and the demands of time, pitting individual survival against collective conscience.... When women say, *"no tenemos hambre de comida, tenemos hambre de justicia,"* they reconcile this fictive split between the struggle for survival and the search for justice. When dignity and daily bread are brought together so that justice overtakes the (not unimportant) struggle for wages, in contexts where they are miniscule to begin with, women give voice to a deeper, existential yearning: the desire to make themselves intelligible to themselves and to each other, to make domination transparent, and to *practice* new and different ways of being. In this process there is no opposition between the demands of survival and the needs of time. Rather, the very force of existential necessity propels the desire to know, the desire to make sense of existence. Theorizing, therefore, becomes an existential necessity. (105-106)

In Alexander's text, definitions of pedagogy seem to be extended outside of the classroom to the working women, rather than the working women who are propelled by this "desire to know" in a classroom. Yet, I recognize my students in her writing. Often they enter the classroom already mobilized into action about their exploited labor in low-paying jobs or under the fear of family deportation, police brutality, or other state violence.[17] They are overcoming tremendous familial, economic, and personal challenges to pursue their education—synonymous with freedom and opportunity; they juggle full-time jobs,

---

17   It should go without saying that the level of fear—as well as activism—among my students and our community have drastically intensified over this first year of the Trump Administration.

children, sibling or parent care, and numerous other layers of responsibility. Many may be double-timing their studies to "catch up" to certain standards after their neighborhood school failed to prepare them or they are intervening in cycles of incarceration. They bring multiple learning styles, needs, and strengths, and produce strong academic work while teaching us to expand and diversify the metrics of success we should be using in higher education.

Community college students are already survivors and thrivers, already fully capable of "making the world intelligible to themselves and to each other." Our pedagogical practices and curricula should therefore teach us to unlearn detrimental misassumptions, so that we can avoid reduplicating them as educators. Rather, we should be opening up spaces for dignity and daily bread to be brought together to feed our students' own hunger for justice. At the same time, our work should amplify their voices across the borderlands of higher education.

## Achieving *Consientizacoa*: Some Strategies for Re-Reading/Re-Writing Antiracist Feminist Pedagogies Through a Community College Lens

As Paulo Freire has famously said, "World and human beings do not exist apart from each other, they exist in constant interaction.... Just as objective social reality exists not by chance, but as the product of human action, so it is not transformed by chance" (51). According to his writings, neither theory without action nor activism without theory are effective methods of achieving *consientizacoa*; only a true synthesis of theory and action in students' engagement will lead to real change, a revolution *with* the people, through "co-intentional education" (Freire 69). In his model, a liberatory educator determines content only as a method of sharing a real dialogical discussion about a topic from the world, as a means of ensuring students' movement from an object of an oppressive structure to a subject acting—through praxis—to rehumanize themselves and their communities. Similarly, Anzaldúa explains, "Nothing happens in the 'real' world unless it first happens in the images in our heads" (109).

In re-framing pedagogical theory for community college spaces, I have gained some insight and tools from Tema Okun's book *The Emperor Has No Clothes: Teaching About Race and Racism to Students Who Don't Want to Know.* Assuming her students to be majority white, Okun shares strategies for meeting their early resistances head-on. The vast majority of my students, though, have intimately experienced the oppressive brunt of racist, sexist, and classist structures, or carry painful legacies of enslavement and colonization across generations and physical borders; they have been embodied and emboldened by these formative encounters. And, typically, they *do* want to talk about it. They do not have the resistance Okun describes. However, Okun's historical account and methods are valuable for feminist educators who are also aiming to be antiracist because she encourages us to address whiteness directly in our class discussions. Okun names the characteristics of white supremacy, which we have been taught to see simply as the "values" of American society (4). Coupled with her reference to the historically specific moment when "whiteness" was constructed as a racial/supremacist category, she leaves us with 16 tangible and easily recognizable "values" to deconstruct with our students (e.g. individualism, paternalism, defensiveness, the right to comfort).[18]

To remember what is at stake in naming white supremacy in the classroom, I return to writers like Anzaldúa:

> The dominant white culture is killing us slowly with its ignorance. By taking away our self-determination, it has made us weak and empty. As a people we have resisted and we have taken expedient positions, but we have never been allowed to develop unencumbered—we have never been allowed to be fully ourselves. The whites in power want us people of color to barricade ourselves behind our separate tribal walls so they can pick us off one at a time with their hidden weapons; so they can whitewash and distort history. Ignorance splits people, creates prejudices. A misinformed people is a subjugated people (108).

---

18 For historical specificity, see also Jacqueline Battalora's *Birth of a White Nation: The Invention of White People and Its Relevance Today.*

In the immediate wake of a Trump presidency, Anzaldúa's words here felt like a premonition; now they read like a narrative of the first year of the current administration.

AnaLouise Keating, in *Teaching Transformation: Transcultural Classroom Dialogues*, grounds the interconnected spirit of *Borderlands/La Frontera* into an inspiring and practical handbook on critical pedagogy, what she calls "transformative multiculturalism." Like Okun, she provides guidance in preparing syllabus statements and how to unfold a topic with sensitivity to the nuances of timing—the opening and shutting of windows of reception sometimes experienced in a group who might be resistant to making connections with each other. While Okun and Keating emphasize shaking students out of their complacency or lack of systemic thinking, doing so at a community college also requires deep care and attention to the personal narratives and traumas that are rattled up by this undertaking, as well as celebration of the joys to be found in real connection with an "intimate other," as hooks phrases it. At community colleges especially, we must be exceedingly careful in designing class plans that strike a productive balance.

For seeking such a balance, I have re-discovered hooks's emphasis on personal storytelling. hooks says, "… I have seen the way essentialist standpoints can be used to silence or assert authority over the opposition, but I most often see and experience the way the telling of personal experience is incorporated into classrooms in ways that deepen discussion. And I am most thrilled when the telling of experience links discussions of facts or more abstract constructs to concrete reality" (*Teaching to Transgress* 85). While strengthening their writing and confidence in their own voices, students' own personal stories also become a collective political narrative.

Applying the wisdom of generations of peacemakers, I also now try to establish an environment in which my students and I engage with one another in justice circles, during which everyone in the room has an equal opportunity to speak and listen. This focuses our collective attention on each other and the center of the room rather than the whiteboard and the white professor.[19]

---

19  I am indebted again to Dr. Ann Russo and Prof. Ana Arredondo for modeling how to be "in circle." For a great, accessible handbook on using circles as a pedagogical tool, see Kay Pranis, *The Little Book of Circle Processes*.

In using discussion circles and embracing the role of facilitating participant, an educator also places herself in a position to share. As we see cautioned in hooks's observations, we must aim to balance revealing just enough of an educator's personal story to establish common ground, alleviate fears of isolation, and make real some of the differences and connections that a class may be theorizing. Anymore and the authority of an educator's position is exploited into a dominant voice in the room which silences student voices. Sharing of ourselves should be done as part of a larger commitment to authenticity, accountability, humanity, and love. As feminist educators activated by transformative pedagogies, we stand/sit *with* our students, not in front of them.

While a focus on interconnectivity is echoed throughout all of these texts on transformative pedagogy, I have found the ways in which Keating centralizes interconnectedness as her primary guiding principal in pedagogy and curriculum to be extremely relevant, particularly for my urban community college classrooms. She explains, "One of my primary goals as an educator is to awaken in my students a sense of our radical connectedness, for I am convinced that this awareness can play a crucial role in working toward social justice. At the very least, I offer relational worldviews as alternatives to the highly celebrated belief in an entirely independent 'American' self" (30-31). In traditional curriculum building, we are taught to compartmentalize various intersecting identities—even the activist arts that express them—into separate "units" or "movements" (if not merely as tokens.) Alternatively, theorizing a "mestiza consciousness," Anzaldúa also gives voice to the experience of educators and students in/from the borderlands:

> These numerous possibilities leave *la mestiza* floundering in un-
> charted seas. In perceiving conflicting information and points of
> view, she is subjected to a swamping of her psychological borders.
> She has discovered that she can't hold concepts or ideas in rigid
> boundaries…. Rigidity means death. Only by remaining flexible
> is she able to stretch the psyche horizontally and vertically. *La
> mestiza* constantly has to shift out of habitual formations; from
> convergent thinking, analytical reasoning that tends to use ratio-
> nality to move toward a single goal (a Western mode), to diver-
> gent thinking, characterized by movement away from set patterns

and goals and toward a more whole perspective, one that includes rather than excludes.... It is work that the soul performs. That focal point or fulcrum, that juncture where the *mestiza* stands, is where phenomena tend to collide. It is where the possibility of uniting all that is separate occurs.... A massive uprooting of dualistic thinking in the individual and collective consciousness is the beginning of a long struggle, but one that could, in our best hopes, bring us to the end of rape, of violence, of war. (101-102)

Although it shakes my own resistances, I aim to avoid curricula that reinforce binary thinking. I now try an intersectional approach in which interlocking oppressions are named as such and then analyzed systemically, with space left open for this "work that the soul performs."

To help, Keating provides her students with a series of presuppositions— "social injustice exists," "our educations have been biased," "racism is real; race is not," etc.—as a framework for their academic community, without assuming that students already share these perspectives nor imposing them forever. She then relies on "relational patterns" to structure class materials, starting with commonality and then taking "multiple interlocking directions" (42). Careful analysis of students' own preconceived assumptions about each "voice" in a text, for instance, works to denaturalize the construction of race, power, whiteness, masculinity, binary thinking, hierarchy, consumerism, and dominance. In writing and applying my own social justice presuppositions, I can attest that even the act of reading them in circle on the first day can be immensely powerful. These bypass some of the anxieties (or dismissiveness) students often feel about being "political" in the classroom; they too have been taught that personal and political stories are not "academic." Such transparent class frameworks immediately legitimize the practice of social justice as a valuable academic outcome in itself, though not often valued in an increasingly corporatizing system.[20]

---

20  I realize that I may be enjoying the privilege of a relatively supportive college administration, which may be uncommon in my colleagues' environments where some of the practices I describe could be perceived as "too radical" and be unwelcome. There is work yet to be done at the administrative level in being accountable to the reality of community colleges as the academic centers of the majority of students from marginalized and targeted communities.

Ultimately, re-framing antiracist feminist pedagogies for an urban community college has encouraged me to activate the following transformative practices, however imperfectly:

- providing students more autonomy with creative projects and self-evaluations;
- collectively setting class values on the first day, rather than pre-set "policies" in the syllabus;
- sitting *together* with my students in the room;
- making more space for the sharing of our personal stories and emphasizing that these narratives are essential for academic analyses;
- engaging in active learning that equalizes power dynamics;
- sharing our preferred gender pronouns and names ... and using them;
- naming our own privilege, white supremacy, and heteropatriarchy, and working toward accountability;
- talking openly about experiences of oppression, racism, and sexism in both personal and systemic language;
- emphasizing community-building over competition and grading, "measuring" students' learning in much broader/multiple ways;
- and building curricula that challenge the status quo within our disciplines.

Doing so encourages a shift in thinking: to value personal/collective transformation—and preparation to actually *make* social change—as the most important measures of success.


## Embodied Theory: Stories and *Testimonio* from the Urban Community College Classroom

To share highlights of these practices, I offer a few stories. Numerous times over the years in my classes on women in film, we have screened documentaries like Lourdes Portillo's *Señorita Extraviada*, on the mass disappearances and brutal murders of young Mexican women working in the *maquilas* in Ciudad Juarez. I used to stand at the front of the room, provide as much "information" as I could about the "issues," and then facilitate a discussion of the film with those students who raised their hands to react. I quickly learned that a discussion such as this should not be relegated to a unit on activist film and therefore "othered" in my syllabus. Early on, I was unprepared for those students with a real and personal connection to the film and would simply "present" the facts of the heartbreaking situation, facilitating an abstract discussion of the film as a documentary. I was missing the opportunity to engage with my students in what Aurora Levins Morales, in *Medicine Stories*, calls "*testimonio.*" Several of my students who resisted these silencing pedagogies managed to share their memories of the disappearances in their families, people they knew, the news they heard before leaving a border city in Mexico and how they were cautioned as girls. Morales powerfully reminds us that, "Recovery from trauma requires creating and telling another story about the experience of violence and the nature of participants, a story powerful enough to restore a sense of our own humanity to the abused" (15).

Now, I use interconnectivity more explicitly in my course design *and* we discuss the film in circle, allowing every single voice to be heard, should they choose. My students' stories now juxtapose with the film, opening up many more layers of deeply personal *and* critical analyses. We often expose how the same systemic forces that allow for such murders in the borderlands work in similar ways in Chicago neighborhoods, for instance, where brutal violence by those in power goes uninvestigated and unprosecuted. The sexual violence against women in Ciudad Juarez also empowers women in the room to add their own stories—silently or vocally—to the interrogation of misogyny as a global toxin. This process also begins to reveal how we have *all* internalized mass media representations designed to make Mexico and other Other(ed) spaces seem uncivilized, uninhabited, and exploitable. Decentralizing the classroom dynamics allows the stories in the documentary to share commonality with those in the room. Practicing accountability means recognizing that my students literally embody the images that are most often disfigured by white supremacist capitalist imperialist heteropatriarchy.

Additionally, these more engaged discussions often open up space for students to critically reflect on their own educational experiences in more traditional classrooms in which they have felt their voices as Mexican American students silenced. Or, in other discussions, how it had never occurred to their white male professors of sociology, for instance, to provide a trigger warning when assigning an article on rape until his students' traumas were indeed triggered (and his journey to self-reflect and be more accountable started). Or, what a different *feeling* it is in a WGS classroom which actively aims to be transformative around intersecting identities, revealing not only the feminist content that has been omitted in their other classes, but also the recognition and valuing of our students' lived experiences of embodied theory.

When Philando Castile and Alton Sterling were killed by police during the summer of 2016, I was immensely grateful that my students and I had already built our community to include routinely sitting in transformative circles. As the footage of murdered black and brown men and women continues to escalate, these decentered learning spaces, eliminating the traditional power dynamics of the classroom, allow our educational community to care for one another in our emotional and intellectual processing of such terror. Documentations of violence such as we have seen with these killings crystallize what so many students at urban community colleges already know in their bodies and souls, the real fear that they could be the next victim the next time they are inevitably harassed by police. Who would dare ask them to check that experience at the door of a classroom?

During our discussions of Sterling and Castile, rather than abstractly echoing the philosophies of Black Lives Matter or discussing the principles of racial justice, I listened, internally taking stock of my own shock that my African American (and Latino) students were *actually* counseling each other with specific instructions on how to avoid being killed. Sitting in circle opened space for those in the room with the most at stake to dominate the discussion, giving me, along with the few white students in the room, the opportunity to listen deeply, to check my privilege, and to turn on my heart and empathy and to be more accountable to my students.

Discussions of violence, even screenings of films from the women's and gender studies "canon," can be triggers for so many other lived experiences of trauma. As hooks demonstrates, if we are to voice and discuss these experiences, we must also remain *loving* social justice educators (*Teaching Community* 163). Living at the borderlands, our students arrive in our classroom also having been taught that their emotions should be left outside. One former student, Dychea Johnson, whose son was attacked by police officers on his own college campus, later shared with me her apprehension at the social justice theme of my class. She wrote,

> When I began your class, my son's assault was still at the forefront of everything I did. And affected me in many ways, yet I tried to push those feelings aside as I had just begun classes ... and wanted to focus on class. When I entered your classroom and found out that we would be discussing citizenship and reading *Black Girl Dangerous*, I was a bit nervous because I felt the topic of social justice would come up. And I wanted to avoid having the conversation because I knew it would upset me. I had yet to find a way to deal with my son's attack, and.... I still felt the pain that he was going through deep in my belly. But he was being strong and so I wanted to try and be strong as well...[21]

Sadly, her comments make clear that the language of trauma is universal and instigating:

> When the discussion of police brutality came up in the classroom, hearing all these young men and women describe different incidents in which they were harassed or assaulted angered me and saddened me. While I didn't want to talk about my son's assault in class, I felt compelled to share his story and explain why I ran out the room crying.... I continue to advocate for my son in hopes that some changes will be made within the agency that refused to prosecute the officers who assaulted him.

We must be able to hold our students and their stories with care and patience, to accompany the healing space with a vision toward systemic analysis, with opportunities for inter-connections that build a stronger community in the room. Community college students build communities despite *and* due to experiencing their classroom as a microcosm of the whole picture of interlocking oppressions. We are all here, in one place, at one time. People in a community

---

21    Excerpted from an email correspondence with Dychea Johnson. Feb. 26, 2016.

made up of people who "actually occupy different locations" as hooks describes it, are likely to say anything, and we all must practice what it means to listen, hear, respond, encourage, and negotiate conflicts (*Teaching to Transgress* 112).

If we are teaching with an attempt at accountability and transformation, we are turned inside out. Seeing our work through a social justice lens, the transformations that begin here also ripple out into all of the many marginalized communities from which my students boundary cross. They are constantly carving out a space and a voice; I think this is essential practice for their future survival in—and dismantling of—the academic hierarchies they will encounter after transfer, as well as the many other spaces they will occupy in life and work.

## Remaining Vigilant, Standing in Solidarity with Community Colleges

In a community college environment, facing all of the many pressures that we do, it is especially important to avoid letting our own voices as educators coopt an educational space, further reinforcing status quo behaviors. It might feel like we "have no time" to teach transformatively, but, contrary to what we may be told, the borderland educational spaces we occupy demand that we do, despite the tremendous emotional work it requires. Doing so can insert joy, connection, excitement and meaning into environments that might otherwise be painful sites of trauma revisited, *una herida abierta,* the scab picked off the wound.

Ideally, an institutional emphasis on teaching is what distinguishes the faculty experiences of educators at community colleges from our colleagues at four-year schools.[22] An assumption that this prevents "real scholarship" leads some of our feminist and social justice colleagues to ignore the voices of community college educators. Understanding the pain of this erasure, I would urge all of us who teach for social justice at community colleges to resist the temptation to sacrifice our "commitment to service" in order to be "taken seriously." As hooks asserts,

---

22  Setting aside that this often translates into an overwhelming course load!

> Commitment to teaching well is a commitment to service. Teachers who do the best work are always willing to serve the needs of their students. In an imperialist white-supremacist capitalist patriarchal culture, service is devalued. Dominator culture pointedly degrades service as a way of maintaining subordination. Those who serve tend to be regarded as unworthy and inferior. No wonder then that there is little positive discussion of the teacher's commitment to serve. (*Teaching Community* 83)

We should develop a strong record of transformative teaching practices with "measurable outcomes," and immeasurable outcomes, while using alternative ways of voicing our communities' experiences of marginalization. Rather than becoming more like mainstream academia, community college teaching and learning should re-inform social justice/feminist theorizing, modeling ways in which systems of interlocking oppression can be chipped away through these transformative mini communities in our classrooms. It is precisely because community colleges often operate as borderland spaces that they are most in need of, and most conducive to, vibrantly exciting pedagogical practices.

# Works Cited

Alexander, M. Jacqui. *Pedagogies of Crossing: Meditations on Feminism, Sexual Politics, Memory, and the Sacred.* Duke University Press, 2006.

Anzaldúa, Gloria. *Borderlands/La Frontera: The New Mestiza.* 4th Edition, Aunt Lute Books, 2012.

Battalora, Jacqueline. *Birth of a White Nation: The Invention of White People and Its Relevance Today.* Strategic Book Publishing, 2013.

"Community College Fast Facts." American Association of Community Colleges (AACC). 2015-2018, https://www.aacc.nche.edu/research-trends/fast-facts/. Accessed 18 Apr. 2018.

"Higher Education Leaders from Across the U.S. Commit to Boost College Access and Success for Low-Income, Minority Students." The Education Trust, 3 Dec. 2009, https://edtrust.org/press_release/higher-education-leaders-from-across-the-u-s-commit-to-boost-college-access-and-success-for-low-income-minority-students-2/. Accessed 18 Apr. 2018.

Freire, Paulo. *Pedagogy of the Oppressed.* 30th Anniversary Edition, Bloomsbury Academic, 2000.

hooks, bell. "Choosing the Margins as a Space of Radical Openness." *Yearning: Race, Gender, and Cultural Politics.* South End Press, 1989.

———. *Teaching Community: A Pedagogy of Hope.* Routledge, 2003.

———. *Teaching to Transgress: Education as the Practice of Freedom.* Routledge, 1994.

Johnson, Dychea. "Re: When I began your class." Received by Amanda Loos, 25 Feb. 2016.

Keating, AnaLouise. *Teaching Transformation: Transcultural Classroom Dialogues.* Palgrave MacMillan, 2007.

Levins Morales, Aurora. *Medicine Stories: History, Culture and the Politics of Integrity.* South End Press, 1998.

Loos, Amanda. "Invisible Battlefields: A Call to Stand with Community Colleges on the Frontlines of Resistance." *Praxis: Journal of the Arcus Center for Social Justice Leadership.* 2 Mar. 2016, http://www.kzoo.edu/praxis/invisible-battlefields/

Okun, Tema. *The Emperor Has No Clothes: Teaching About Race and Racism to People Who Don't Want to Know.* Information Age Publishing, 2010.

Portillo, Lourdes. *Señorita Extraviada.* Women Make Movies, 2001.

Pranis, Kay. *The Little Book of Circle Processes: A New/Old Approach to Peacemaking.* Good Books, 2005.

# The Community College as an Enabling Institution: Women's Studies Programs Resisting the Neoliberal Severing of the Personal and Political

Sara Hosey

> "Feminist education—the feminist classroom—is and should be a place where there is a sense of struggle, where there is visible acknowledgment of the union of theory and practice, where we work together as teachers and students to overcome the estrangement and alienation that have become so much the norm in the contemporary university." (bell hooks, *Talking Back*, 51)

## Introduction: Enabling and Disabling Contexts

Early in her first semester at a large state university, Ellie[23] was sexually assaulted in a dorm room. Although she felt the campus officers she spoke to about the assault were helpful and sympathetic, she was unwilling to face what she understood would be a lengthy and difficult ordeal and decided not to pursue a complaint. As the semester continued, however, Ellie found herself struggling. She was failing all of her classes and ultimately stopped attending, leaving school two weeks before the beginning of winter break.

---

23   Student names have been changed. Quoted material is from personal interviews.

Ellie is white and upper-middle class. She describes her parents as supportive of her; when she told them what had happened to her they encouraged her to go to therapy, to move back home, and, a few months later, to enroll in classes at Nassau Community College (NCC). Ellie says she initially imagined NCC would be a "shithole," as that was its reputation among many of her friends, so she was happily surprised when she found herself connecting deeply with other students in her Introduction to Women's Studies class. As a result of those relationships, she became involved with and subsequently took on a leadership role in NCC's women's student group. In addition, over three semesters at NCC, she has earned high grades, revised her career goals, begun and maintained a long-term romantic relationship with another student, and looks forward to transferring to a four-year school. For Ellie, the community college became a safe place to recover from trauma, to pursue her interests, to develop meaningful relationships, and to prepare for the next steps in her academic career.

Ellie's perspectives and experiences are not unique. Anecdotally, those of us who teach community college know that, while there are some students who are happy and proud to enroll in a community college, many, like Ellie, perceive community college as a last resort, as a dumping ground for underprepared students, as not "real college" or as an extension of high school (O'Keefe). Perhaps more problematically, these assumptions seem to be shared by some faculty at many four-year schools. What does it say about our democracy if "democracy's colleges"[24] are widely imagined to be "shitholes"?

However, like Ellie, those of us affiliated with community colleges have also found—or already knew—that the community college with a commitment to women's studies and a strong feminist ethos is a site of resistance to the neoliberal severing of the personal and the political that has taken place at many "corporate universities" within the "academic industrial complex."[25]

---

24  The term "democracy's colleges" was originally used to refer to the land-grant colleges of the 19th century that provided access to education to many farmers and industrial laborers. See Earl Ross's 1942 book, *Democracy's Colleges: The Land Grant Movement in the Formative Stage*. However, the term is now popularly applied to open-access community colleges. See, for example, the American Association of Community College's 2010 report "Democracy's Colleges: the Evolution of the Community College in America" (Boggs).

25  See Felicia Lee's "Academic Industrial Complex" for a discussion of this term.

Whereas many four-year colleges function as disabling contexts, or spaces in which students must conform to bourgeoisie conceptions of the "traditional" student or risk exclusion, open-enrollment institutions can function as "enabling contexts": learning environments which create the conditions for all students to feel a sense of belonging, to access the support they need to succeed, and to nurture not only academic accomplishment, but personal growth and empowerment.

Using a feminist disability studies-informed perspective,[26] I will discuss data about community colleges nationally as well as from my home institution (NCC), in addition to information obtained through interviews with several current and former NCC students, in order to argue that the ideals of the community college are compatible with feminist thinking in exciting and potentially fruitful ways. NCC is an example of a community college grounded in feminist ethos in that the college has created the conditions for the sharing of diverse perspectives and for true student engagement. NCC's Women's Studies Project[27] has succeeded in embracing the concept of the "personal is political" in our theory and our practice, fulfilling hooks's call to overcome the "estrangement and alienation" so common in higher education. I conclude this essay with a discussion of how entrenched heteropatriarchy and the pervasive myth of "postfeminism" threaten our mission, as well as how and why faculty at four-year colleges should embrace the project of the feminist community college.

---

26  While feminist scholarship engages with the construction of all social hierarchies and, in particular, forwards critiques of ableism, feminist and disability studies scholarship too often remain discrete disciplines. Thus, "feminist disability studies" as practiced by Rosemarie Garland-Thomson and Alison Kafer makes central the intersections of gender and disability identity, challenging naturalized hierarchies based on perceived "difference" or inferiority and insisting on the importance of context. In *Feminist Queer Crip*, for example, Alison Kafer argues for a departure from the cultural model of disability in order to suggest that those within the disability community can acknowledge the difficulties that might accrue to physical conditions without succumbing to a medical model which casts disability as inferiority, as self-evidently deficient, and as apolitical. I draw on Kafer here when I argue that we can be realistic about the challenges some community college students face without casting those challenges as unilaterally negative, insurmountable, or useless.

27  At NCC, "projects" are interdisciplinary programs that have significantly less clout than official departments, but are generally well-supported by the institution.

## "I Could Connect with Everything": Forging Conceptual and Personal Relationships at the Community College

Identifying crucial overlaps between postfeminist and neoliberal sensibilities, Rosalind Gill writes,

> First, and most broadly, both appear to be structured by a current of individualism that has almost entirely replaced notions of the social or political, or any idea of the individual as subject to pressures, constraints or influence from outside themselves. Secondly, it is clear that the autonomous, calculating, self-regulating subject of neoliberalism bears a strong resemblance to the active, freely choosing, self-reinventing subject of postfeminism. (Gill)

I follow Gill in arguing that the neoliberal and postfeminist emphasis on the autonomous individual relies upon a severing of the personal from the political, an understanding which refuses to acknowledge the impact of larger systems and hierarchies on the individual's lives and experiences. Much recent rhetoric surrounding higher education reflects this thinking in its assumptions that college is a private benefit for hard-working citizens, rather than a public good that should be truly accessible to all.[28] A neoliberal postfeminist sensibility in higher education naturalizes those mechanisms which continue to exclude marginalized groups, including those with physical, emotional, or intellectual impairments, people of color, females who provide care to family members, and poor people, by casting these groups as "nontraditional," unworthy of education, or incapable of learning. A feminist disability studies-informed perspective enables us to analyze and lay bare the ableist, racist, and classist underpinnings of the neoliberal postfeminist understanding which undervalues the experiences of and expectations for "nontraditional" students.

---

28　See Sara Hebel's "From Public Good to Private Good" and Chris Davidson's "Public vs. Private Good: How Neoliberalism has Changed the Role of Higher Education and Created Issues of Access."

Rhetoric about "traditional" and "nontraditional" students is a neoliberal euphemism that is inaccurate and injurious.[29] "Traditional students" signifies individuals who are white, able-bodied, middle and upper class and 18-21 years old. Traditional students often do not work full-time in addition to going to school and they generally do not have dependents. Nontraditional students may have some of these characteristics but fail to conform in some crucial category. Thus, when an individual's circumstances sets her apart from the traditional model—if she has children or parents that need care, if she is part of an underrepresented minority group, if she is over the age of 25, if she is a veteran—she is often made to feel that her personal challenges are just that: personal, rather than political. The neoliberal university relies upon ignoring systems which create inequality, in order to persist as institutions that pretend to challenge inequality at the same time that they replicate the status quo: those with means and support are enabled to succeed while those without are expected to fail. Students risk exclusion if they are unable to grapple with educational obstacles silently and independently.

The community college's negative reputation is inextricable from representations that position traditional and nontraditional students as discrete categories in opposition to each other, effectively erasing the challenges "traditional" students might be facing, while casting "nontraditional" students as deficient is some respect and therefore an "undesirable" population. However, the alternative to the disabling model of the neoliberal university is not one in which "we meet students where they are," a perhaps well-intentioned but nevertheless patronizing cliché often batted around by community college professors that suggests that "where" community college students are is a place that

---

29  According to the National Center for Educational Statistics: "Exactly what constitutes a nontraditional student has been the source of much discussion in recent research. Most often age (especially being over the age of 24) has been the defining characteristic for this population ... Age acts as a surrogate variable that captures a large, heterogeneous population of adult students who often have family and work responsibilities as well as other life circumstances that can interfere with successful completion of educational objectives. Other variables typically used to characterize nontraditional students are associated with their background (race and gender), residence (i.e., not on campus), level of employment (especially working full time), and being enrolled in nondegree occupational programs" (*Nontraditional Undergraduates*). Over 70% of undergraduates, however, may be considered "nontraditional" (Sheehy), further suggesting how this designation tends to obscure rather than illuminate.

is somewhat removed from where other, "normal" students are. This approach to "nontraditional" students suggests that even in attempts to be inclusive, to recognize that students have a variety of needs and interests, we often succumb to a kind of thinking that measures students using white middle-class norms, consistently and implicitly understanding "difference" from these norms as inferiority. This too, of course, is an ableist model. In this model, the (often white, non-disabled, middle-class) community college professor is the long-suffering do-gooder who works with undesirable populations in order to lift them up and mold them into proper able-bodied workers.[30]

Of course, many students do come to community college rather than attending four-year schools because they are in some respect "disadvantaged." Many of the students who attend community college have been previously failed by educational systems, their families, their communities and/or the United States more generally.[31] Many students of color attend community colleges, as do many students from low-income backgrounds.[32] Many are older, have families, and must work full-time (Perna).[33] While acknowledging the difficulties that many of these students face in the racist, heteropatriarchal, ableist United States of the early 21st century and how these difficulties might negatively affect their ability to "perform" academically, we can no longer countenance the defining of community college students by their adversity.

---

30   For a discussion of the "white hero teacher" narrative, see Christopher Emdin's *For White Folks Who Teach in the Hood ... and the Rest of Y'all Too: Reality Pedagogy and Urban Education*.

31   Seventy-five percent of students in open-enrollment two-year institutions are placed in one or more remedial classes. *See Beyond the Rhetoric: Improving College Readiness Through Coherent State Policy* (2010). Additionally, according to the American Association of Community College's 2012 report, *Why Access Matters: The Community College Student Body*, "Community college students have a greater proportion of students with various risk factors when compared to all of higher education" (Mullin).

32   According to the American Association of Community College's 2014 factsheet, 56% of Hispanic undergraduates and 48% of black undergraduates were enrolled at community colleges. Additionally, the Association of Community College's 2012 report, *Why Access Matters: The Community College Student Body*, claims that community colleges "provide access to nearly half of all minority undergraduate students and more than 40% of undergraduate students living in poverty."

33   According to the American Association of University Professors' report *Understanding the Working College Student*, community college students are employed at the same rates as four-year college students despite the belief that community college students must work more (Perna, 2010).

Instead, we can overcome the "estrangement and alienation" of the contemporary college if we use feminist and disability studies perspectives in order to remember the political in the personal and the personal in the political as we attempt to forge enabling institutions.

An enabling context is one that not only emphasizes the importance of learning the tools and the vocabulary to demand justice for oneself and for others, and to identify and resist disabling contexts, but is also one that does not seek to "fix" the student. Rather, an enabling, feminist context seeks to analyze and "fix" the environment, combatting racism, classism, sexism, and ableism both in the institution and in the larger community. As always, professors have much to learn from students. Thus, many of the community college students that I've worked with report that they don't necessarily wish their lives had been "different." Rosie, a former NCC student, is Deaf. She reports that she does not wish to be hearing, although she does wish that more of her peers and professors knew sign language. Another former NCC student, Lila, who was encouraged by her dysfunctional family to drop out of school at 15, reports that she does not wish she had a different family, although she does wish there had been more supportive systems in place that would have enabled her mother to better care for her children.

Rosie and Lila are not "deficient" students, although each had unique needs when she began studying at NCC. Lila, for example, arrived with profound gaps in her academic knowledge and skills. Yet, again, while she is frank about the suffering she experienced as a young person, Lila nevertheless maintains that her family's poverty and homelessness has made her a more empathetic person. She says that she wants "to do good in the world, to help people." While it is likely that Lila would have felt a calling to socially important work even if she had not attended college, her decision to pursue an education enriched her life as well as the lives of her classmates and professors. For example, Lila often used class discussions as opportunities to reconsider her experiences of disempowerment, including racism and economic and educational disenfranchisement. In this way, she raised awareness of these issues as well as modeled thoughtful feminist analysis for her peers at the same time that she developed a perspective on how her life has been impacted by larger, often dysfunctional, systems. As a caseworker advocating for homeless individuals in New York City, she now acts on that knowledge. She has moved beyond analyzing her own experiences of injustice and enacts feminist practice in her work.

The analysis of experiences of adversity can lead to enlightenment and empowerment for all participants. A strength of community colleges generally, especially in contrast to many public and private four-year schools, is the racial, ethnic, class, and age diversity of community college students. NCC, for example, is located in Nassau County, New York, in what is the most racially segregated suburb in the United States (Lambert). As of 2016, our student population was 41% white, 21.5% black, 20.7% Hispanic, 6.3% Asian, 5.6% unknown, 4.1% American Indian, and 1.3% "Non Resident Alien" (Petersen). Anecdotally, I know that some white students are in fact uncomfortable with the diversity of NCC; I suspect too, that some of NCC's reputation as a "shithole" might arise from many white students' basic inexperience and wariness of multi-racial situations. Again, however, what may be perceived by some from dominant groups (i.e. white, affluent, able-bodied, US citizens) as a shortcoming of the institution is ultimately one of its greatest offerings: in an increasingly stratified society, sites including NCC's classrooms, club meetings, teams, and childcare center often provide safe spaces for individuals of different racial/ethnic backgrounds, social classes, ages, and abilities, to interact and connect.

For example, we discuss segregation in the women's studies and composition classes I teach and it is not uncommon for students to share that before NCC, they had never taken a class with or meaningfully engaged with a student of a different race. In this simple fact, NCC provides a unique situation in which students from various backgrounds whose lives have been impacted by historical and systemic racism (that they are often unaware of), have the opportunity, for the first and perhaps only time in their lives, to engage in rigorous and respectful discussion with individuals of different races and socioeconomic backgrounds. Further, moving beyond the identification of segregation and racism, together as a class we grapple with the historical and political contexts that have created the neighborhoods we call home, deal honestly and critically with our responses to our histories, and develop understandings, coalitions, and strategies for overcoming the political forces that have kept us separate. Women's studies classes provide an opportunity for us to carefully begin this work in theoretically informed ways.

Another example of a site on campus which has encouraged the development of sustaining relationships across age, race, class, and social position is the childcare center, NCC's Children's Greenhouse.[34] The Greenhouse offers a sliding-scale payment plan (and many students received subsidies). Between 70-75% of Greenhouse parents are NCC students; the vast majority are mothers, and many are low-income. Beyond providing childcare, which is itself crucially important,[35] the Greenhouse, by offering an on-site mentoring program that pairs professors with students, facilitating a club for student parents, and providing informal opportunities for parents to socialize and connect, has evolved into a site of feminist struggle and mutual aid. Thus, imagine meeting a young mother and commiserating with her over the "terrible twos" at a pizza party; then imagine seeing that individual as a student in your class or in the college writing center. Rather than "meeting students where they are," perhaps we should simply "meet students" and find out who they are. From there we can begin to better construct learning environments to best meet their needs.

Authentically meeting students as individuals is a challenge to hierarchies in higher education and a source of feminist activism. One "nontraditional" student, Julia, was a fifty-year-old wife, mother, and hairdresser when she enrolled in her first college class in 1993. She'd not gone to college earlier because, she explained, her Italian American family did not value education for girls and women; when she considered pursuing a degree later, around the time her own children were attending and graduating from college, her husband opposed the idea of her taking classes at NCC. Julia insisted, pushing back against her own self-doubt and internalized sexism. In her Introduction to Women's Studies class Julia felt she could "connect with everything." The class provided her with a critical framework for analyzing many of her experiences, including her termination of a pregnancy before Roe V. Wade and

---

34  The Greenhouse was established in 1979 through the work of women's studies faculty and allies who recognized childcare as a social justice and feminist issue.

35  One crucial aspect of supporting community college students is ensuring that parents of young children have access to affordable and excellent childcare. The American Association of University Women report notes that 25% of all women in community colleges are mothers; half of those mothers are not married. The AAUW report notes that "Student parents consistently cite child care responsibilities as a chief reason for dropping out."

her unquestioning acceptance of her husband's emotional abuse. For Julia, as for many women's studies students, the discovery of the personal as political was empowering and energizing. At NCC, Julia was not made to feel that she was too old, too unsophisticated, "just a mom" or simply a hairdresser. The women's studies faculty and, in particular, the program coordinator at that time, Dr. Barbara Horn, recognized and encouraged Julia's intellectual curiosity and emerging activism. She became a student aide in the women's studies office and later, when pursuing higher degrees at other institutions, she worked as the women's studies "administrative assistant" or secretary.

Julia is now a poet and an associate professor of English and women's studies at a community college. She is beloved by her students, many of whom she connects with deeply. Julia would have been an insightful and compassionate person whether or not she'd ever taken a women's studies course. However, the opportunity to immerse herself in feminist theory and practice allowed her to understand her experiences of oppression, violence, and shame as not private or separate from larger social issues. In addition, she was provided with the opportunity to communicate to others how the personal is, ultimately, political, and to embody the feminist principal that all individuals, regardless of race, class, age, gender, or ability, have the right to learn, to speak, and to be heard. Where else but in a women's studies program does the secretary have the support and mobility to become the professor? Perhaps Julia would have persisted regardless of the institution where she began her higher education; however, the structures in place at NCC, including a strong women's studies program which employs full-time professors, which keeps class size small, and which encourages and works to retain a truly diverse student population, clearly provides the kind of environment in which a student like Julia would be more likely to succeed.

Julia's story is not simply one of private benefit. Julia enriches the lives of her colleagues and students. (She reports, too, that her husband's life has been improved by feminism. They are still happily married, but like his wife, his understandings have evolved). Thus, Julia's successes demonstrate the opportunities and possibilities of the community college generally, but also the community college with a strong, vibrant women's studies program that emphasizes feminist pedagogy and practice.

## Conclusions: "Cultivating Accountability"

Recently at NCC, some women's studies faculty began to question the appropriateness of enrolling students in women's studies courses if those students had not yet completed their remedial course work.[36] These faculty members articulated a reasonable fear that the content of our women's studies courses was too sophisticated for students struggling to read and write at a college level and that allowing students to enroll created the conditions for failure.

In order to understand how our students were performing in classes, we asked the Office of Institutional Research to gather data comparing outcomes for students in Introduction to Women's Studies (WST 101) classes who had been placed in one or more remedial course and those who had no remedial courses. What we discovered was that the WST 101 pass rates for students in multiple remedial courses were comparable to those of students in no remedial classes; during one semester, in fact, "remedial" students out-performed students who had no remediations.[37]

These results suggest to me that, rather than creating conditions for failure, women's studies courses can promote success, as the material we cover in these courses is at once challenging and relevant. More precisely, while clearly college students should and do grapple with material that at first blush might not seem relevant (Kant, for example, or chemistry), a level of disengagement coupled with weak skills, under-preparation, and/or general alienation in college might lead to higher withdrawals and failures, whereas the content of women's studies courses may be sophisticated or even to some degree upsetting, but is almost always immediately applicable in student's lives. Pedagogies that blend academic and popular material, invite students to draw on

---

36    From fall 2008 through fall 2011, 70-71% of NCC's incoming students were placed in remedial courses (*SUNY Finds*).

37    According to our research, in the fall 2012 semester, 81% of students with one remedial class passed WST 101 and 60% of students in no remedial courses passed. Remedial students were less successful in subsequent semesters, but still remained competitive: in spring 2013, 34% of remedial students passed and 64% of non-remedial students passed; in fall 2013, 55% of remedial students passed and 82% of non-remedial students passed; in spring 2014, 63% of remedial students passed and 70% of non-remedial students passed.

their own experiences and observations, ask students to think creatively and allow them to draw on their areas of expertise build confidence and engagement not only in women's studies courses, but potentially across all of their college experiences. Thus, through embracing active learning pedagogies and multiple learning modalities, community college women's studies programs can continue to trouble academic hierarchies as well as serve as models across the campus.

Further, it is both a challenge and a gift of academic women's studies that we are definitionally required to continue learning and evolving, remaining aware of the "ways in which we may consciously and unconsciously reproduce the dominant social order in our own classrooms" (Crabtree and Sapp 132). Consistent with many aspects of feminist pedagogy, this self-reflection keeps us honest as feminist practitioners. In "cultivating accountability" we are "encouraging faculty and students in women's studies to recognize our structural relationship to one another and our involvement in maintaining systemic hierarchies" (Russo qtd. in Adsit 30). In doing so, we can resist succumbing to the fear that in order to secure and maintain academic legitimacy, we should abandon experiential and experimental research, publications, and pedagogies.

But just as we must continue to hold ourselves accountable in the community college, our colleagues and allies at selective four-year colleges and universities must also answer for their neglect of community college students. That is, to truly embrace diversity, academic feminists affiliated with four-year colleges and universities must begin to grapple with the racial segregation that they countenance at their home institutions, to resist transforming women and gender studies classes into places "where revolutionary feminist thought and activism are submerged and made secondary to the goals of academic careerism" (hooks 51), and to continue the project of historical, political, and personal analysis of their situations.[38] It must be part of the larger feminist agenda to more fully support the work that goes on in community colleges. Ignoring community college students, faculty, and work reflects a larger surrender to

---

38  Many four-year schools continue to lack diversity; see Ben Wolfgang's "Report: Racial Divide Still Exists on College Admissions" in which he discusses Georgetown University's Center on Education and the Workforce's study showing that since 1995, 80% of white students enroll at "elite and competitive" schools, while 70% of black and Hispanic students enroll at community college and open-access institutions.

a neoliberal postfeminist severing of the personal and the political. That is, if you don't see and struggle with and for students in community colleges, you become one of the voices telling these individuals, you are not real students, you are on your own, your voices, stories, and needs are not important.

Those of us who are affiliated with community colleges, of course, have our own work to do as well. Despite many of the strengths of my home institution, for example, we still struggle with the more general neoliberal devaluing of education, which we feel most acutely in the form of diminishing support from the county and state. Most particularly, despite years of handwringing, NCC's faculty remains shamefully racially homogenous, especially given the demographics of our community and our student population.[39] In addition, in 2016, NCC's administration published a public "Performance Improvement Plan" which grossly misrepresented female faculty's contributions to and motivations for teaching at NCC, suggesting that female faculty in particular are drawn to NCC because of a light teaching load and minimal publication expectations. Further, specific female faculty have felt discriminated against and, in particular, those faculty who dedicate service in areas traditionally coded feminine, such as our campus daycare, have found their work dismissed and devalued during promotion considerations. Finally, several sites on campus which employ largely female work forces—including the childcare center, which has an all-female staff—are marred by abysmally low wages.[40]

Unsurprisingly, these problems are inextricable from the issues we review in women's studies classes and which affect student's lives. These are the challenges we must confront at NCC, but they are not challenges unique to NCC and as feminists we must face them together, insisting that persistent racial and gender discrimination, the devaluing of women's work inside and outside of the academy, and the lack of support for caregivers (be they parents, adult children, or daycare staff), are understood as political issues which affect all of our lives. In this way, in addition to functioning as emblematic of the gains

---

39   According to the *SUNY Report Card-Nassau* for 2010-11, 83% of NCC's faculty and staff are white.

40   The faculty of the Women's Studies Project has mobilized to draw attention to the issue of the low wages at the childcare center.

feminists have made in recent decades, women's studies programs at community colleges can provide us with a sense of what work remains to be done.

# Works Cited

Adsit, J. & Doe, S. & Allison, M. & Maggio, P. & Maisto, M. "Affective Activism: Answering Institutional Productions of Precarity in the Corporate University." *Feminist Formations*, vol. 27 no. 3, 2015, pp. 21-48.

*Beyond the Rhetoric: Improving College Readiness Through Coherent State Policy*, National Center for Public Policy and Education and the Southern Regional Education Board, 2010.

Boggs, George R. *Democracy's Colleges: The Evolution of the Community College in America*, Washington, D.C.: American Association of Community Colleges, 2010.

Crabtree, Robbin D. & Sapp, David Allan. "Theoretical, Political, and Pedagogical Challenges in the Feminist Classroom: Our Struggles to Walk the Walk." *College Teaching*, vol. 51, issue 4, Fall 2003, pp. 131-140.

Davidson, Chris. "Public vs. Private Good: How Neoliberalism has Changed the Role of Higher Education and Created Issues of Access." *RE: Reflections on Experience*. 12 February 2015, www.blogs.lt.vt.edu

Emdin, Christopher. *For White Folks Who Teach in the 'Hood ... and the Rest of Y'all Too: Reality Pedagogy and Urban Education*. New York: Beacon Press, 2016.

Garland-Thomson, Rosemarie. "Integrating Disability, Transforming Feminist Theory." *NWSA Journal* vol. 14, issue 3, 2002, pp. 1-32.

Gill, Rosalind. "Postfeminist Media Studies: Elements of a Sensibility." *European Journal of Cultural Studies*. vol. 10, issue 2, 2007, pp. 147-166.

hooks, bell. *Talking Back: Thinking Feminist, Thinking Black*. NY: Routledge, 1989, 2015.

Kafer, Alison. *Feminist Queer Crip*. Indiana University Press, 2013.

Lambert, Bruce. "Study Calls L.I. Most Segregated Suburb." *New York Times*, 5 June 2002, http://www.nytimes.com/2002/06/05/nyregion/study-calls-li-most-segregated-suburb.html?mcubz=0

Lee, Felicia. "Academic Industrial Complex." *New York Times*, 9 June 2003, http://www.nytimes.com/2003/09/06/arts/academic-industrial-complex.html?mcubz=0

Mullin, Christopher M. "Why Access Matters: The Community College Student Body." American Association of Community Colleges, Washington D.C.: 2012.

*Nontraditional Undergraduates*, National Center for Education Statistics, https://nces.ed.gov/pubs/web/97578e.asp

O'Keefe, Kristin. "The Community College/ 'Real' College Divide," *New York Times*, 11 February 2015. The Motherlode. https://parenting.blogs.nytimes.com/2015/02/11/the-community-collegereal-college-divide/?mcubz=0

Perna, Laura W. *Understanding the Working College Student*, American Association of University Professors, 2010.

Petersen, Carrie. 2016. "Nassau Community College," Stateuniversity.com

Ross, Earl D. *Democracy's College: The Land Grant Movement in the Formative Stage*. Iowa State College, 1942.

Sheehy, Kelsey. "Three Common Questions from Nontraditional Students Answered," *US News and World Report*, September 30, 2013, https://www.usnews.com/education/best-colleges/paying-for-college/articles/2013/09/30/3-common-questions-from-nontraditional-students-answered

St. Rose, Andresse and Catherine Hill. *Women in Community Colleges: Access to Success*, Washington, D.C.: The American Association of University Women. 2013.

"SUNY Finds Too Many Not Ready for College," *Newsday*, 17 January 2012, http://www.newsday.com/opinion/suny-finds-too-many-not-ready-for-college-1.3456637

*SUNY Scorecard: A Competitive SUNY, Including 2010-11 Report Data for Campus: Nassau*, https://www.suny.edu/media/suny/content-assets/documents/excels/SUNY-Excels-PIP-Narrative_Nassau_20151223.pdf

*2016 Fact Sheet*. American Association of Community Colleges, Washington, D.C., 2016.

Wolfgang, Ben. "Report: Racial Divide Still Exists on College Admissions." *Washington Times*, 12 August 2013, http://www.washingtontimes.com/news/2013/aug/5/report-racial-divide-still-exists-on-college-admis/

# Student Voices: Jimmy Lynch, Jefferson Community and Technical College

Louisville, Kentucky

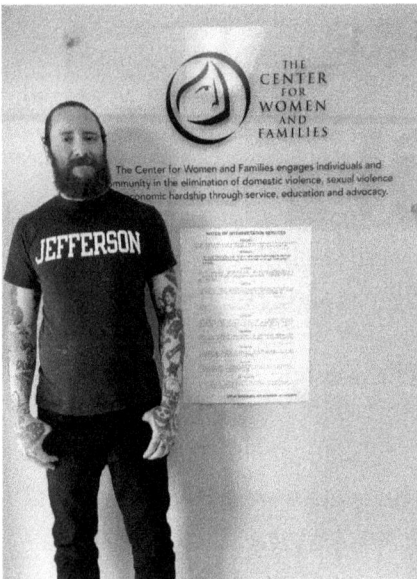

Jimmy Lynch completed an AA and a Certificate in women's and gender studies from Jefferson Community and Technical College. He will graduate magna cum laude from the BSW program at the University of Louisville's Kent School of Social Work in May 2019 and intends to pursue a MSSW. Jimmy has been involved with the Center for Women and Families in various roles as a volunteer and practicum student providing trauma-informed advocacy and support for individuals, families, and communities affected by intimate partner violence and sexual assault.

*How did your women's and gender studies course contribute to your career goals? How did the course prepare you for the workforce?*

"After reading 'I Am Not a Rapist!' by John Stoltenberg for my coursework I was motivated to take part in a group similar to the one described in the article. After meeting with my professor, I became active with the Own It initiative of the Center for Women and Families (CWF) in Louisville, Kentucky. I also believe that my women's and gender studies certification will make me a more desirable applicant for employment with the CWF or an organization with similar values and goals. The coursework in general has taught me to better understand and provide service to groups and individuals at risk for gender-based violence."

*How did the course help you in your private life (interpersonal relationships, parenting, self-esteem, self-love, etc.)?*

"Taking these courses has increased my awareness of power differentials in my interpersonal relationships and I no longer pursue less healthy relationships. The relationships I do maintain are more fulfilling on an individual basis. Although the focus of these courses was to raise awareness of oppression of varied groups, I was personally made aware of my own privilege. Being fully aware of my own privilege has empowered me to take responsibility for the world around me and to use my own privilege to empower the oppressed."

*Would you recommend the course(s) to other students? If so, why?*

"I would and do recommend these courses to every student I can. As the world becomes increasingly diverse and interconnected, I consider it a necessity to understand the differences in the life experiences of individuals. I have taken no other course that has increased my ability to understand these differences and to work for and with others as my WGS courses have."

*How was/were your women's and gender studies course(s) different from the other courses you took in college?*

"I can recall no point in my WGS courses where I was told the correct answer to a question. My WGS coursework was designed to [make me] think about and come to some personal comprehension of a topic and communicate my own answers of a question while considering differing situational perspectives."

*How did taking the women's and gender studies course(s) help you understand other courses better? In what ways did you notice connections between what you learned and studied in women's and gender studies and the other course(s)?*

"Because of my own awareness of other individuals as stakeholders in different issues I am now better able to understand their expectations and meet them in my other courses. I am also able to be more diplomatic in framing an issue of equality or social justice in a way so that others may recognize their role as stakeholders and see a personal benefit in working toward a more equitable culture."

# Our Stories to Tell: Situating Activism in the Intersections of Class, Women's/Gender Studies, and Community Colleges

Jill M. Adams

## Introduction

On February 25, 2015, almost 100 people attended a teach-in at Jefferson Community and Technical College in Louisville, Kentucky. In response to, and in solidarity with National Adjunct Walk-Out Day, two English Department adjunct faculty members opted to conduct a teach-in instead of walking out. They wanted to create a learning opportunity that shed light on the plight of contingent faculty facing issues such as low pay, lack of benefits, limited if any office space, last-minute contracts, and more. The national walk-out made headlines leading up to and after the event, in a range of online and print publications from *Inside Higher Ed* to *The Washington Post*. Jefferson's teach-in was the cover story of Louisville's local alternative publication *LEO Weekly* which covered the teach-in and activities at Jefferson and the University of Louisville.

Activism at Jefferson—or community colleges in general—doesn't always look as familiar as a teach-in. The more common forms of activism on campus like talking about bias and privilege, supporting LGBTQ rights, hosting Love Your Body Day events or voter registration drives, and holding vigils for interpersonal violence awareness, rarely garner media attention, but are nevertheless significant. For example, students in a leadership program at Jefferson launched Students 4 Change ($4C) in order to raise money to buy grocery cards for students who don't have enough food or gas money for the week; if students are hungry or can't get to campus, then they can't learn. These acts of social change at Jefferson are often performed by students who attend part-time while holding down full-time jobs, and who typically have caregiving responsibilities at home. And, quite frankly, for many of these students, attending college is in itself an act of resistance and social change.

These forms of activism aren't flashy and don't usually receive media coverage. Yet, the actions *do* reflect the mindset and realities of many community college students. Women's and gender studies colleagues who teach at community colleges around the country recount similar experiences, but these stories and social movement aren't readily visible in scholarship or popular culture. The narratives of unrest and large protests on the storied campuses of Berkeley, Harvard, Kent State, and Columbia in the 1960s and 1970s have shaped the cultural expectations of how students, and institutions of learning, participate in activism. It makes sense then, that less flashy, smaller actions on community college campuses are overlooked: they don't look like the stories we've come to expect. For example, fifty years after Vietnam and anti-war protests, it's similar larger-scale acts such as the #BlackLivesMatter movement at the University of Missouri in 2015, or the walkouts and #MarchForOurLives actions by Marjory Stoneman Douglas students in 2018, that capture news feeds and the attention of researchers. Those are the narratives woven into our collective consciousness, and although important, those representations of campus activism don't tell the full story or reflect the dynamics and actions at many community colleges.

Activism at Jefferson doesn't look like mass movements, so it becomes invisible. To create an alter-narrative that makes visible the activism on community college campuses, we need to examine the historical context for campus activism and the ways in which class dynamics impact who within higher education participates in social action. Within women's and gender studies, we also need to understand the ways in which the discipline intersects with the identities of community college faculty and students to support or resist campus movements. For the purposes of this discussion, "activism" is defined as *an action designed to bring about social change*. This definition affords flexibility for the myriad ways that activism may show up on different campuses and the ways it reflects the community being served by community colleges.

## (A Brief) History of Community Colleges

Community colleges (CCs) are often referred to as "democracy's colleges," as institutions that meet local and regional needs for equitable access to higher education, training, and economic growth (Young; Rhoads and Valadez; Shaw, Valadez and Rhoads; Boggs; Delmont). DeBard and Rice suggest that community colleges' adaptability bridges geographic and political borders and is reflected in how they create pathways between higher education and surrounding communities for myriad types of learners. With open admissions policies that essentially advocate for accessible, affordable education for everyone, community colleges in many areas across the United States were created as a result of coalitional politics and wrangling. Local and state governments, school boards, universities and four-year colleges, business leaders, and community groups often found mutual interest in creating CCs that would serve their various needs and reflect community conditions, even while they sometimes vied for control of the new colleges (Delmont; Brown and Muller; Dowd). At Jefferson, for instance, the early months of the college's opening in 1968 were fraught with the challenges of negotiating joint oversight by both the University of Kentucky and the University of Louisville along with input by state legislators. For example, since hiring faculty and approving curriculum was initially the responsibility of the appropriate chairs and deans at the University of Louisville, "many of the [Jefferson] faculty rebelled at the constraints on their teaching" (Ecker 9-10). However, despite these challenges in leadership, the college worked to build a sense of community and collegiality while encouraging student engagement inside and outside of the classroom (Ecker 9, 11, 36). In this way Jefferson represents the promises and challenges that characterized a lot of community colleges at the time. For example, Delmont's case study of the origins of the Community College of Philadelphia recounts the tensions and collaborations of local organizations and leaders who were working to address issues of social inequality and racial diversity—framing the new CC as a means of increasing opportunity especially for students of color.

With roots in the early 20th century when junior colleges emerged to support enrollment and operational challenges at small, typically private colleges, the more systemic role of community colleges as we think of them today evolved as part of a national movement heralded by President Truman's 1947 Commission on Higher Education. The Commission called for the expansion of post-secondary education to help meet the emerging industry and workforce needs that followed World War II, and the Commission specifically called for increased access to higher education for minority populations (Cohen and Brawer; DeBard and Rice).

Because the Commission specifically focused on increased access for minority populations, the very formation of community colleges can be viewed as an act of social change within specific communities because they were focused on improving economic and social circumstances through education. Van Dyke suggests that activism early in an institution's history plays a role in shaping a subculture that encourages later activist movements on campus. Therefore, because they were originally envisioned as spaces of advocacy to support educational access, the nature of community colleges makes them potential sites of activism and social justice work in the 21st century.

Similarly, the development of women's studies as a discipline was a direct result of activism. With its "historical roots in activist movement, its social justice mandate, and its reflective approach to its own knowledge production" activism (as social change) is considered a principle of women's studies (Berger and Radeloff). In addition to challenging academe itself, the women's (and gender) studies curriculum teaches social change for the next generation of student activists to "make their classroom learning relevant, worthwhile, and, in the best cases, truly transformational for themselves and others" (Berger and Radeloff). Indeed, "women's studies without activism is like the ocean without salt.... The act of claiming the identity of 'feminist' demands that we take action for there is no separation between women's studies and activism" (Bart et al. 258, 260). Therefore, with the combined activist origins of both discipline and institution, women's and gender studies programs *at* community colleges create unique opportunities for marginalized and hyper-marginalized[41] groups (e.g., students who are marginalized in terms of identity markers like race or class and who face additional obstacles by virtue of

---

41    I use this term cautiously, not to suggest a measuring stick of marginalized groups, but to emphasize concomitant oppressions that aren't typically mentioned. Adding incarceration, substance use/recovery, and homelessness to "gender, race, and class" creates a more inclusive awareness of whose bodies are seated in CC classrooms.

having been formerly incarcerated, being in recovery, or by living in halfway houses or homeless shelters, etc.). These programs teach about oppression and emphasize the role of education in bringing about social change. In working with historically non-traditional students, the sixty-five community colleges with women's and gender studies offerings (ranging from full degrees to stand alone courses) can create possibilities for activism even for students and institutions with little or no previous experience with activism (Stoehr).

These expectations shape the outcomes of the discipline, especially with regard to the WGS introductory course (which is the most commonly offered WGS course at community colleges). Building on the groundbreaking work of Luebke and Reilly, Berger and Radeloff note the general outcomes of women's and gender studies. They identify the primary concepts of the discipline, according to WGS graduates, as gender, intersectionality, inequality, equity, and empowerment; and the salient skills as critical thinking, knowledge, communication, awareness, and empowerment. Kimmel argues that there are four pedagogical themes within women's and gender studies: power (the awareness and mutations of it within the classroom as well as societally); diversity (addressing the complexity of issues surrounding race, sex, class, and gender as well as privilege and oppression); emotions in learning (accounting for and including the affective domain); and, social responsibility and action (where "social action fosters a sense of agency and connects ideas to action, keeping feminism alive and evolving to meet the changing conditions of women's lives") (67).

If teaching women's and gender studies is partially intended to disrupt the dominant patriarchal narrative of higher learning and help foster activism, then it follows that students may be encouraged, and supported, to participate in activism on campus, including at community colleges. The challenge for us in the WGS field and on CC campuses is making (more) visible the work being done and challenging the scholarly and popular writings that omit our narratives.

## Visibility and Historical Contexts of Campus-Based Activism

With the roots of activism at post-secondary institutions reaching back to the 19th century, politics and rebellion have consistently found a home *somewhere* on college campuses. From political and social issues to curricular protests, from challenging exclusionary policies to the student demonstrations in the 1930s, student groups and students affiliated with organizations such as the American Student Union, the Student Christian Volunteer Movement, the Young Men's Christian Association, the Young Women's Christian Association, and the Young Socialists to name only a few, have reacted to and organized about injustices on campus and in their communities (Cohen and Brawer; Horowitz; Altbach).

Levine and Wilson mark three specific eras of collective student action: the period before World War I; the economic upheaval and social shift in the 1930s; and of course, the 1960s. The tools and tactics across the century are similar: "[S]tudent activism in each period is identified and characterized by what have become the familiar forms of student dissent: demonstrations, strikes, boycotts, and the like" (Levine and Wilson 628; Sahlins; Cohen and Brawer). In the 1960s, for instance, these strategies also served to merge the interests and participants of both the anti-war and counterculture movements at the time (Sahlins). This bridging of campus and community-based interests defines the most successful social movements of the mid- to late-20th century including the civil rights movement, the antiwar movement, the black power movement, and the women's liberation movement (Barlow; Cunningham; Franklin; Swank and Fahs; Renn).

Although the 1960s and 1970s typify or constitute the hegemonic narratives about student mobilizations, the 1980s witnessed strong and pervasive anti-apartheid and nuclear disarmament movements. Current 21st century campus activism has focused on issues related to undocumented students, the new student movement, labor and anti-sweatshop work, Occupy (Wall Street, etc.), rape/rape culture and sexual assault prevention, and certainly identity politics including Black Lives Matter, LGBTQ rights, and Native American rights. While the news of these movements makes its way into mainstream and social media feeds, community colleges are missing from these narratives and the scholarship that analyzes these movements. Why are CCs invisible in these writings? Perhaps because of the marginal role that CCs occupy within the hierarchy of higher education, they aren't locations where activism is expected, so they're overlooked for important, historic research.

Because these movements connect across community and campus boundaries, it's also important to contextualize community colleges and activism within their respective communities. With visions and collective cultural memories of *campus* activism, research too often minimizes campus-community coalitions, and instead characterizes social activism as a "student" movement *or* a "social" movement. The difference creates an unnatural binary that obscures activist identities that are *both* "student" and "community member." The implications for community college activists are complicated because they typically live full-time in their communities rather than on campus, and often their role as a student is only a small piece of their identity. In contrast, students residing on campus at four-year institutions are immersed in a culture that foregrounds their identity as student, and there is less need to juggle multiple expectations of self. Where Franklin asserts that students in the civil rights movement in the United States and in anti-apartheid South Africa were "willing to sacrifice their education" for these larger social changes, community college students often sacrifice their education in making choices to survive (214). These become choices and opportunities framed by class and intersected with race, sex, gender, and more. Chen and Crossley argue the significance of class in understanding why and how individuals may choose to advocate for change, but also the significance of class in contesting power to bring about that change. Students commuting to campus a few times a week have less time for interacting on campus to build networks and coalitions to support change.

Barlow's work suggests four traits common to campus movements: a heightened awareness of politics and a concomitant awareness of self; strong critical thinking spurred by liberal arts education; easily mobilized students who socialize in groups; and students "relatively free of the social constraints of jobs and families" (Barlow 2). While Barlow's assessment is useful in understanding campus activism at four-year schools, it doesn't provide an adequate framework for understand activism at CCs. For example, it doesn't adequately account for the role that class plays in shaping activist identities, the level of participation in movements, or the forms of protest that are enabled or prevented. Whether in the 1960s or in the present day, working-class students—

those often enrolled at community colleges—face multiple constraints of jobs, caretaking, and other commitments. Thus, they aren't "relatively free from the constraints of jobs and family." Additionally, community colleges are largely non-residential campuses, meaning many students remain on campus only for classes and are less likely to socialize or hang out on campus; consequently, they are not "easily mobilized students who socialize in groups," as Barlow asserts. Their "mobilization" occurs in commuting between home, campus, work, and other commitments. They don't often have the benefit of "free" time on campus to take part in student life or a movement.

Similar to Barlow, Gill and DeFronzo assert that the "social circumstances characteristic of being a student somewhat independent of both parental supervision and the pressing financial requirements of family life, permit idealism to temporarily flourish" (205). This description of student life essentializes a student experience, thus reinforcing class (and potentially race and gender) biases. The description of student activists' "social circumstances" disregards the reality and precarity experienced by working-class students, those with caretaking responsibilities, and those who juggle academic and employment commitments who do not have the time or resources for other activities. For instance, "evening students," who may take classes after a full day of childcare responsibilities or workforce employment are a distinct sector of community college student bodies and represent students CCs were designed to serve.

The narratives offered by Barlow, Gill and DeFronzo work to make CC student activism invisible. The model of student activism proffered by these researchers overlooks the role of class and how it may impact activism at community colleges. Because this type of research forms our definition of student activism, the dominant narratives around activism on college campuses remain focused on daytime protests of students gathering in groups (e.g., Black Lives Matter in Missouri).

## Stories and Scholarship About Community Colleges and WGS

Despite the activist missions of CCs, there is little research on community colleges, gender/class, and activism. The near invisibility of community colleges within research studies and discussions of higher education in general

further obscures the presence of social action at these institutions, including that stemming from women's and gender studies programs, which are similarly under-examined at community colleges. For example, in a recent three-year period, the journal *Research in Higher Education*—dedicated specifically to issues and institutions of postsecondary education—published only eight articles about community colleges out of more than 100 total, and *Gender and Education* did not publish any. Despite a focus on women's and gender studies as a discipline, *Feminist Formations* published no articles discussing community colleges during the same three-year window. Conversely, although the *Community College Journal of Research and Practice* specializes in community colleges, only 2% of their published articles deal with activism at CCs, and none discuss WGS programs.

This invisibility can be interpreted as a class issue, a sign of insignificance or lack of value, which is particularly troubling for the students, faculty, and community members of community colleges. Without research on activism at CCs, there's a risk of further marginalizing these institutions and their student bodies. Such erasure defaults four-year institutions as the primary site of campus activism, suggesting that only certain student bodies are willing and capable of being activists.

Indeed, the students who comprise most community colleges don't seem to meet a historically stereotypical "student activist" profile. Nationally, 36% of CC students are first-generation. Many are Pell eligible. Some are academically underprepared. An overwhelming number of CC students are balancing academics with employment: 62% of full-time students, and 73% of part-time students also work. Our colleges represent the diversity of the United States with enrollments of approximately 50% students of color, 17% single parents, and significant immigrant and refugee populations (AACC Fact Sheet). Founded with a mission of open enrollment and to help level the playing field for marginalized groups, erasure of these campuses underscores continued elitism within higher education.

The issue is further complicated by the general elision of class within women's and gender studies. In three recent years, for instance, the subject index of the National Women's Studies Association conference program omitted "class" as a subject of scholarship at the primary conference for the discipline (Rellihan). The implication is that class, like community colleges in general, is less significant and thus under-theorized, despite its ubiquitous role in the "gender, race, and class" triad that undergirds much of feminist intersectional scholarship.

## Defining and Making Space for Class

The fact that the default images of campus activism center white, middle-class students associated with much of the 60s and 70s activist student movements as well as national and transnational social movements beyond campus, does a disservice to people of color and low(er)-income students, and others who have financial/employment constraints yet engage with social movements while navigating those competing needs. The "middle-class" moniker was also largely drawn on economic lines alone, as students who had the economic privilege to spend their time taking part in protests. "Class" can be more expansively defined as financial/economic (in how finances are impacted by family structure/parenting/caregiving responsibilities, and how employment affects opportunities for "free time" that could be used to engage in activism); cultural (rules, expectations of spaces, communities, institutions, and social structures); physical (the "marking on the body" of speaking, walking, stance, body language, etc.); and psychological (self-concept, and managing competing and different expectations). These aspects work together to form class or a "class identity" as Bettie uses the term: "Conceiving class as an identity rather than a consciousness reveals two important points: first, that such an identity may not necessarily be a politicized one, and second, that class is only one among many identities that might mobilize people" (43). Bettie's work is particularly informative in differentiating between "inherited" (class) identity—that into which one is born and/or reared—and "chosen" (class) identity, which is the public identity her students perform at school. For community college students and faculty, the performative character of class similarly highlights the potential tension between expectations of "college self," and their upbringing, or "home self." Thinking more expansively about the definition of class may help us understand if, how, and to what degree students and faculty at community colleges engage in activism. Discussions of activism within women's and gender studies readily take race and gender into account but seem less focused on class identity.

Institutionally and individually, higher education reinforces middle-class values and shapes institutional cultures based on those values: "middle-class groups ... skillfully, assiduously, and strategically use the sphere of education to their advantage in the process of class formation" (Dowling 836). This plays out institutionally when, despite their open admissions policy to increase access to higher education, community colleges replicate middle-class values in certain ways such as faculty expectations of "successful" student mannerisms and professionalism. At the personal level, being "successful" for many working-class students and faculty necessitates "passing" as middle class to meet expectations. Navigating those expectations and challenges is part of the class performance demanded of working-class bodies especially in educational settings (Bettie; Walkerdine and Ringrose). Their struggle is how to utilize social capital (access to higher education) in order to build economic capital without sabotaging their *existing* social capital vested in their relationships with families and neighborhoods. Through this process, students illustrate the duality of class as both a fluid and fixed identity, what Bettie differentiates as the performance (fluid) and performative (fixed) nature of class. Performing class can shape expectations of their own worth, voice, and power to make change (Bettie; Adair, "Branded").

Tokarczyk and Fay assert that working-class women in academe pay a particular price for class transformation: although higher education can be a path toward economic stability, "it offers hope even as that hope is complicated by pedagogies and policies that are ultimately detrimental to poor women." Black suggests that working-class women are dually othered as women and then as working-class women. She makes clear the connection between identity, place, and class by asserting the multiple layers of oppression which working-class women experience in academia. For instance, Black argues that working-class women have "failed against middle-class standards of femininity," and observes that their "ability to succeed in an unfamiliar world with a set of rules which remain alien, and are implicit until transgressed, depends upon learning to read, understand, and 'pass' according to those rules" (131).

Student stories may illustrate how to better understand class dynamics and student activism. Extending a class analysis, Leondar-Wright poses specific organizational questions: "What could be seen by looking through a class lens? If members' class life stories were known and discussed, what mysteries in activist groups would be cleared up? If class-culture differences were named and understood, what new solutions to voluntary-group troubles would be possible?" (27).

Thinking about the collaborative nature, or at least mutual interest, of activist work, collective action could benefit from organizing strategies that understand and create space for classed, intersectional identities (Kennelly, "Youth Cultures" and "Learning to Protest"). How, for instance, might a classroom or campus environment function as an *organization* that contributes to shared identities, or perhaps points of solidarity, that foster or discourage activism? How might we look differently for, and at, activism happening at community colleges and the ways in which it's shaped by class identity in terms of time, resources, comfort level/experience with activism, and sense of activist agency (feeling knowledgeable, capable, and willing to engage in activism)?

Because poverty-class and working-class identities can be a source of *dis*empowerment in our broader communities, understanding how campus communities interpret and operationalize class is essential to any consideration of activism at community colleges. Obvious challenges faced by poverty- and working-class students such as working full- or part-time while also taking courses, not feeling included, and lack of previous exposure to activism can pose barriers for engagement. Although limited student life experiences are a/n (unintended) consequence of being a commuting, often part-time student with responsibilities beyond the campus, it's paramount that we recognize less traditionally "visible" forms of activism. Expanding our definition of what counts as activism to include less-traditional forms of student movements will help make visible the activism at CCs. Community colleges are defining activism for ourselves. How we listen for and document this movement on our campuses begins (re)locating that alter-narrative within the dominant story of activism. Women's and gender studies classrooms and programs at community colleges are pivotal points for teaching about social justice; for practicing intersectional pedagogy that truly interrogates and embraces gender, race, and class identities in activism; and creating a space for telling these stories— our stories.

# Works Cited

Adair, Vivyan C. "Branded with Infamy: Inscriptions of Poverty and Class in the United States." *Signs,* vol. 27, no. 2, 2002, pp. 451-471. *Jstor,* www.jstor.org/stable/3175788.

———. "Class Absences: Cutting Class in Feminist Studies." *Feminist Studies*, vol. 31, no. 3, 2005, pp. 575-603. *Jstor,* www.jstor.org/stable/20459051.

American Association of Community Colleges (AACC). "2016 Fact Sheet." *American Association of Community Colleges*, 2016, www.aacc.nche.edu/AboutCC/ Pages/fastfactsfactsheet.aspx. Accessed 2 Feb. 2017.

Altbach, Philip G. "From Revolution to Apathy: American Student Activism in the 1970s." *Higher Education,* vol. 8, 1979, pp. 609-626. *Jstor,* www.jstor.org/stable/344. Accessed 17 December 2015.

Altbach, Philip G. and Robert Cohen. 1990. "American Student Activism: The Post-Sixties Transformation." *Journal of Higher Education,* vol. 61, no. 1, 1990, pp. 32-49. *Jstor,* www.jstor.org/stable/1982033. Accessed 17 December 2015.

Barlow, Andrew. "The Student Movement of the 1960s and Politics of Race." *The Journal of Ethnic Studies*, vol. 19, no.3, 1991, pp. 1-22. *ProQuest*, eric.ed.gov/?id=EJ435252.

Bart, Pauline B., Lynn Bentz, Jan Clausen, LeeRay Costa. "In Sisterhood? Women's Studies and Activism." *Women's Studies Quarterly,* vol. 27, no. 3/4, 1999, pp. 257-267. *JSTOR*, www.jstor.org/stable/40004495. Accessed 7 November 2014.

Berger, Michele Tracy and Cheryl Radeloff. *Transforming Scholarship: Why Women's and Gender Studies Students are Changing Themselves and the World*. Kindle, 2nd ed., Routledge, 2014. Accessed 31 March 2015.

Bettie, Julie. *Women Without Class: Girls, Race, and Identity*. U California Press, 2003.

Black, Paula. "Class Matters in UK Higher Education." *Women's Studies International Forum*, vol. 28, 2005, pp. 127-38. *JSTOR*, www.jstor.org/stable/23212083.

Boggs, George. *Democracy's Colleges: The Evolution of Community Colleges in America*. American Association of Community Colleges, 2010.

Brown, Raymond and Gilbert Muller, eds. *Gateways to Democracy: Six Urban Community College Systems*. Josey-Bass, 1999.

Chen, Chris. "'We Have All Become Students of Color Now:' The California Student Movement and the Rhetoric of Privilege." *The South Atlantic Quarterly*, vol. 110, no. 2, 2011, pp. 559-564. Duke, saq.dukejournals.org/content/110/2/559.full.pdf.

Cohen, Arthur M. and Florence B. Brawer. *Confronting Identity: The Community College Instructor*, Prentice-Hall, 1972.

Crossley, Nick. "From Reproduction to Transformation: Social Movement Fields and the Radical Habitus." *Theory, Culture & Society*, vol. 20, no. 6, 2003, pp. 43-68. *Sage*, doi.org/10.1177/0263276403206003.

Cunningham, Hilary. "The Ethnography of Transnational Social Activism: Understanding the Global as Local Practice." *American Ethnologist*, vol. 26, no. 3, 1999, pp. 583-604. *JSTOR*, www.jstor.org/stable/647439.

DeBard, Robert and Tamara Rice. "Modeling Social Justice Through the Community College." *Community College Models,* edited by Rosalind Latineer Raby and Edward J. Valeau, Springer, 2009, pp. 117-134.

Delmont, Matthew. "Working Toward a Working-Class College: The Long Campaign to Build a Community College in Philadelphia." *History of Education Quarterly,* vol. 54, no. 4, 2014, pp. 429-464. *Wiley Online Library,* DOI: 10.1111/hoeq.12078. Accessed 2 February 2016.

Dowd, Alicia C. "From Access to Outcome Equity: Revitalizing the Democratic Mission of the Community College." *Annals of the American Academy of Political and Social Sciences,* vol. 586, 2003, pp. 92-119. Sage, http://www.jstor.org/stable/1049722.

Dowling, R. "Geographies of Identity: Landscapes of Class." *Progress in Human Geography,* vol. 33, no. 6, 2009, pp. 833-839. doi: 10.1177/03019132508104998.

Ecker, Pat. "A History of Jefferson Community College, 1960-1977: The Promise and the Complications of 'La Porta.'" Dissertation, University of Kentucky, 1991.

Franklin, V. P. "Patterns of Student Activism at Historically Black Universities in the United States and South Africa, 1960-1977." *The Journal of African American History,* vol.88, no. 2, 2003, pp. 204-217. *Jstor.* DOI: 10.2307/3559066. Accessed 15 October 2014.

Gill, Jungyun and James DeFronzo. "A Comparative Framework for the Analysis of International Student Movements." *Social Movement Studies,* vol. 8, no. 3, 2009, pp. 203-224. Taylor & Francis Online, dx.doi. org.ezproxy.uky.edu/ 10.1080/ 14742830903024309. Accessed 15 October 2014.

Horowitz, Helen Lefkowitz. 1986. "The 1960s and the Transformation of Campus Cultures." *History of Education Quarterly*, vol. 26, no. 1, 1996, pp.1-38. *JSTOR*, http://www.jstor.org/stable/368875.

Kennelly, Jacqueline Joan. "Learning to Protest: Youth Activist Cultures in Contemporary Urban Canada." *Review of Education, Pedagogy, and Cultural Studies*, vol. 31, no. 4, 2008, pp. 293-315. *Routledge*, dx.doi.org. ezproxy.uky.edu/10.1080/ 10714410903132865. Accessed 2 February 2016.

———. "Youth Cultures, Activism and Agency; Revisiting Feminist Debates." *Gender and Education*, vol. 21, no. 3, 2009, pp. 259-272. *Routledge*, eric.ed.gov/?id=EJ866246. Accessed 2 February 2016.

Kimmel, Ellen. "Feminist Teaching, An Emergent Practice." *Coming into Her Own*, edited by Sara N. Davis, Mary Crawford and Jadwiga Sebrechts. Jossey-Bass, 1999, pp. 57-76.

Leondar-Wright, Betsy. *Missing Class: Strengthening Social Movement Groups by Seeing Class Cultures*, Cornell University Press, 2014.

Levine, Arthur and Keith R. Wilson. "Student Activism in the 1970s: Transformation Not Decline." *Higher Education*, vol. 8, no. 6, 1979, pp. 627-640. *JSTOR*, JSTOR, www.jstor.org/stable/3446223.

Luebke, Barbara and Mary E. Reilly. *Women's Studies Graduates: The First Generation*, Teacher's College Press, 1995.

Rellihan, Heather. "Community College Students Need Women's Studies! Why There Needs to Be More Institutional Support for These Programs." Paper presented at NWSA Conference, 2014.

Renn, Kristin A. "LGBT Student Leaders and Queer Activists: Identities of Lesbian, Gay, Bisexual, Transgender, and Queer Identified College Student Leaders and Activists." *Journal of College Student Development*, vol. 48, no. 3, 2007, pp. 311-330. *Muse*, msu.edu/~renn./JCSD48.3renn. pdf. Accessed 7 November 2014.

Rhoads, Robert A. and James R. Valadez. *Democracy, Multiculturalism, and the Community College*, Routledge, 1996.

Sahlins, M. "The Teach-Ins: Anti-War Protests in the Old Stoned Age." *Anthropology Today*, vol. 25, no. 1, 2009, pp. 3-5. Jstor, www.jstor.org/ stable/20528196. Accessed 17 December 2015.

Shaw, Kathleen M., James R. Valadez, and Robert A. Rhoads, eds. *Community Colleges as Cultural Texts: Qualitative Explorations of Organizational and Student Culture*, State U of NY Press, 1999.

Stoehr, Alissa. "The Status of Women's and Gender Studies Programs at Community Colleges." Dissertation, Iowa State University, 2015.

Swank, Eric and Fahs, Breanne. "Students for Peace: Contextual and Framing Motivations of Antiwar Activism." *Journal of Sociology & Social Welfare*, vol. 38, no. 2, 2011, pp. 111-136. Univ. of Western Michigan, www.scholarworks.wmich.edu/jssw/vol38/iss2/7.

Tokarczyk, Michelle and Elizabeth A. Fay. *Working-Class Women in the Academy: Laborers in the Knowledge Factory*, U Mass. Press, 1993.

Van Dyke, Nella. "Hotbeds of Activism: Locations of Student Protest." *Social Problems*, vol. 45, no. 2, 1998, pp. 205-220. *Jstor,* www.jstor.org/ stable/3097244.

Walkerdine, Valerie and Jessica Ringrose. "Femininities: Reclassifying Upward Mobility and the Neo-Liberal Subject." *The Sage Handbook of Gender and Education*, editors Christine Skelton, Becky Francis & Lisa Smulyan. Sage, 2006, pp. 31+. Sage, dx.doi.org/ 10.4135/9781848607996

Young, Robert B. "The Identity Crisis of the Community College: A
   Dilemma in a Dialectic." *The Journal of Higher Education,* vol. 48, no.
   3, 1977, pp. 333-342. *Jstor,* www.jstor.org/stable/1978685. Accessed 17
   December 2015.

# Student Voices: Ibiene Minah, Nassau Community College

Garden City, New York

Ibiene Minah graduated from Nassau Community College with an associate's degree in creative writing. She is now pursuing a double major in literature and gender studies at Purchase College, part of the State University of New York system. She is very active in social advocacy on her campus. As an undocumented student her utmost priority is to occupy space that has systemically been denied to people in her communities. She actively advocates for student rights including fair and accessible education.

*What are your career goals?*

"I'm a creative writing major and it's always been my dream to work in an editorial capacity with any top literary journal or magazine. Being an editor-in-chief for the *Paris Review, Granta*, or *Ms. Magazine* seems rather nice. I of course want to publish my own work and the ultimate goal is to launch my own literary magazine that centers immigrant voices and is centered on stories caught between home and safety. The diaspora of the transient is how I imagine it."

*How did your WGS course contribute to your career goals?*

"I'm really grateful for the questions [my professor] asked because they pushed me to thoughtfully engage with my own ideas and the world in ways I don't think I was previously doing. Furthermore, her class prepared me a lot in informal ways for what it will look like for me as a black woman with a lot of opinions and passion to be entering spaces not designed for me in mind, case in point the literary industry. Engaging with our class taught me a lot in what it means to navigate environments and conversations that are not attuned to my experience or amplifying my voice.... [My professor] didn't just push us as students. She pushed us as human beings, as people who are responsible to one another as well as to ourselves. Because of the Women's and Gender Studies Program the list of things I'd like to write my dissertation on is now two pages long and growing, and because of the professors I had in the WGS program, I know without a doubt that I want to teach at the collegiate level. Seeing such amazing women doing their thing—literally changing lives by meeting every student from a place of compassion and respect—showed me that heroes really don't wear capes or get the recognition they deserve ... but they still change the world."

*How did the course help you in your private life (interpersonal relationships, parenting, self-esteem, self-love, etc.)?*

"Upon the ending of [the] class, all of the Intro students made a group chat to stay in contact and exchange ideas. That's the first and only time I've ever had that kind of experience. Due to the level of intimacy and community [my professor] had fostered in her class there was a genuine desire from everyone to continue to hold space together even after the end of the semester. Our class established a group chat to continue to engage with each other on a personal and analytically sociocultural level and to this day we still message each other. We are close by virtue of the deeply nuanced places the class allowed us to go with each other, something I have yet to encounter in any other class or department."

# Assessing Student Learning in Gender, Sexuality, and Women's Studies: Curricular and Faculty Development in the Two-Year College

Jessica Van Slooten, Amy Reddinger, Holly Hassel, and Ann Mattis

The Gender, Sexuality, and Women's Studies Program at the University of Wisconsin (UW) Colleges includes 13 two-year liberal arts transfer campuses and an online campus, with a 25-year history of offering courses in women's studies.[42] Over the past eight years, the program leadership has developed rigorous, strategic, and recursive assessment activities with the goal of assessing shared student learning outcomes across core and cross-listed courses. In this essay, we describe how our assessment program has supported curriculum development as well as faculty development. We also share how data analysis has informed the work of developing a cohesive program across multiple campuses and supported faculty from a dozen home departments. This article details our successful assessment program activities, the impact on our instructors and courses, as well as our next steps in developing program-wide learning objectives; we also reflect on the challenges of this kind of work within a geographically decentralized and open-admissions institution that focuses on general education coursework. As educators in a gender, sexuality, and women's studies (GSW) program that is situated in a two-year institution, we have sought to tailor our assessment projects to the pedagogical imperatives that are specific

---

42    In 2014 the program members voted to change our name to gender, sexuality, and women's studies to better align with national trends while also being more inclusive of our growing LGBTQIA focus.

to both GSW programs, and institutions of access. In integrating these two missions, our assessment projects strive to elucidate key concepts and learning outcomes in the GSW discipline in ways that will best serve the students and faculty at our institution.

Like many large programs, ours has core or stand-alone courses—housed only in the GSW program—as well as cross-listed courses with 13 classes shared with housing academic departments. As a multi-campus, open-admission institution, the GSW program of the UW Colleges serves a wide range of students with diverse levels of preparation, including many first-generation, academically at-risk, and/or non-traditional students. Logistically, our program faces some challenges. With 13 physical campuses, plus an online campus, managing the multiple responsibilities of program coordination is amplified. The GSW program director receives a one-course release per academic year in addition to some summer funding; within that set of resources, they must review curriculum proposals from campuses proposing GSW core or cross-listed courses; review and approve credentials from instructors; communicate with multiple program committees; and develop a process for ensuring adequate evaluation and monitoring of instructors. Further, because UW Colleges offers academic-transfer level coursework that is parallel to the baccalaureate-granting University of Wisconsin system, our courses are focused on a curriculum that transfers seamlessly to those institutions. This necessarily frames our work in developing program and course-level goals as well as in the assessment of student learning.

While we have developed a strong assessment program within the GSW program, and assessment is an institutional priority for the UW Colleges, individuals and departments embrace this part of our program work to varying degrees. There remains a significant subculture of resistance to assessment across our institution. One sentiment articulated by colleagues in our institution is that assessment is a top-down and administratively driven mandate that has little meaningful impact on, or even relationship to, teaching. This may be the result of the institutional history that led to our present-day focus on assessment. In 2003, a Higher Learning Commission (HLC) review found that "University of Wisconsin Colleges still faces challenges regarding the Assessment of Academic Achievement" (Assurance Section 7). This led to significant institutional emphasis on building and enhancing an institutional general education assessment program as a step to ensuring our re-accreditation as an institution. In particular, the HLC report asked the Colleges to focus on assessment of student achievement, closing the loop,[43] and the high rates of students failing to meet stated learning outcomes (Assurances Section 16). Every semester, to fulfill institutional and accreditation requirements, we participate in (usually with some customizing) an institutional-level assessment focused on general education outcomes in five areas: communication skills, analytical skills, quantitative skills, aesthetic skills, or intercultural skills. Additionally, academic departments and programs are required by the institution to create discipline-specific assessment projects every semester to measure outcomes of their choosing. Departments and programs have a great deal of latitude in creating meaningful projects. These projects may or may not be aligned with the general education assessment outcomes and may focus on narrow or broad disciplinary concerns.

The assessment program in the UW Colleges GSW program began with a broad focus on general education outcomes in order to fulfill the institutional assessment requirements. We assessed student learning using shared institutional proficiencies as well as through program-specific projects. This evolved into more pointed focus on student learning of threshold concepts in our program assessment projects (discussed later). By focusing on these core concepts, we aimed to articulate learning goals that are at the heart of interdisciplinary learning in GSW across lower division, core, and cross-listed courses regardless of home discipline *and* to fulfill an institutionally mandated focus on general education outcomes. These concepts were therefore selected to meet both programmatic and institutional goals that are tailored to the learning needs of students at our two-year institution. Our assessment projects were meant to facilitate students' proficiency in concepts that are both foundational to GSW and highly transferable.

Past GSW program assessment projects have focused on outcomes like patriarchy as a system, the social construction of gender, and intersectional-

---

43   Closing the loop is the application of assessment results in classrooms and the larger institution, followed by additional assessment of the use of the assessment results. A question often asked when thinking about how to close the loop is "how can we use or respond to this data?" In this way, we are encouraged both to identify and use the results—but also use results to improve the assessment process or methodology.

ity (concepts selected based on instructor feedback regarding what concepts instructors prioritize, or failed to prioritize, in their courses). We found that, prior to our projects, most instructors comfortably and consistently covered patriarchy as a system (or androcentrism) and the social construction of gender, but few directly addressed intersectionality in their courses. Subsequent assessment projects, then, have analyzed student understanding and application of these concepts in short written responses to shared texts; we reported the results of our assessments back to instructors and used our findings as the foundation for faculty development activities.

In other words, prior to 2009, the GSW program did not participate in any type of assessment of student learning. Starting in 2009, we initiated assessment work by launching general education assessment of student learning, ultimately moving through several projects increasingly focused more on our GSW program assessment outcomes—what is called program-level assessment. We found this method significantly more meaningful from the standpoint of continually evolving program work and faculty development activities. Even though we are institutionally required to conduct both types of assessment (general education and program-level assessment), our growth as a program has been driven by the GSW-focused assessment we have done, even as the general education assessment results are filtered up to our institution's assessment office as one data point for assessing general education outcomes across the associate's degree and all departments and programs. In this essay, then, we describe our movement from general education assessment work to program-specific (disciplinary-focused) student learning outcomes, a series of assessment projects in which we undertake both general education and discipline-specific work to assess student learning.


## Data Analysis and Faculty Development

Starting in 2009, we began designing targeted program assessment projects that were distinct from the general education outcomes that had been the starting point of our assessment work, even as we continued to conduct both types of assessment, per our institutional mandate. Our earliest projects emerged from scholarship of teaching and learning (SoTL)[44] work by program members, and the assessment was a way to learn about our strengths and weaknesses as a program, as well as provide context and further data for these program-member projects that developed out of instructor concern about student learning. Our assessment of student learning has been dialogic, an evolving conversation between collection of data, refining of the process, and continued use of results to inform our curriculum, program, and faculty development.

Our initial approach, in 2009-2010, linked our institutional assessment of a general education proficiency with our program-specific assessment; we identified what we saw as a core program learning goal: "After taking any course in women's studies, students will recognize the ways that patriarchal values are reinforced or challenged in the dominant culture." Our institutional assessment focused on analytical skills, proficiency defined as interpreting and synthesizing information and ideas. The institutional assessment asked instructors across the program to evaluate student understanding of patriarchy as a threshold concept by applying the institutional, generic rubric to a final project, essay, or exam of their choosing. For our GSW program-specific assessment, we measured this by crafting a program assessment project developed around a small lesson study project drawing from SoTL methodologies,[45] (detailed below). Although the general education assessment was broader than our program-specific assessment, both forms of assessment measured students' analytical skills but with different emphases. Our general education assessments focused on broader and more transferable analysis skills while our GSW program assessments focused on discipline-specific content.

---

44   By SoTL, we refer to pedagogical and classroom research that was undertaken systematically—starting with a research question, evidence that is collected using an established methodology, and conclusions drawn from that evidence of student learning. See "Inquiry: A Brief History of SoTL and Some Definitions," by co-author Hassel for a basic definition of systematic teaching and learning research, as well as the website of the International Society for the Scholarship of Teaching and Learning.

45   "Lesson study" has its origins in the Japanese educational system and is a mode of pedagogical assessment in which a small group of instructors collaborate to discuss learning goals, to plan an actual classroom lesson, to observe how it works in practice, and then to revise and report on the results so that other instructors can benefit.

Our program-specific assessment project focused on student understanding of patriarchy as a system in two sections of WOM 203: Women in Popular Culture.[46] This was our earliest effort to distinguish general education assessment from discipline-level learning. The learning goal of our lesson study was student comprehension and application of the threshold concept of patriarchy as a system to specific visual text/artifacts. After a two-day lesson, which included reading, an out-of-class quiz, an in-class PowerPoint presentation, and group work, students were asked to demonstrate their grasp of the concept of patriarchy through the analysis of a popular cultural artifact. They had to apply sociologist Alan Johnson's four core concepts of patriarchy, as defined in *The Gender Knot: Unraveling Our Patriarchal Legacy*. The authors of this study and volunteers observed the student group discussions and their processing of information through small group discussions to better understand the efficacy of the lesson.[47] A benefit of using a small-scale lesson study as part of assessment was the ongoing impact of our lesson and findings. We were able to share our lesson materials, as well as our analysis of the lesson, with our women's studies colleagues at program meetings. Our own ongoing tweaking of the lesson and thinking about best practices for teaching threshold concepts became part of a larger program discussion about what concepts we teach, as well as resources and materials for how to teach them across our interdisciplinary program.[48]

The next phase of our growth in program assessment took place over three years and focused intensively on feminist theory and feminist analysis. The benefit of this focus in shaping program conversations across our geographically dispersed two-year transfer institution was the assessment *process*, in-

---

46   Prior to 2015, our program was women's studies (WOM). After much discussion, we changed our program name to gender, sexuality, and women's studies (GSW).

47   For example, observers were prompted to record responses to questions aimed at capturing how students were processing the concept: "What kinds of emotions do students express when they talk about patriarchy? How do students make sense of competing ideologies (support of and simultaneous challenging of patriarchal values) if they encounter them? Do individual interpretations change during the lesson? Do students avoid discussing particular features of the artifact?"

48   For a more detailed discussion of this lesson study please see Hassel, Reddinger, and Van Slooten, "Surfacing the Structure of Patriarchy."

cluding the collaborative creation of the assessment tool through committee work and discussion at program meetings. Because we are a two-year college program (not a department in terms of our institutional structure), few of our instructors have an advanced degree in women's studies; most members have women's studies coursework, research foci, and/or teaching experience in the field. Hence, program-wide discussions about what students should be learning in women's studies courses are crucial in creating a community of shared disciplinary understanding and commitment to assessment. Since we are geographically dispersed, and with various qualifications for teaching in the program, it is particularly challenging and important for us to work from a shared vision and framework that answers the perennial disciplinary question: "what is women's studies?" Our program members value assessment, for the most part,[49] and are ready to learn from the important discussion of the difference between core and cross-listed courses in our program, and about the discrepancy in student learning in these two different kinds of courses. Because of the discussions about feminist theory and analysis, it became increasingly clear that instructors desired more resources to help enhance their understanding of women's studies as a discipline, and subsequently align their knowledge of what needs to be covered in cross-listed as well as core courses.

---

49   This will be addressed more fully in the next section of this essay.

*Table 1*

|  | *2010-2011 Project* | *2011-2013 Project* |
|---|---|---|
| *Institutional assessment* | Communication skills: read, observe and listen with comprehension and critical perception | Analytical skills: interpret and synthesize information and ideas |
| *Program assessment focus* | Feminist theory (aligned with institutional assessment) | Feminist analysis (aligned with institutional assessment) |
| *Learning outcome* | After taking any course in women's studies, students will be able to recognize and explain feminist theory. | After taking any class in women's studies, a student will possess the ability to conduct a feminist analysis of a reading. |
| *Assessment tool* | Students read a two-page explanation of six kinds of feminism described in Gwen Kirk and Margo Okazawa-Rey's textbook, *Women's Lives: Multicultural Perspectives*, and then analyze one of their course readings. | Students apply feminist analysis to a short excerpt from Helen Gurley Brown's 1963 book *Sex and the Single Girl*. |
| *Form of analysis* | The assessment coordinator and program director evaluated the student work. | The assessment coordinator and a program member evaluated the student work. |

Our examination of feminist theories and feminist analysis took place over three years (see Table 1) and supported the development of both content/ theory expertise and assessment expertise in our faculty. In the two years that we assessed feminist analysis (2011-2013), the assessment tool and rubric were revised midway in response to both program-member feedback and our own evaluation of the tools over time. This clarification of the rubric language (and identifying more precisely what we were measuring) allowed us to apply the rubric in a more consistent way and with greater levels of agreement among instructors about what was being assessed.

We also found through these projects the importance of a clearly defined and disciplinary-specific rubric; in program conversations after the first year (2011-2012) using the feminist analysis rubric, instructors agreed that the rubric did not appropriately describe students' responses demonstrating feminist analysis at the "exceeds expectations" level. After the first semester using the rubric, we revised the rubric to refine and narrow the definition of an essay that "exceeds expectations" and illustrates deep understanding and application of this threshold concept. This recursive approach to assessment design, and willingness to revise assessment tools to most accurately measure student learning and reflect program members' concerns has made our assessment program responsive, collaborative, evolving, and inherently feminist in nature (rubric example below).

*Table 2*

| A student who *exceeds expectations*: | A student who *meets expectations*: | A student who *fails to meet expectations*: |
|---|---|---|
| Can apply feminist analysis by addressing issues of sex and/or gender in the context of at least one of the following: power, oppression, equality, and/or intersectionality. The analysis makes specific reference to the passage, and demonstrates insight, depth, and nuance. | Can begin to apply feminist analysis by pointing out issues of sex and/or gender in the context of at least one of the following: power, oppression, equality, and/or intersectionality. The analysis demonstrates a topical understanding; it might include analysis of the personal but will also reference the passage in some way. | Fails to demonstrate an understanding of the issues of sex and/or gender in the context of at least one of the following: power, oppression, equality, and/or intersectionality in any meaningful way. The response may include summary with no analysis, or an analysis that is not feminist. The response may also be entirely personal with no reference to the passage. |

## Enhancing Disciplinarity

Research has shown that students learn better when core disciplinary concepts are identified and integrated into a curriculum. In their study, "Threshold Concepts, Student Learning and Curriculum: Making Connections between Theory and Practice," Sarah Barradell and Mary Kennedy-Jones discuss the synergy among threshold concepts, students' learning outcomes, and curriculum. Reorienting disciplinary curriculums around threshold concepts—as opposed to content and amorphous skill-sets—requires instructors to re-evaluate content in relation to what students need to know as meta-learners within the discipline (539-541). This, of course, makes effective assessment essential as it points out gaps in knowledge that prevent students from realizing their own expertise in a discipline. As Barradell and Kennedy-Jones also discuss, the process by which instructors are able to identify the threshold concepts of a particular discipline is by no means easy (538). In fact, the lesson studies we have conducted ourselves reflect just how much trial and error is involved in the process of identifying the liminal spaces of novice students' learning. The process requires us to break down disciplinary knowledge so that it is compatible with student learning.

The most recent phase of our assessment program has honed in on specific core outcomes derived from "interdiscipline-specific" threshold concepts that are applicable across courses. The term "threshold concept" was coined by educational theorists Jan Meyer and Ray Land in order to distinguish between "core learning outcomes that represent 'seeing things in a new way' and those that do not" (xv). According to Meyer and Land, threshold concepts "can be considered as akin to a portal, opening up a new and previously inaccessible way of thinking" (1). Crossing a threshold of understanding, then, affords a student "a transformed way of understanding, or interpreting, or viewing something" (xv). The notion of a threshold operates here because the theory proposes that unless students have grasped and crossed this "threshold," they cannot advance conceptually in their understanding of the field (see Launius and Hassel for threshold concepts in women's and gender studies). Whereas our earlier assessment emphases were methodologically and theoretically focused, more recent projects have aligned with the trend of "threshold concepts" even more intensively. This work began with a survey of program members in spring 2013 (see Appendix) to better understand what disciplinary concepts and skills they were teaching. We used these results to inform our next two cycles of program assessment, focusing first on concepts that most program members incorporated—sex and gender—and then on the concept that the fewest members incorporated—intersectionality. At this time, we also separated institutional and program assessment projects; institutional assessment focused on more general skills application, while program assessment continued our focus on threshold concepts program-wide, rather than in small, select SoTL groups, to better gauge student learning of these concepts across our curriculum, and across our geographically dispersed institution.

*Table 3*

| | *2013-2014 Project* | *2014-2015 Project* |
|---|---|---|
| *Institu-tional as-sessment* | Analytical skills: interpret and synthesize information and ideas (separate project from program assessment) | Intercultural skills: apply an under-standing of different cultures to an analysis or interpretation of course content (separate project from pro-gram assessment) |
| *Program assess-ment focus* | Sex and gender | Intersectionality |
| *Learning outcome* | After taking any course in wom-en's studies, students will be able to understand and analyze the concepts of sex and gender, as well as the relationship between the two. | After taking any course in women's studies, students will be able to un-derstand and apply the concept of intersectionality. |
| *Assess-ment tool* | Analysis of a textual passage: George Packer's *New Yorker* arti-cle, "Narcissism in Pink and Blue," about gender reveal parties | Analysis of a "case study" narrative |
| *Form of analysis* | The assessment coordinator evaluated student work. | The assessment coordinator evalu-ated student work. |

As with previous projects, we valued program input on our assessment projects. We were able to use feedback members had provided in the afore-mentioned survey to guide our creation of projects, adding another layer of member feedback. The survey showed many instructors in both core and cross-listed courses simply were not familiar with, or utilizing, the concept of intersectionality, though this is increasingly an important lens for the field. As a result, we decided to build professional development into our spring 2014 meeting. We asked program members to complete several readings on intersectionality,[50] including prior to the biannual face-to-face meeting, and in small group work and large group discussion during the meeting, to facilitate deeper understanding of the topic and hopefully encourage more robust inclusion of the topic into all women's studies courses.

After reflecting on our previous six years of program assessment, it was clear that we needed to move forward with the conversation about shared program concepts and skills. We decided to take a different approach to our program assessment in 2015-2016 and build a year-long conversation around program learning outcomes. This work was timely, as our institution was also revising its associate's degree standards at the same time. This work connects to our previous program assessment projects, which focused on specific disciplinary threshold concepts (patriarchy, social construction of gender, and intersectionality), and our interest in building an even stronger and more cohesive program that is in sync with the field. To gather program member feedback, we created a survey using our institutional subscription to Qualtrics, an online research software platform. We administered this survey in fall semester and used the results to guide a discussion and activity at our spring meeting. Overall, there is support for developing program-wide learning outcomes, with some concerns about academic freedom and flexibility given our diverse array of courses and home disciplines. However, there are also strong feelings about the benefits of developing learning outcomes for disciplinarity, cohesion, and rigor.

## Resistance and Challenges

As noted in the opening section, the academic departments and programs in the Colleges responded to the institutional mandate to conduct assessment in a variety of ways. The Gender, Sexuality, and Women's Studies Program has taken a proactive approach, creating the comprehensive assessment program (detailed in the previous section) that serves to enhance our program

---

50   This included a prepublication chapter, "Intersectionality" from *Threshold Concepts in Women's and Gender Studies* (Launius and Hassel) and "Mapping the Margins" by Kimberlé Crenshaw; other readings included chapters from *Critical Race Theory: An Introduction* by Delgado and Stefanic.

identity and the quality of our teaching within a two-year transfer institution. The methods of data collection and analysis have varied according to the type of assessment (institutional/general education or program-specific) we have undertaken and have been met with different levels of support or critique from our program members.

A specific concern that has emerged from among our program membership is that some of our assessment projects and activities have been prescriptive and could limit the instructor's academic freedom. For example, we have had discussions at program meetings about the ways in which focusing on a threshold concept such as "intersectionality" or "patriarchy" might then impact how and what an instructor includes in her course content. Is this too prescriptive? Is it necessary? To what end should all instructors be incorporating specific terms and ideas into their courses? Must all GSW courses teach the concept of patriarchy? What if an instructor is teaching the concept, but using different terminology or frameworks (e.g. androcentrism or structural inequality)? We have taken these concerns very seriously, making them central to our biannual day-long program meetings. These discussions have led to complex, messy, and engaging ongoing conversations that have ultimately been productive and generative for us as a program. Specific benefits include:

- Enhanced instructor understanding of threshold concepts
- Specific and enhanced understanding of patriarchy, the difference between gender and sex, and intersectionality
- Increased focus on these above concepts in our core and cross-listed courses
- Commitment to creating program-wide learning goals

The challenge of teaching—and thus assessing—threshold concepts across all of our courses is also complicated by the number of cross-listed courses we offer (we currently have thirteen cross-listed courses in our catalog). While our program requires that all instructors of our core and cross-listed courses go through an approval process, we recognize that for most of our instructors of cross-listed courses their primary scholarly training has been in the area of their home discipline. We work to address this concern through workshops, shared readings, and program discussions. One of the questions is whether all threshold concepts are equally relevant across different coursework. For example, it was suggested that it is easier to address a concept like intersectionality in an introductory (core) course than it would be in a science-based cross-listed course. However, our collaborative study and discussion of Kimberlé Crenshaw's meaning of "intersectionality" suggested to us the deep need to make the connection that intersectionality must be thought about and taught when talking about all aspects of women's and gender studies. Indeed, this is precisely what Crenshaw means when she says we must move away from a "single-axis framework" of analysis to a deeper, intersectional analysis (139).

Another challenge to building a successful assessment program is participation. While it is required that instructors on the tenure track participate in assessment in their home departments, this mandatory participation becomes a little more murky when talking about affiliation with a program that does not weigh in on the tenure decision. As an institution, it is harder to get tenured faculty and adjunct faculty (who are often over-taxed by the pressures of being adjunct—teaching more classes than faculty, sometimes at multiple institutions, etc.) to participate in assessment in general. Our assessment projects usually require an additional hour of work at the end of the semester when most instructors are incredibly busy and tired.

We have worked tirelessly to build participation through multiple approaches: designing assessment projects through collaboration and program member input; reviewing the assessment project in person so that instructors fully understand what is being asked of them; multiple emails and reminders encouraging participation; and the creation of projects that seem valuable and meaningful to our colleagues. Despite these efforts we have seen participation in assessment wane dramatically when we are experiencing periods of institutional stress.

Indeed, perhaps the most significant challenge to the success of our assessment program is institutional instability. Since 2010, the UW Colleges (and the UW System as a whole) have been under significant strain due to unprecedented budget cuts and subsequent restructuring in the UW Colleges. The stress that this has put on faculty, and particularly adjunct faculty, has been enormous, and this has impacted our collective emotional well-being. In semesters of particular crisis there has been a noticeable downturn in program meeting attendance and assessment participation.

The longitudinal impact of our assessment projects on our program has been multi-fold. The first and most significant success has been in the creation of our assessment program itself. Because GSW is a program and not a department, we were not required by our institution to have an assessment program. We voluntarily created this assessment program as a way of furthering our program cohesion, student learning, and our full participation in the institution. We have also made progress in the quality of assessment projects we have conducted, progressing from vague/amorphous assessments that were not clearly defined to well-designed and thoughtful assessments that tackle threshold concepts and program learning goals. We have moved towards closing the loop—an institutional and Higher Learning Commission (our accrediting body) focus—which has led us to deeper understanding about how and what students are learning in our courses.

For example, after several iterations of assessment projects we now see that there tend to be different rates of success in cross-listed versus core courses. Some semesters, depending on what was being assessed, our core classes had higher rates of "exceeds" and "meets" results than the cross-listed courses; however, this was not a consistent result across each semester or year. We attribute this to a variety of factors: the concept being assessed; students' prior coursework; participation rates; and other variables. The process of creating yearly assessment projects, significantly informed by discussions at our program meetings, has helped to shift our program culture to focus more deeply on student learning and, subsequently, course development, as well as open up conversations with cross-listing instructors who tend to have less GSW-specific background than core-course instructors. This is not to suggest that these conversations are simple or without conflict. As mentioned above, program members disagree about what threshold concepts are central to which courses, what those concepts mean, and how to best teach them. These conversations are ongoing, and they build program cohesion and a shared focus on learning. As we move forward, we are especially invested in taking what we have learned through the implementation of our assessment program and using that knowledge strategically to develop and strengthen our learning outcomes for our GSW program.

## Feminist Program Building

The challenges faced while implementing an assessment agenda have created a program culture that revolves around inquiry, dialogue, and support. The productive conversations we have had—and continue to have—about our disciplinary identity and programmatic outcomes are in line with our vision as feminist educators in a community college. We believe that a feminist ethic is also at the heart of establishing a strong assessment program and, in turn, clear standards for interdisciplinary competencies insofar as they make vital feminist concepts more accessible to all our students, including underprepared or at-risk students. By articulating a common set of learning outcomes and providing opportunities for faculty to revisit their pedagogy, we are working toward the goal of making the intellectual resources of feminist theory more available to our student body. If we want to maximize student success at a two-year institution where there is a wide range of student preparedness, we need to develop a keen understanding of core disciplinary knowledge in our GSW program.

Assessment has helped us articulate student learning needs and course emphases that require us to retool our pedagogy to more effectively meet our students where they are—a refrain that we know many instructors at open-admissions institutions embrace. By revising our curriculum so that it privileges student learning as opposed to the top-down delivery of content, we draw the focus away from our expertise even while we clarify the concrete disciplinary knowledge that will facilitate student success in the GSW classroom. Assessment projects centered on threshold concepts allow us to illuminate the sophisticated disciplinary maneuvers that we use as experts in a way that is in sync with students' needs. Because the threshold concepts model requires the teacher to view content through the eyes of the student, we believe this approach will allow us to infuse a feminist ethic into our curricular approach. Feminist praxis is thus a driving force behind a pedagogy and curriculum that revolves around threshold concepts.

Feminist pedagogy has always sought to challenge traditional modes of content delivery and classroom relationalities. In the introduction to *The Politics of Women's Studies: Testimony from 30 Founding Mothers*, Mari Jo Buhle provides a summary of the various ways feminist pedagogues have sought to distinguish their practices from the standard classroom. Feminist pedagogy involves a cooperative, anti-hierarchical, student-centered ethic, which includes group work activities, student-led discussions, and student reflections. Student experience and testimony have historically been privileged in the women's studies classroom, as they mimic the dynamics of consciousness raising (xxiv). Likewise, Lori Amy articulates the extent to which a feminist ethic can be cultivated by the "dialogic" dynamics of traumatic testimonial and witnessing in the classroom. Amy provides an effective rejoinder to critics who argue that feminist classroom dynamics are more therapeutic than academic (57-59). Personal dynamics will inevitably complicate and invigorate the GSW classroom. The content of our courses will draw out the personal and even the traumatic in our students, particularly for the demographics we serve as a two-year college. We understand that it is essential that students sort through their messy experiential knowledge in order to acclimate themselves to a feminist critical paradigm that will allow them to examine the world in a different way. And, we are further aware that the emotional labor of teaching GSW courses to at-risk students, often in rural and impoverished areas, and within a woefully underfunded institution carries a particularly heavy burden.

Yet, as instructors, we are keenly aware of the unique emotional labor of the GSW classroom that must be balanced with academic rigor. At our program meetings, we often discuss how we struggle with negotiating these personal and social dynamics during our classes and office hours. A coherent curriculum and structured learning activities can help us manage that emotional labor by providing a productive pedagogical context for student testimonial. We have found that the threshold concept model is an effective way to preserve academic rigor in the GSW classroom, as these concepts allow students to view social phenomena—including their own personal experiences—through a theoretical lens. In organizing classrooms around a curriculum that privileges key concepts, students are more likely to be able to situate their experiential knowledge within disciplinary terms that will serve them scholastically as well as personally in the long run. Threshold concepts thus allow us to preserve the feminist classroom's ethical focus on students' experience while linking that knowledge more closely and intuitively to students' academic needs. At two-year institutions such as ours, the content needs to be adapted to meet the needs of a wide range of students. The threshold concept model makes the conceptual footholds of the discipline more available to at-risk students whose learning needs complicate their experience in the traditional classroom. However, curricular adaptations have more than scholastic implications for at-risk students. Because this group is likely to have life obstacles and personal crises that alienate them from a traditional classroom, a student-learner-centered pedagogy further makes the emancipatory potential of the GSW paradigm available to individuals who need it the most. Adapting our curriculum so that it is targeted to learning outcomes is an essential aspect of student retention and a transformative feminist pedagogical practice.

## Conclusion

Ultimately, we argue for the importance of developing a disciplinarily rigorous program for two-year college students using faculty development activities emerging from thoughtfully conceived assessment work. Through trial and error, the program assessment projects have made us aware of pedagogical and institutional challenges that impede quality assessment. Over time, the recursive studies have provided us with solid information for constructing activities that will effectively facilitate our students' knowledge of key concepts or, more particularly, threshold concepts that can be honed and tracked across a variety of disciplines. More than anything, we have learned that assessment leads us to think critically about our students' learning needs as we reconfigure our programmatic goals. We have found that assessment studies enhance our mission as a GSW program that is situated in a two-year institution. In an institutional context that caters to many students who are not college-ready, it is essential that we establish a curriculum that clarifies a path to academic success in every discipline. With specific assessment data on the GSW program, we are able to pinpoint gaps in disciplinary learning and then begin to work with one another to find the best way to proceed as a collaborative community of feminist educators. Program assessment projects have illustrated differences in types of courses, degrees of difficulty for different threshold concepts, and the importance of ongoing conversation and collaboration among program members to enhance our disciplinary identity and student learning. Disciplinary rigor thus begins with providing instructors with resources and opportunities to hone concrete pedagogical strategies that nourish a cohesive curricular plan. Threshold concepts facilitate that cohesion as they promote a deep understanding of disciplinary knowledge among students of various backgrounds and levels of preparedness, such as those who attend two-year institutions.

Tensions among faculty in an interdisciplinary program prompt us to underscore the importance of collaboration in developing a curricular and assessment agenda. Whether it is by setting aside time for assessment discussions or workshops at a department meeting or by providing incentives for developing SoTL projects, GSW programs can benefit greatly from initiatives that foster scholarship and professional development focused on pedagogy. SoTL projects and related assessment create an institutional climate in which pedagogy is regarded as an intellectual enterprise. These activities inspire colleagues to reflect individually on their pedagogy, and they can help us to coordinate a curriculum and pedagogical praxis that ultimately enables a deeper learning of core GSW concepts, especially at two-year institutions.

# Appendix

Spring 2013 Survey of Women's Studies (now GSW) Instructors

1. What types of women's studies courses have you taught?
- Core courses only
- Cross-listed courses only
- Both core and cross-listed courses

2. Please mark all WOM core concepts that you regularly teach/address in your courses (select all that apply):
- Feminism/feminist critique
- Patriarchy/androcentrism
- Sex vs. gender
- Intersectionality
- Privilege/oppression
- Difference vs. inequality
- Structures and systems of power and inequality
- Heterosexism/heteronormativity
- Male/female gaze
- Biological determinism/social constructionism
- Other (please specify)

3. Which of these strategies do you regularly use in your WOM classes? (Please select all that apply.)
- Lecture
- Small group work
- Class discussion
- Student presentations
- Collaborative assignments
- Personal response writing (e.g. blogs, journals, informal responses)
- Instructor PowerPoint presentations

- Video, web content, other media
- In-class writing
- Field trips
- Student-faculty conferences
- Online discussion forums (D2L, Twitter, etc.)
- Tests and/or exams
- Research papers and/or project
- Service-learning projects
- Other (please specify)

4. What is most rewarding to you about teaching women's studies courses?

5. What is most challenging for you about teaching women's studies courses?

6. What topics would you be interested in for future women's studies workshops? (Pedagogical issues? Women's studies issues? etc.).

# Works Cited

Amy, Lori E. "A Pedagogy of Witness." *Transformations: The Journal of Inclusive Scholarship & Pedagogy*, vol 17, no. 1, 2006, pp. 57-69. *Education Research Complete*.

Assurance Section. "Report of a Comprehensive Evaluation Visit to University of Wisconsin Colleges." Madison, Wisconsin, March 10 - 12, 2003. The Higher Learning Commission. A Commission of the North Central Association of Colleges and Schools.

Barradell, Sarah, and Kennedy-Jones, Mary. "Threshold Concepts, Student Learning and Curriculum: Making Connections between Theory and Practice," *Innovations in Education and Teaching International,* vol. 52, no. 5, 2015, pp. 536-45.

Brown, Helen Gurley. *Sex and the Single Girl.* Barricade Books, 2003.

Buhle, Mari Jo. "Introduction." *The Politics of Women's Studies: Testimony from 30 Founding Mothers,* edited by Florence Howe and Mary Jo Buhle. The Feminist Press at CUNY, 2000. xv-xxvi.

Crenshaw, Kimberlé. "Demarginalizing the Intersection of Race and Sex: A Black Feminist Critique of Antidiscrimination Doctrine, Feminist Theory and Antiracist Politics." *The University of Chicago Legal Forum*, Issue 1., article 8, 1989, 139-67.

Crenshaw, Kimberlé W. "Mapping the Margins: Intersectionality, Identity Politics, and Violence against Women of Color." *Stanford Law Review,* vol. 34, no. 6, 1991, 1241-1299.

Delgado, Richard, and Jean Stefancic. *Critical Race Theory: An Introduction.* New York UP, 2012.

Hassel, Holly. "Inquiry: A Brief History of SoTL and Some Definitions." *Teaching English in the Two-Year College*, vol 41, no. 2, Dec. 2013, pp. 178-181.

Hassel, Holly, Amy Reddinger, and Jessica Van Slooten. "Surfacing the Structures of Patriarchy." *International Journal of Scholarship of Teaching and Learning*, vol. 5, no. 2, 2011. https://digitalcommons.georgiasouthern.edu/cgi/viewcontent.cgi?article=1303&context=ij-sotl

International Society for the Scholarship of Teaching and Learning. "Welcome to ISSoTL." Web. http://www.issotl.com/issotl15/.

Johnson, Allan. *The Gender Knot: Unraveling Our Patriarchal Legacy.* Temple UP, 2005.

Kirk, Gywn and Margo Okazawa-Rey. *Women's Lives: Multicultural Perspectives.* McGraw-Hill. 5th ed, 1994.

Launius, Christie and Holly Hassel. *Threshold Concepts in Women's and Gender Studies: Ways of Seeing, Thinking, and Knowing.* 2nd edition New York: Routledge, 2018.

Meyer, Jan H.F. and Ray Land. "Threshold Concepts: Issues of Liminality." *Overcoming Barriers to Student Understanding: Threshold Concepts and Troublesome Knowledge*, edited by Jan H.F. Meyer and Ray Land, eds. Routledge, 2006. 19-32.

―――. "Threshold Concepts and Troublesome Knowledge: Linkages to Ways of Thinking and Practising within the Disciplines." *Improving Student Learning―Ten Years On*, edited by C. Rust. Oxford, 2003.

Packer, George. "Narcissism in Pink and Blue." *The New Yorker* 23 Apr. 2012. newyorker.com/news/daily-comment/narcissism-in-pink-and-blue

# Petticoats, Pumps, and Pantyhose: Creating Student Success through a Women's Studies Learning Community

Donna M. Thompson and Paquita L. Garatea

"All human beings are practicing historians. As we go through life we present ourselves to others through our life story; as we grow and mature we change that story through different interpretations and different emphasis. We stress different events as having been decisive at different times in our life history and, as we do so, we give those events new meanings. People do not think of this as 'doing history'; they engage in it often without special awareness. We live our lives; we tell our stories. It is as natural as breathing." (Gerda Lerner from *Why History Matters: Life and Thought*)

"I am not a historian. I happen to think that the content of my mother's life—her myths, her superstitions, her prayers, the contents of her pantry, the smell of her kitchen, the song that escaped from her sometimes parched lips, her thoughtful repose and pregnant laughter—are all worthy of art." (August Wilson from "A Note from the Playwright" in *Seven Guitars*)

In spring 2010, Chandler-Gilbert Community College (CGCC), a college in the Maricopa Community College District located in the greater Phoenix, Arizona, metropolitan area, offered a team-taught student learning community (LC) which combined HIS 201: History of Women in America with a section of ENG 102: First-Year College Composition. Although the college has a long history of developing learning communities, this pairing was the first to include a gender-focused course. Both instructors were full-time residential faculty with appointments and teaching assignments in multiple academic disciplines including history, humanities, women's studies, literature, and composition.[51] The LC aimed to provide an introduction to the study of history, specifically women's history, through the discussion of primary and secondary historical sources, the analysis of literary and cinematic texts, attendance at campus co-curricular events, extensive writing assignments, and the real world application of theory. We entitled the LC "Petticoats, Pumps, and Pantyhose: Do Women Have a History?" This was partly done as a marketing strategy but also to reference the content of the class and the many ways throughout history in which women's lives have been constrained, confined, and curtailed not only by clothing but by laws, policy, and cultural expectations.

The LC embodied multiple High-Impact Practices (HIPs) as defined by the American Association of Colleges & Universities including:

1. Common Intellectual Experiences: A set of common required courses or campus programming for students
2. Learning Communities: Linked or team-taught courses which integrate learning across disciplines
3. Writing Intensive Courses: The practice of writing across the curriculum to deeply engage students in critical thinking in information literacy
4. Collaborative Assignments and Projects: Active learning assignments and assessments designed to promote problem solving and student interaction
5. Diversity and Global Learning: Classroom and co-curricular programs through which students explore cultures and worldviews different from theirs (Kuh)

These practices have proven successful at engaging students, increasing retention, and aiding the development of underserved and underprepared students (Kuh). Reflection on our course practices and pedagogy and a review of quantitative and qualitative student data demonstrate that our use of HIPs with women's studies content increased student success in two academically

---

51   In the Maricopa Community College District, the term residential faculty refers to faculty who have taught full-time at the college for five or more years and received satisfactory evaluations throughout their employment. In contrast, those faculty who have taught full-time for less than five years are termed probationary. Residential status conforms to Arizona's version of tenure.

challenging courses while encouraging deeper level thinking and active/collaborative learning. An examination of this learning community provides a useful opportunity to analyze best practices in teaching women's and gender studies at community colleges, particularly the use of learning communities as an effective tool for teaching and learning as well as for developing, growing, and sustaining women's and gender studies programs.

In the narrative that follows we initially focus on one half of the learning community, HIS 201: The History of Women in America. First, we discuss student misconceptions about women's history, and how we revised the curriculum of the course to both interrogate the construction of "America," and privilege the lived experiences of women, particularly women of color. Next, we discuss the other half of the learning community, ENG 102: First-Year College Composition. As a gateway course, ENG 102 is an important marker in students' paths to graduation. We analyze the effects of offering a gateway course like ENG 102 through a learning community and suggest that this effort increased student success, particularly for minority students. Finally, we talk about how we've built on the success of the HIS 201/ENG 102 learning community. The success of this first gender-related LC encouraged us to develop more learning communities, and the increased visibility and stronger cross-campus relationships resulting from the learning communities helped us expand our women's studies program.

## "There Is No Life That Does Not Contribute to History"[52]: Addressing Student Preconceptions about Women's History

At the beginning of the semester, we asked students to complete a brief questionnaire about their reasons for taking the class, their prior knowledge of American history and gender studies and how they attained it, and what they hoped to learn from taking the course. To enroll in the ENG 102 half of our LC, students needed to have successfully completed English 101 with a C or better. Based on this, we could assume some basic preparedness in writing. However, HIS 201, the other half of the LC, has no prerequisites. Because there are no

---

52    Quote appears in *The Living Is Easy* by Dorothy West.

prerequisites, the makeup of this class is often varied and diverse with many students having completed no coursework in history outside of mandatory high school requirements.[53] We also found that many students came to our learning community with no background in gender analysis or women's studies as these topics are rarely covered in high school curricula or in required introductory-level courses at the community college. Regardless of age, ethnicity, gender, or area or year of study, the responses to our questionnaire were similar: The students presented an idea of American history that reflected the course content of a traditional high school class. They assumed women's history focused on notable women or the small role females played in "male" history. For example, they expected women's history to explore women's roles in the Civil War, or to learn about the suffrage movement. Their notion of women's history was based on fitting women into traditional histories or only looking at women-focused events.

This first assumption maintains the regular curriculum while adding a few exemplar women to showcase the significance of the female role in American history. This places these women in the role of being exceptions. While this strategy was a common approach in the early days of teaching women's history, it's now seen as problematic because it encourages students to see the lives of ordinary women as unworthy of study while clinging to the exceptionalism of a select few. The second assumption often presupposes that what is important in history happens in the military and political spheres. History, as a character in Jane Austen's *Northanger Abbey* complains, concerns itself with, "The quarrels of popes and kings, with wars or pestilences, in every page; the men all so good for nothing, and hardly any women at all" (1014). This approach assumes that women's lives are anecdotal side notes in a story focused on men in the fields of war and on the floor of congress. Indeed, in

---

53    The state's Arizona General Education Curriculum (AGEC) does mandate that students take one course focusing on ethnicity, race, or gender, and one course emphasizing contemporary global/international or historical awareness to satisfy the general education requirements in cultural awareness and global/international/historical awareness. However, even for the students who have already completed this requirement, this may be their first course in the history department because the historical awareness area competency can be met through courses in disciplines outside of history. For example, completion of both the gender and historical awareness requirements can be satisfied by taking HUM/WST 209: Women and Films.

many history textbooks the stories of women are set aside in boxed sections as if they are outside the "real" history.

As Purdue University professor Melinda Zook asserts in her article "Integrating Men's History into Women's History: A Proposition," a focus on female history in domestic spheres separate from the broader society also allows historians to ignore the gendered status of men. Zook writes of manhood that "it is a construction of cultural meanings and prescriptions that is forever changing and reactive, in part, at least, due to changing definitions of femininity" (377). In traditional history courses, men function solely as agents in society while women are restricted to the home. Challenging this restrictive view affords us an opportunity to examine the full lives of American men while also allowing our analysis of women to shift from mere descriptions of notable personages to critiques of their participation in our cultural and political histories.

By reading the students' answers on the questionnaire and through our interactions with them at the beginning of the semester, we also realized that the students tended to view history as a static set of dates and facts rather than as a collection of events that influence current laws, behaviors, and mores. For example, while many students claimed a familiarity with the contemporary abortion debate, for most this knowledge extended solely to Roe v. Wade, news reports, and their own beliefs. Students understood such policy discussions as modern inventions outside of a historical context. To address this, we assigned Cornelia Hughes Dayton's "Taking the Trade: Abortion and Gender Relations in an Eighteenth-Century New England Village," James Mohr's "Abortion in America," and Leslie Reagan's "When Abortion Was a Crime: Reproduction and the Economy in the Great Depression." These texts highlight an ongoing focus on this issue and demonstrated the constantly shifting mores around the practice of abortion. We deepened this discussion by examining, both locally and globally, broader issues including access to information, birth control, and maternal healthcare. From this the students could see the dynamic connections between the past and the present and move away from the idea of history as merely a set of dates and facts.

## "Our Liberation Is Bound in Each Other's"[54]: The History of Women in America Can't Just Be about Us/US

Prior to the development of our learning community, History of Women in America focused solely on women in the United States. This is consistent with how the course is often taught throughout the country, and general textbooks on American women's history usually emphasize the US experience. However, through the selection of new course materials we were able to broaden the construction of America by fully including all of North, South, and Central America as well as the Caribbean and US territories. This allowed us to add an understanding of America and Americanism as a learning outcome, which is in line with the intellectual traditions in women's and gender studies that emphasize intersectional theory and encourage the interrogation of social and political hierarchies. With the new materials the course could then respond to what Mary Frederickson proposes in her essay "Going Global: New Trajectories in U.S. Women's History":

> Now is the time to build on the extensive work that has been done
> in U.S. women's history and expand the field even more by shift-
> ing the emphasis from "American exceptionalism" to an approach
> that analyzes U.S. women's history in a global context—one that
> focuses on international connections, facilitates comparisons, and
> traces personal, cultural, and intellectual relationships across na-
> tional borders and cultural boundaries. (171)

Similarly, we ensured that the scope of American history was not limited to the arrival of Europeans in the New World by exploring histories of indigenous peoples before their first contact with Europeans.

In addition to interrogating Americanism, the new LC readings—which included primary documents, scholarly articles, memoirs, and novels—provided a comprehensive exploration of women from diverse backgrounds.[55]

---

54 Quote appears in a speech by Dr. Martin Luther King, Jr.

55 Because the LC was fully integrated, there was one set of reading assignments that were discussed in both courses. These readings included both historical and literary texts.

For the most part, we selected women-authored texts to reinforce the idea of women voicing their own lived experience. We also elected to focus on texts by women of color or those with clearly defined ethnicities. Even within the field of women's history, these figures remain less recognized and studied than their white counterparts. We found the inclusion of fiction particularly useful in exposing students to the history of groups that were different from them. The use of literature rather than a traditional history text or reader allowed students to engage with a different representation of history. Students connect with people and their stories, which can inspire their curiosity. While the characters' lives might be centered in unfamiliar cultural, economic, or historical worlds, the literary texts allow students to connect to vastly different people and groups. Literature helps fill the gaps between dry historical facts and create authentic engagement with women's lives.

The LC centered on five texts covering multiple eras and peoples in American history. The first was the novel, *Family*, by African American author J. California Cooper which explores the life of an enslaved woman and her family in the years before and after the Civil War. The film, *Jefferson in Paris,* was used to complement and augment Cooper's narrative by discussing the tradition of slave owners, like Jefferson, who fathered children with their enslaved women. The film presents the Jefferson-Hemmings relationship as a romance of sorts. This allowed us to delve into difficult discussions about rape, consent, and power relations between masters and slaves. Students were encouraged to think critically about these contrasting histories and written assignments included a critical review of both the novel and the film.

We then assigned *Bread Givers* written by Anzia Yezierska and published in 1925 to show students the experience of an orthodox Jewish family who immigrated from Poland at the turn of the 20th century and settled in the lower east side of New York City. Due to significant population growth in Europe, tens of thousands of non-English speaking, non-Protestant immigrants from eastern and southern Europe entered the United States, thus creating an extreme sense of xenophobia. This resulted in the 1924 Native Origins Act which restricted further immigration from these countries. In this novel, students read a narrative about a young woman's struggles, defeats, and achievements within a community built upon both Old World and New World standards. Students researched immigration laws, life in tenements, and the gendered experiences of new Americans. The history of immigration patterns to the United States were discussed in depth, creating a better understanding of the current debate surrounding immigrants. Students were asked not only to learn about the life of immigrants in the United States but to address the lives, experiences, and cultures of the places they left.

Continuing this vein of women and their impetus in searching for self, students read *Esperanza's Box of Saints* by Mexican author Maria Amparo Escaldon. The novel provides students with a present-day, modern view of Mexican women in the context of current immigration policies. The students follow Esperanza's journey through Mexico, her life in a border town, and her experience crossing the US border while hidden in the trunk of a car. The novel encouraged students to ask questions about what choices women have when confronting the dangers awaiting them as undocumented border crossers. This novel led to important discussions among students regarding the current debates surrounding immigration, particularly involving women. For example, Arizona's SB 1070 legislation passed in the same year we taught our LC. Students saw firsthand the consequences of this policy change. They experienced these changes through the lives of their classmates, friends, and in some cases within their own families. We used this current event to discuss both sides of the immigration issue, the real-life outcomes of government actions, and women's roles in social activism.

*Lakota Woman*, an autobiography by Mary Crow Dog (a.k.a. Mary Brave Bird), gave the class an inside look at life on a desolate American Indian reservation in South Dakota. Published in 1990, the memoir chronicles Mary Crow Dog's youth and adulthood which occurred during the establishment of the modern American Indian movement. In particular, it focuses on her participation in the Native American stand at Wounded Knee in 1973. Arizona has the largest American Indian population in the United States and CGCC is bordered by the Gila River reservation. However, this close proximity to Native lands and people had little impact on most students who were unaware or quite ethnocentric in their opinions of the indigenous peoples of the Americas—even those in their own communities. In addition to the text, students viewed the documentary, *We Shall Remain: Siege at Wounded Knee*, which highlights Crow Dog's involvement in this Native resistance movement. Slowly, after many discussions, students began to understand the plight of Native peoples who were essentially their neighbors. The important role of indigenous women to their respective communities became more apparent to the students. This helped create an increased interest in the role of women in the students' own historical and ethnic backgrounds.

Additionally, students read Julia Alvarez's *In the Time of the Butterflies*. The book emerged out of interviews conducted by Alvarez with people involved in the revolution to overthrow the long-standing dictator Rafael Trujillo in the Dominican Republic. The book focused on three sisters who became involved in the revolution and were executed by Trujillo's forces. We required students to read the novel, view a film based on the book, and critique each. Students tackled issues of race, class, and gender in the Dominican Republic through the lives of the Mirabel sisters. In addition, students learned of the US support for the Trujillo regime and of the consequences of our country's foreign policies with dictator states.

Additional resources came from primary historical documents—journals, letters, speeches, legal rulings, etc. These were augmented by readings from contemporary scholars like bell hooks, Hunani-Kay Trask, Nellie Wong, Kimberlé Crenshaw, and Jennifer Morgan. The learning community utilized films such as *A Midwife's Tale, Twilight in Los Angeles, Ida B. Wells: Passion for Justice, Around the World in 72 Days*, and *The Life and Times of Rosie the Riveter* to highlight specific social and political movements or eras. Contemporary poets, artists, and performers like Kara Walker, Betye Saar, Sarah Jones, Lois-Ann Yamanaka, Maggie Estep, Kristina Wong, Alix Olson, Sunni Patterson, Yellow Rage, and Good Sista/Bad Sista filled out the curriculum to link the students' developing historical knowledge with current topics of interest to them. Students participated in co-curricular campus projects related to the United Nations Millennium Goals. One of these initiatives called for improving the status of women. We addressed this by focusing on excerpts from texts like *Half the Sky: Turning Oppression into Opportunity for Women Worldwide* which compelled students to reflect on their connection to women in the global community and to challenge themselves to become agents of change. The variety of course materials allowed for points of access for students with different learning styles and enabled us to cover a broader range of regions and time periods.

## "I Am the Keymaster ... Are You the Gatekeeper?"[56]: The Women's Studies Learning Community as a Pathway to Student Success

At CGCC, as at many other institutions, ENG 102: First-Year College Composition is a gateway course. The successful completion of gateway courses such as pre-college English and math, ENG 101/102, reading, and/or lower level math courses, provide an academic foundation for future learning and are required for most degrees and certificates. According to the John Gardener Institute for Undergraduate Learning, "These courses merit focus and transformation because they enroll large numbers of students and lack of success in these courses is directly correlated with poor performance in higher education and, in many cases, failure to complete a postsecondary degree or credential all together" (Gateway). Since many students attend community colleges unprepared for college-level classes, gateway courses pose a particular threat to their academic advancement. When a course like First-Year College Composition is integrated into a learning community it provides an opportunity for students to tackle required, gateway courses through a unique learning experience. The combination of classes in the learning community provides students with a true interdisciplinary learning experience while allowing them to develop necessary skills. In this instance, our course paired a two-hundred-level history class with a skills course (research writing). Students strengthened their overall writings skills and learned how to employ the voice of a specific discipline. Students earned the same grade for both classes. For many, this lessened their apprehensions about the skills course because they viewed it as a critical component in their acquisition of historical knowledge rather than as roadblock to their college success. Students received written feedback from both instructors on almost every assignment. The team-taught approach allowed instructors to provide more comprehensive instructional support for the students. There was greater interaction with instructors, genuine community with peers, and focused content-based writing assessments, all of which engaged students at a deeper level while helping them develop critical thinking skills and other college-level competencies. Students spend a considerable amount of time with each other in a learning community. Research shows that

---

56    Quote taken from the 1984 film *Ghostbusters*.

when students, particularly at-risk students, feel welcomed and supported by their instructors and classmates, they feel stronger bonds with the institution (Otto 3). This leads to higher retention and completion rates.

Our student success data supports this argument. For our HIS 201/ENG 102 learning community in 2010, initial enrollment was 78.26% female and 21.74% male. The students self-identified from a variety of ethnicities, genders, ages, and with a range of academic goals. Approximately 83% of the students identified as freshmen. Based on first-day enrollment numbers, the course retention rate, where retention is the number of students who remained in the class all semester, was 85.19%.[57] Of these students, 70% earned a grade of C or better for both classes. The 70% successful completion rate in our learning community is comparable to stand-alone sections of ENG 102.[58] However, if we focus on students of color, the data shows that the students enrolled in the ENG 102 that was a part of our learning community had a higher success rate than the average for stand-alone sections of ENG 102. For example, while Hispanic students completed ENG 102 at a rate of 68% in stand-alone courses, the rate was 75% in our learning community. Increasing success rates among this demographic is particularly significant because Hispanic students make up 22% of our total student population (Fact Book).[59] In fact, the college is in the process of receiving its designation as a Hispanic-Serving Institution (HSI), a process which includes developing infrastructure, pedagogy, and support for this growing population of students. Learning communities which focus on gender, global awareness, and social justice would provide opportunities to engage these students with content related to their lived experiences and with issues taking place in their communities.

We also saw increased success for other minority groups. During this same period, African American students completed stand-alone sections of

---

57    This number does not include students who were administratively withdrawn.

58    Completion for most CGCC courses is a D as this is the grade a student must receive to pass a course. Arizona public universities accept grades of C or better as transfer credits to their institution. For our purposes, successful completion is a C because students must receive this mark in ENG 102 to complete most degree and certificate programs for which first-year composition (ENG 101 and 102) is a required class.

59    This number is for fall 2015 enrollments. At the time of the LC, the percentage was approximately 17%. The percentage has since increased to over 22%.

ENG 102 at a rate of 64% while there was a 100% successful completion rate for our learning community.[60] Eighty-five percent of Native American students successfully completed ENG 102 in other sections while our course had 100% completion. Although we worked with a small sample of students, we believe that if this learning-community model was expanded to larger populations we would see a similar increase in success rates. Our data demonstrates that the content and structure of the course effectively met the needs of a broad range of individuals with varying degrees of preparedness. These statistics show an increased level of first-year success for students who participate in learning communities and particularly minority students.

In addition to increasing student success through course completion, we believe our learning community—and other gender-focused learning communities—have the additional benefit of developing students' understanding of diversity, and therefore we believe the learning community contributes to a positive and inclusive campus climate. Both the Maricopa Colleges District's and CGCC's missions focus on developing civic and global awareness as part of each student's academic growth. CGCC's student body primarily identifies as white (50.3%). Therefore, creating spaces of security and comfort for students of color and for open dialogue about controversial issues can be a tricky endeavor. Educational research demonstrates that minority and developmental students experience different stressors and roadblocks to success than their majority college-ready counterparts, including feelings of discrimination and alienation on campus ("Untold Barriers" 16; Horton 85-86). Additionally, students who are not actively engaged or participating in campus activities are more likely to withdraw from school (Tinto 69). Learning communities can help mitigate these issues by providing both formal and informal moments of engagement.

Learning communities in women's studies provide students with an educational model through which to critically explore issues central to the study of gender and society, and opportunities for understanding different experiences and worldviews. This focus allows us to delve into current events and conditions that impact the quality of all of our students' lives in an effort to

---

60    Data provided by the Chandler-Gilbert Community College Office of Institutional Research.

further develop a campus climate that is inclusive of all student backgrounds and experiences. The framework of the learning community—two combined classes which provide more time for the students to build relationships and develop trust—grants us the time and space to understand and reflect on gender and social justice, and to work on creating and sustaining dialogue around the issues of our times. This strengthens students' critical thinking, cultural awareness, and sense of community. Additionally, learning communities provide a sustainable mechanism for assisting minority and developmental students in adjusting to our college and having positive academic and social interactions with other students and faculty. Therefore, we believe that learning communities like the one we developed will lead to increased student success and retention as well as a transformation of our campus into a learning environment which is inclusive, welcoming, and accommodating for students from all backgrounds. CGCC's physical location situates us at the intersection of many national debates including immigration, ethnic studies, ethnicity, citizenship, democracy, racial profiling, and equity (economic, educational, gender, etc.). The focus on race, class, gender, and sexuality allows us to challenge preconceived notions about the world, to provide effective methods of student support, and to utilize the current debates as an opportunity for community building.

## "I Have a Thing for Things That Last"[61]: Developing and Maintaining Effective Educational Programming in Women's and Gender Studies

Since the development of our learning community in 2010, the college has offered two other LCs that contained gender studies courses. In planning these courses, we attempted to make use of trends in student scheduling and to collaborate with already thriving programs on campus. In 2013, we offered a learning community that combined PSY 101: Introduction to Psychology with WST 209: Women and Films. The Social and Behavioral Sciences Division offers approximately 25-30 sections of PSY 101 each semester. Each section

---

61   Quote appears in Criss Jami's book *Killosophy*.

enrolls thirty-two students. Based on information from the college's Learning Community Committee and the Office of Institutional Research, we elected to link the women's studies course with a class that students commonly take as freshmen. While new students lack a working knowledge of women's studies, we create an advantage for our discipline by pairing it with a popular course. The PSY 101/WST 209 LC enrolled twenty-two women and eight men. The LC had a 77% course completion rate with 80% of the course completers receiving passing grades. Through this pairing of courses, students applied major psychological theoretical perspectives to gender, and film, utilizing their understanding of psychology to examine and explain the effect of gender on social issues, behaviors, and representations in cinema.

In 2016, we offered an honors-only learning community of HIS 111: World History since 1500 and WST 100: Introduction to Women's and Gender Studies. Interestingly, this learning community, which focused on global economic and gender inequity, enrolled an equal number of male and female students. The LC had a 100% completion rate, and 95% completed the course with a C or better. Course texts included John Perkins's *The New Confessions of an Economic Hitman*, Lynn Nottage's *Ruined*, Rigoberta Menchu's *I, Rigoberta*, Catalina de Erauso's *Lieutenant Nun, and Threshold Concepts in Women's and Gender Studies by Christie Launius and Holly Hassel*. The final project for the course required students first to demonstrate what they learned about global interconnectedness and gender issues and, second, to engage in an activity promoting equality and/or social justice while learning more about the intricacies of democracy, politics, and social change. This LC demonstrated to us that the conscious pairing of courses may help increase the number of men enrolled in women's studies courses.

The Women's Studies Program at CGCC has grown significantly and we think part of this success can be attributed to our use of learning communities. In 2005, only one section of the introductory class was offered each semester and it was taught by an adjunct faculty member. Until 2011, we offered only two courses with WST (women's studies) prefixes—WST 100 and WST 290: Women and World Religion. Since then, we have added three courses (WST 285: Contemporary Women Writers, WST 200: Essential Feminist Writing, WST 209: Women and Films) as well as online sections for our previously existing courses. The successful implementation of gender-focused learning communities demonstrated the viability of women's studies courses which allowed us to expand offerings to both of our college campuses and to add courses in online formats. As interest in WST courses grew, faculty worked collaboratively to increase enrollments. We raised the visibility of the discipline on campus through marketing, sharing assignments, attending new student orientations, sponsoring campus events, and conducting talks in other classes. This allowed us to build a recognizable presence on campus and to compile a significant pool of data establishing the growth possibilities for a full-fledged program. In 2014, the college curriculum committee allowed us to institute a 15-credit academic Certificate in gender studies. Since a certificate program already existed at one of our sister colleges, we used their framework as the foundation for our certificate. The certificate requires the completion of the introductory course (WST 100) and then allows students to meet the remaining twelve credit requirements by selecting courses from a list of electives. Some of these courses include: HIS 201, PSY 235: Psychology of Gender, Anthropology 211: Women in Other Cultures, Sociology 212: Gender and Society, English Humanities 261: Native Women's Literature, WST 200: Essential Feminist Writing, and English Humanities 285: Contemporary Women Writers. Because these electives are offered in a variety of divisions, we garnered support from other faculty as the success of our program increases enrollments in their courses. Due to these practices, enrollments in WST courses on our campus continue to grow and we have seen an increase in support from faculty and administration.[62]

As a discipline, women's and gender studies is perfectly suited to provide quality educational services while engaging students in thoughtful dialogue. Women's and gender studies provides an interdisciplinary approach to learning and as such is useful for a variety of degrees and career fields at the community college level. Each course focuses on critical thinking, problem solving, and community engagement. Course content focuses on diversity and global awareness. As such, the field is uniquely positioned to tackle questions of social justice, difference, and democratic engagement. When delivered as part of

---

62   While they are not required by any major at CGCC, all WST courses contribute to the completion of the AA and AAS degrees by providing course credits in the social and behavioral sciences, and humanities as well as satisfying transfer tags in humanities, cultural diversity, history, and humanities and fine arts.

learning communities, these courses provide a safe but academically challenging space for students at all levels of preparedness. When combined with foundational classes, it enables students, particularly minority and developmental students, to find the course content and institutional support which provides necessary scaffolding for their continued success and retention at institutions of higher learning. Combining women's and gender studies courses with other disciplines supports students while developing a new brand for the field, shifting WST out of the "boutique course" category.

Emma Perez suggests that we create new norms by studying history. She writes, "If history is the way in which people understand themselves through a collective, common past where events are chronicled and heroes are constructed, then historical consciousness is the system of thought that leads to a normative understanding of past events" (qtd. in Jacobs 587). Learning communities in women and gender studies create a space for faculty and students to develop new norms about their lives and their culture. The LC provided an effective method of increasing student success for students of color in both content and skills courses. Additionally, it demonstrated that women's and gender studies is a dynamic field through which students of diverse backgrounds and interests can learn to think critically, synthesize materials, and increase their cultural awareness.

# Works Cited

"201 Best Martin Luther King Jr. Quotes — The Ultimate List." *Christian Animal Ethics*, https://christiananimalethics.com/martin-luther-king-jr-quotes/, Accessed 8 August 2016.

Alvarez, Julia. *In the Time of the Butterflies*, Algonquin Books, 2010.

"Arizona General Education Curriculum." *AZ Transfer*. www.transfer.com/generaleducation. Accessed 3 August 2016.

"Around the World in 72 Days." *American Experience*, Directed by Mel Bucklin and Christine Lesiak, PBS, 1997.

Austen, Jane. *The Complete Novels*, Penguin, 2006.

Brave Bird, Mary. *Lakota Woman*. Harper Perennial, 1991.

Cooper, J. California. *Family*, Anchor, 1991.

Dayton, Cornelia. "Taking the Trade: Abortion and Gender Relations in an Eighteenth-Century New England Village," *Women's America: Refocusing the Past*, Edited by Linda K. Kerber et al, Oxford UP, 2011, pp 116-133.

Escaldon, Maria Amparo, *Esperanza's Box of Saints*, Touchstone, 1999.

Erauso, Catalina de, *Lieutenant Nun: Memoir of a Basque Transvestite in the New World*, translated by Michele and Gabriel Stepto, Beacon Press, 1996.

*Fact Book 2016.* Chandler-Gilbert Community College Office of Institutional Research, 2016.

Frederickson, Mary. "Going Global: New Trajectories in U.S. Women's History," *The History Teacher,* vol. 43, no. 2, 2010, pp. 169-189.

"Gateway Courses Definition." *John N. Gardner Institute for Excellence in Undergraduate Education.* www.jngi.org/gateway-courses-definition. Accessed 3 August 2016.

*Ghostbusters.* Directed by Ivan Reitman, performances by Bill Murray, Dan Akroyd, and Sigourney Weaver, Columbia Pictures, 1984.

Horton, Joann. "Identifying At-Risk Factors That Affect College Student Success," *International Journal of Process Education,* vol. 7 no.1, June 2015, pp 83-101.

*In the Time of the Butterflies.* Directed by Mariano Barroso, performances by Salma Hayek, Lumi Cavazos, Edward James Olmos, Mía Maestro, and Demian Bichir, MGM, 2014.

Jacobs, Margaret D. "Getting Out of a Rut: Decolonizing Western Women's History," *Pacific Historical Review,* vol. 79, no. 4, 2010, pp. 585-604.

Jami, Criss, *Killosophy,* CreateSpace Independent Publishing Platform, 2015.

*Jefferson in Paris.* Directed by James Ivory, performances by Nick Nolte and Gwyneth Paltrow, Touchstone Pictures, 1995.

Kristof, Nicholas D. and Sheryl WuDunn, *Half the Sky: Turning Oppression into Opportunity for Women Worldwide,* Vintage, 2010.

Kuh, George D., "High-Impact Educational Practices: A Brief Overview," *High-Impact Educational Practices: What They Are, Who Has Access*

to Them, and Why They Matter. *American Association of Colleges &*
*Universities*, www.aacu.org/leap/hip. Accessed 3 August 2016.

Launius, Christie and Holly Hassel, *Threshold Concepts in Women's and*
*Gender Studies: Ways of Seeing, Thinking, and Knowing*, Taylor &
Francis, 2015

Lerner, Gerder. *Why History Matters: Life and Thought*, Oxford U P, 1998.

*The Life of Rosie the Riveter.* Directed by Connie Field, Direct Cinema
Limited, 1980.

Menchu, Rigoberta. *I, Rigoberta Menchu: An Indian Woman in Guatemala*,
2nd ed., Verso, 2010.

"A Midwife's Tale." *American Experience*, Directed by Richard P. Rogers,
PBS, 1998.

Mohr, James C. "Abortion in America," *Women's America: Refocusing the*
*Past*, Edited by Linda K. Kerber et al, Oxford UP, 2011, pp 205-214.

Nottage, Lynn, *Ruined*, Theatre Communications Group, 2009.

Otto, Sheila. "Learning Communities in Higher Education: Best
Practices," *Journal of Student Success and Retention*, vol. 2, no. 1,
October 2015, http://www.jossr.org/wp-content/uploads/2015/10/
Learning-Communities-in-Higher-Education-JoSSR-submission-
revised-10-26-2015.pdf, Accessed 10 August 2016.

Perkins, John, *The New Confessions of an Economic Hitman*, Berrett-
Koehler Publishers, 2016.

Reagan, Leslie C. "When Abortion Was a Crime: Reproduction and the
Economy in the Great Depression," *Women's America: Refocusing the*
*Past*, Edited by Linda K. Kerber et al, Oxford UP, 2011, pp 506-511.

Tinto, Vincent. *Leaving College: Rethinking the Causes and Cures of Student Attrition*, 2nd ed., U Chicago P, 1994.

Townsend, Robert B. "What the Data Reveals about Women Historians." *Perspectives on History*. vol. 48, no. 5, 2010, p 14.

"Twilight: Los Angeles." *Great Performances*, Directed by Marc Levin, performances by Anna Deveare Smith, PBS, 1994.

"Untold Barriers for Black Students in Higher Education: Placing Race at the Center of Developmental Education." Southern Education Foundation, www.SouthernEducation.org, 2017.

"We Shall Remain: Siege at Wounded Knee (Part V)." *American Experience*, Directed by Stanley Nelson, PBS, 2009.

West, Dorothy. *The Living Is Easy*, Feminist Press at CUNY, 1996, p 114.

Wilson, August. *Seven Guitars*. Penguin, 1997.

Yezierska, Anzia. *Bread Givers*, 3rd ed., Perseus, 2003.

Zook, Melinda. "Integrating Men's History into Women's History: A Proposition," *The History Teacher*. vol. 35, no. 3, 2002, pp. 373-387.

# Student Voices: Chara Andrews, Sacramento City College

## Sacramento, California

Chara Andrews attended Sacramento City College (SCC) where she was a women's and gender studies major before transferring to the University of California, Davis in fall 2018. Her major is now cinema and digital media. Chara thrives on creativity and creating something that is her own. With her innate feminist views, along with the education she gained from the women's and gender studies major, she feels confident that she can contribute a new lens in which to view women and gender.

*What skills did you learn in your WGS course(s)?*

"Some of the classes I took had to do with societal views of women pertaining to film and media, while other courses discussed human sexuality and the analysis of gender. For example, I took a course called Sex and Gender in the U.S. that delved deep into the complexities of America's view of gender roles while also shedding light on the experiences of LGBTQIA members of society. What I found most interesting about taking all the courses for the women's and gender studies major was the multiple layers that make up this academic discipline. For instance, the term 'intersection,' when used in the context of women's and gender studies, can be described as the following: being a woman of color and gay means that this individual not only faces sexism and racism in our society, but also the prejudices of homophobia and the ignorance that accompany a culture which views heterosexuality as 'the norm.' The intersections are: being a woman, being a woman of color, and homosexual."

*Would you recommend your WGS course(s) to other students? Why do you think it's important for college students to take women's and gender studies courses?*

"I would highly recommend students enrolling in at least one course pertaining to women's and gender studies. Taking these classes really helped me develop my critical thinking skills and gave my already passionate views of women's rights a stronger foundation. I feel like a veil has been lifted and I'm viewing the world with new eyes. In my opinion, I believe it is critical for all students to have an open mind and allow themselves to be exposed to subjects outside of what they already know because how can a person grow intellectually without learning new things? More importantly, these courses bring empowerment to those that feel, or have felt, they haven't had much power in their lives."

*How did your WGS course(s) contribute to your career goals?*

"When I started SCC in the fall of 2014, I was 30 years old and had no clue what I wanted to major in. Luckily, I spoke with an academic advisor that suggested I look into women's and gender studies as a major, and I'm so glad I did. I was able to be successful at SCC because I was pursuing something, I was passionate about, while gaining invaluable knowledge."

# Chiseling Away at the Foundations of the Patriarchy: On Teaching Masculinity Studies at an American Community College

Richard E. Otten

For several years, I have been teaching a course entitled Introduction to Masculinity Studies at Anne Arundel Community College. I spun the syllabus for this writing-intensive course that satisfies our college's diversity requirement from a masculinities literature review that I produced as I progressed through the George Mason University Cultural Studies program. My doctoral training familiarized me with critical frameworks derived from diverse disciplines that can be applied to examine cultural objects such as the ideology of masculinity. As I state at the top of the syllabus, the course is an examination of masculinity as a social construct loosely tethered to the biology of sexual dimorphism, and almost all of the course readings reinforce the notion that these constructions instill and perpetuate larger hegemonic structures. The backgrounds and trajectories of the students who enroll in the class predispose many of them to be recalcitrant to this curriculum, which should not be a surprise, but community college students uniquely benefit from such a class.

Humbly, I proffer that, while gender and sexuality studies courses broadly represent significant contributions to any community college curricula, a course in masculinity studies provides a singular value within the scope of a course catalog. Mine is a very rare course: a course in masculinity studies is far from a *de rigueur* offering at any typical university's women's studies department, and I am unaware of any like it at any other community college. Even as looming curricular standardization places such courses in peril going forward, the essay that follows asserts that community college students, more than students enrolled in any other institution of higher education, stand to benefit from studying masculinity. May they enjoy more opportunities to do so.

## Masculinity Studies and the Diversity Requirement

Immediately, I can make one broadly accurate generalization about my students: experience has made quite clear to me that I offer a gender and sexuality studies course for students who would otherwise never take a gender and sexuality studies course. Although each semester I can count on a few students who are earning our college's Certificate in gender and sexuality studies, and who may transfer on to take more women's and gender studies courses while earning a bachelor's degree at a four-year college or university, the overwhelming majority of my students take the course only to satisfy their diversity requirement. They likely find the prospect of satisfying this requirement—a requirement that they may perceive as tangential or even onerous within the context of their professional and vocational training—by studying masculinity to be intriguing and attractive, at best, or a means by which to game the system, at worst. When academic advisors lay out for our students their options for how they might satisfy this requirement, with course titles such as Music, Power and Gender, or African American Literature as available options, they choose Introduction to Masculinity Studies. A recent student offered the most earnest explanation of how he thought that he was getting one over when he told the class that, as an army veteran, he assumed that he knew all there was to know about masculinity, but that he quickly realized that the material would be more complex than he ever imagined.

As much as I love that my masculinity studies class produces such pedagogical moments, this situation causes me some consternation, because our diversity courses have been constrained in recent years by pressures exerted upon them from a few sides. Most acutely, these diversity courses have suffered under conditions of declining enrollment that our college, like other institutions of higher learning, has experienced in recent years, so that we as allied colleagues have found ourselves competing with one another for students. Introduction to Masculinity Studies has flourished, while many other vital courses have withered, and herein lies the larger issue. These courses are rare, and community college curricula are being standardized in service of the four-year schools to which our students hope to transfer. Courses that uniquely serve the needs of our students are on the chopping block, so we as faculty must defend our own individual courses while we also fight to defend the value of diversity education itself.

By what logic is Introduction to Masculinity Studies available as a diversity option available to these students? While a diversity requirement might appear to be little more than a liberal mandate for each student to expose oneself to a minority perspective (and some classes that satisfy this requirement might offer little more than that), ideally a diversity course should situate students within the socio-historical power dynamics that render homogeneity pernicious at our present juncture. Most commonly, when critical theorists examine these power dynamics, we study the subordinate side: when we study gender, we study women and transgender people, not men; when we study sexuality, we study homosexuality, not heterosexuality; when we study race, we typically do not study whiteness; and a community college catalog will not likely feature an economics course that offers an explicitly Marxist perspective on wealth. Female, homosexual, transgender, racialized, and poor people clearly suffer from patriarchy, homophobia, racism, and capitalism, so a diversity course will sensibly instill empathy for these social groups.

Such a focus, unfortunately, from the student's perspective, may seem to frame the female gender, homosexuality, gender nonconformity, blackness and other non-white racial categories, and poverty as problems, not the structures of superordinance that produce these categories, while villainizing men, heterosexual people, cisgender people, white people, and wealthy people who benefit from at least a modicum of the privilege expropriated from the subordination of others. Rather than merely empathizing with people unfortunate to be born into a subordinated social group, or even admiring those individuals with the gumption to overcome the bad hand that fate dealt them, students who successfully complete a diversity course should come away understanding that superordinance itself is the problem. They should develop some sense of solidarity with subordinated social groups, and they should walk into their next classroom, workplace, or other social setting armed to provoke any agent or apologist for hierarchical ideologies.

However, it should not be surprising that many students begin the course as enthusiastic defenders of—or even exponents of—patriarchal ideology. As their instructor, I have my work cut out for me.

## Students Who Get It and Students Who Do Not

I have enjoyed an approximately equal distribution of male and female students in my classes, and very early in the semester I make a point to congratulate male students who have chosen to register for the class. One of the first readings that I assign is an essay by Harry Brod, describing experiences in his own pioneering masculinity studies class, in which he quotes the veteran sociologist of masculinity Michael Kimmel to support the observation that such men demonstrate a degree of bravery because, from the perspective of the dominant culture, taking a course in masculinity implies that a man lacks some knowledge of what it means to be a man (Brod).

Whereas Brod raises that issue to underscore his disappointment that few men register for his class, I do not have this problem: I have other problems. It seems obvious to me that, just as a women's studies program is not a finishing school, a masculinity studies class does not offer a primer in how to be more manly, but some of my students seem to be expecting precisely that, or at least they believed that they registered for a course that will validate their own convictions about masculinity. Some men, understandably, bring to the class convictions that certain behaviors and beliefs distinguish a well-adjusted man from lesser men, and may even express this perspective in casually homophobic, misogynistic, or transphobic terms. Without doubt, they have been socialized by their families, by their schooling, and by popular culture to broadly view men and women equally, but they tend to judge people, especially other men, by how well they fit gendered expectations, unconscious that it is these very gendered expectations that gird the superstructures of the patriarchy.

Women who take the course certainly come from many different backgrounds, and, as I have indicated, tend to receive the lessons of the course very well. Surprisingly, like their male classmates, few have ever taken a gender and sexuality studies class before. Although they could have taken Introduction to Women's Studies to satisfy the diversity requirement, they chose to take

Introduction to Masculinity Studies instead. They do not identify themselves as the kind of student, or as the kind of woman, who takes a women's studies course, but they were drawn to a course in masculinity. They often tell me that they have chosen to take this course so that they can learn more about the men in their lives, which strikes me as a very reasonable motivation, though I will respond to it by explaining how their men have been socialized to be the men that they are. If they express interest in learning some innate truth about men, I tell them that in my course they will learn to think critically about that very question, and recommend that they take my colleague's Psychology of Men course next semester to continue their study of the male gender.

As one would expect, women who are taking my course after having already begun to study gender bring a valuable perspective to the course. They are already familiar with patriarchy and how it subjugates women, and they know that men tend to perpetuate that subjugation, with or without intention. Their understanding of masculinity itself, however, tends to be unsophisticated. They may not have considered the pressures that men, especially young men, feel to fit an ideal of masculinity, pressures that include a proscription against expressing any frustration or distress that they feel in response to these pressures. Very likely, these women have not considered that patriarchy is also a hierarchy among men, one in which the type of men who are likely to attend community college do not occupy the highest rungs.

## Why Community College Students Need Introduction to Masculinity Studies

Diversity courses should make students into better citizens and members of society; regardless of their political inclinations, students should learn from diversity courses to at least think critically about, and not become dupes of, dominant ideologies, and some students will come away from these classes both inclined and equipped to actively resist hegemony. Such pedagogical strategies, as we have seen, cause friction when they meet with the dispositions of many of our students. Therefore, diversity courses, and especially Introduction to Masculinity Studies, play a valuable role within the community college curriculum. According to R.W. Connell's concept of hegemonic masculinity, even men who do not collect a significant patriarchal dividend perpetuate structural dynamics that subordinate the women who are their mothers, sisters, girlfriends, wives, and co-workers (Connell). In fact, just as fascists recruit the brown shirts from the working classes, these men who benefit least from patriarchy are the most eager to defend it. These students can play a significant role—passively or actively—in dismantling patriarchy and other dominant ideologies that subordinate them disproportionately. The relative subordination of the class habitus of community college students can be difficult to quantify, but data from the 2011–2012 National Postsecondary Student Aid Study and the College Board suggest that what unifies our diverse student bodies is that they tend to come from families that lack capital, both economic and cultural.

Community college students come from less wealthy families than the families that send their dependent children to four-year colleges and universities. Among students who are enrolled in public two-year schools and who are dependent upon their families, 31% come from families earning less than $30,000 per year, and only 17% come from families earning at least $100,000 per year. Among their counterparts attending public four-year schools, 22% come from families earning less than $30,000 per year, and 29% come from families earning at least $100,000 per year; these figures shift significantly to 18% and 33% for students attending private non-profit four-year schools (Ma and Baum 9).

Likewise, community college students come from less educated families than the families that send their kids to four-year colleges and universities. Among students enrolled in public two-year schools, fewer were raised by parents who themselves completed at least a bachelor's degree (33%) than those who never enrolled in college (36%). In comparison, overwhelmingly more students enrolled in public four-year schools were raised by parents who earned a bachelor's degree (54%) than those with no college experience (24%), and that ratio becomes even more disproportionate for students attending private four-year schools, with 61% growing up with at least one parent who earned a bachelor's degree, and only 19% with parents who never attended college at all (Ma and Baum 9). Here we may find the greatest inequality of all, since parents who attended college prepare their children to themselves attend college, whether or not, under the precarious economic conditions of the early 21st century, they can afford to pay the tuition for their children. Personally, my parents told me that I would be attending the college of my choice from when I was very young. I distinctly remember a day when I came home from kindergarten in a grumpy mood and my mother told me that I would need to get used to going to school, since I would be a student for at least another sixteen years, and even longer than that if I eventually went to graduate school, like she did. Since so many of them represent the first generation of their families to enroll in an institution of higher education, community college students are unlikely to have been supported by such parental pep talks.

Community college students are clearly disadvantaged, economically and culturally, underscoring the real purpose of requiring community college students to satisfy a diversity requirement—not to learn that inequalities exist, but to become familiar with the complex, structural nature of intersectional inequalities, and accept that these power dynamics do not work in their favor. Their reasons for enrolling in a community college instead of a more prestigious institution, and perhaps struggling in their classes, are overdetermined, much like gender and sexuality. Even if some of my male students remain convinced that patriarchy serves their personal self-interest, or that traditional gender roles, though imperfect, serve society's needs, they will not be able to deny that patriarchy oppresses many of their fellow men. Although I cannot reasonably expect all of my students to become feminists—and I cannot fairly assess them based upon their commitment to that or any other cause—successful Introduction to Masculinity Studies students of all genders will learn to think critically about these circumstances.


## Conclusion

Objectively, student recalcitrance is completely understandable. We live in a patriarchal society. Patriarchy is virtually a global phenomenon, and not a recent development. My students and I are all subject to it, and I might be the first person who has ever required them to take the temperature of the water that we all swim in and asked them if it could be warmer. To expect students to unlearn all of this powerful socialization within the span of a few months would be unreasonable, and to expect that I can achieve that as a teacher at a perfect success rate would demonstrate hubris on my part. The ability to recognize the structure at work is more important than the arrival at a disposition antagonistic to the ideology that it delivers. I have never had a student tell me that he or she could not accept the idea that gender is not something instrumentally ordained by a higher power or encoded in our DNA. The recalcitrant student fundamentally believes that patriarchal hegemony serves a virtuous social function by making men better men, and that the social institutions that powerfully shape the construction of masculinity (church, parents, hetero-femininity, the physical culture of sport, the military, schools, etc.) once did so well but have failed recently.

To accept this circumstance would not be so difficult, if not for the material realities of the community college. Frankly, as rational consumers in the higher education marketplace, very few students choose to enroll in a community college simply because it is the most affordable option. It probably is, but the choice is more determined by other factors. Enrolling in a bachelor's degree program at a four-year institution is not an option for most community college students, due to factors such as their age, their prior scholastic achievement, or their finances. Whatever value cultural capital holds, they tend to lack that as well, and the function of the community college is to allow them to conceal this deficit. These students need to understand that their subordination is not their fault, and that even if their education provides them better leverage than that offered by their own bootstraps with which they might lift themselves out of their current station in life, these structures of superordinance will remain in place. Even the students from relatively affluent families, who were raised with the expectation that they, like other family members who came before them, would attend college, whose families chose the community college because it offers a cost-effective means of completing collegiate general education and exploring academic options while living at home, should while immersed in the community college environment become aware of their own relative privilege, and one would hope that they would become allies with their classmates in the struggle against oppression. Studying gender while attending community college should disabuse students of the bourgeois aspirations that community college recruitment marketing promises to realize.

It is precisely in their response to these material conditions of our lives that Introduction to Masculinity Studies and other women's and gender studies courses are valuable. Community college students need to be made familiar with the structures of power that oppress them. Students famously forget whatever they are tested upon very quickly, but I prefer to believe that the lessons students take away from a gender studies course are the type that might not sink in until weeks, months, or even years after we have submitted their final grades. If we can teach them to think critically about how gender shapes their understanding of the world, including helping them to develop the tools to dismantle the patriarchal structures that surround them, we can contribute to the missions of our community colleges to shape students into better members of our local communities and better citizens of our nation and our world.

# Works Cited

Brod, Harry. "Studying Masculinities as Superordinate Studies."
    *Masculinity Studies and Feminist Theory.* Ed. Judith Kegan Gardiner.
    New York: Columbia University Press, 2002. 161-162.

Connell, R.W. *Masculinities.* Vol. 2nd. University of California Press, 2005.

Ma, Jennifer and Sandy Baum. *Trends in Community Colleges: Enrollment,
    Prices, Student Debt, and Completion.* New York: The College Board,
    2016.

# Student Voices: Kayla Calvin, Montgomery College

Rockville, Maryland

Kayla Calvin is a student at Montgomery College where she will be graduating in the spring with an associate's degree in general studies focused in humanities and social sciences. She plans to continue her education at University of Maryland, College Park as an anthropology major. Through the understanding of intersectionality that Kayla learned in the Women's and Gender Studies Program she discovered feminism is about advocating for all injustices. With her diverse multicultural background, she found she could apply the interdisciplinary foundation of women's and gender studies to socio-cultural anthropology and advocate for all the marginalized and overlooked groups she identifies with. Kayla's passion to advocate for herself and others has taken on a life of its own in her anthropology rookie research internship this spring; she has been able to bring more awareness to gender studies within different cultures to the Anthropology Department and hopes to find creative ways that allow her to continue this work.

*How has your study of women's and gender studies been valuable to you?*

"The Women's and Gender Studies Program allowed me to believe in who I am and who I want to become. Due to my multicultural background I believe I have always had a level of openness to understanding what women's and gender studies entails. The program however gave me the language and the history I needed to know to actively promote my passion and my involvement in the study. I believe in the work this program does in standing up for equality, defining what that means in depth, and how it advocates for all types and groups of people. But most importantly, I believe in the people running this program. They have allowed us to have the hard-to-understand, hard-to-explain conversations that lead to change and understanding. I have always believed myself to be a feminist and believed in the word, but this program made me realize how much goes into that word and how much power is behind the phrase 'I am a feminist.' I learned that we all play a role in keeping patriarchy alive. I learned that it's important to almost interrogate yourself in order to unlearn things that allow an unjust society to remain. Something that challenged me in that way was when we went through bystander training. We learned about the different ways to be a participating bystander when forms of sexual violence arise. I learned how to provide support in a way that is safer for everyone involved which required me to form a new thought process in these situations to ensure I am always a participating bystander and not just a bystander."

*What skills did you learn in your WGS course(s)? Why do you think it's important for college students to take women's and gender studies courses?*

"The most important lesson I learned when it comes to participating in change is that as I continue to put in the work for equality, as a feminist, I represent equality in all of its forms and as that change comes about, I myself have to be ready and willing to change as well. That is a lesson one learns only in a course like this one.... This program opened my eyes to how much work needs to be done, but it also opened my eyes to the fact that it can be done. I am a better human with the knowledge I gained from this course because it's more than just a course: it's real life."

# Introduction to LGBTQ Studies: Designing the Course

Grace Sikorski

Lesbian, gay, bisexual, transgender, and queer (LGBTQ) studies is an expanding and dynamic field that examines non-heteronormative sexualities and genders from a transhistorical, cross-cultural, and interdisciplinary perspective. It studies the history of human sexuality and gender identity/expression; cultural and social constructions of sexuality and gender; representations of LGBTQ experience in textual and visual media; legal rights and restrictions; events and sociopolitical issues of current interest; methods of queer theory/ queer studies; and advocacy, activism, and change.

In the summer of 2008, I designed an Introduction to LGBTQ Studies course to enrich the general education curriculum for the associate's degree program at my home institution, Anne Arundel Community College in Arnold, Maryland. Since then, I have taught the course in full and accelerated terms, including summer sessions, both in face-to-face format and online. I would like to share what I learned from these experiences with the hope that this information might help others who are designing such a course now, as well as those who find it necessary to defend an already established course, for instance, if your institution is undergoing general education review.

First, be prepared to meet with some resistance. In light of current mandates to eliminate electives and the restricted number of "boutique" courses being offered at community colleges, how can we say that this course is necessary? It does not respond directly to current trends in workforce development as other courses of study, such as cybersecurity, have done. It does not seem to directly support the learning outcomes of vocational and skills-based training.

However, we can argue that this rigorous academic course does align with the mission and values of the community college: it helps students develop essential knowledge and skills needed for full, informed participation in the complex and volatile world outside of the classroom. This is precisely why many community colleges require students to complete a diversity requirement before graduation, and it stands to reason, Introduction to LGBTQ Studies is well-suited to meet that requirement. Students learn how to analyze complex systems of power, privilege, and oppression that construct and enforce identity categories. They learn about the causes and effects of structured inequality and categories of difference. And they develop cultural literacy as a basis for effective participation in diverse global, national, and local communities. Such learning outcomes are at the heart of diversity curriculum.

If your school does not have a diversity requirement per se, look to the college's mission, statement of values, or strategic plan for any language referring to equity, inclusion, and diversity that may help you to argue that such a course is in line with the college's larger goals. This will support the claim that your course is appropriate and necessary for the students at your institution.

You may also argue that Introduction to LGBTQ Studies has a place within the general education core curriculum. Its multidisciplinary method prepares students for a range of academic and professional pursuits, since LGBTQ studies has its roots in history, sociology, psychology, philosophy, and other well-established academic disciplines. In fact, it possesses what the Middle States Commission on Higher Education calls "Characteristics of Excellence in Higher Education: Requirements for Affiliation and Standards for Accreditation" for general education coursework:

- incorporates essential knowledge, cognitive abilities, and an understanding of values and ethics;
- enhances students' intellectual growth; and
- draws students into new areas of intellectual experience, expanding their cultural and global awareness and sensitivity, and preparing them to make enlightened judgments outside as well as within their academic specialty. (47)

If your institution falls outside of the Middle States region, refer to your regional accrediting organization to discover if you might frame your course within its definition of general education. (See the Council for Higher Education Accreditation website for more information.)

Question may arise regarding the prevalence of LGBTQ studies at other colleges and universities, particularly transfer institutions. Unfortunately, research into LGBTQ studies at the community college level is virtually non-existent, and there is precious little data regarding academic programs/courses in this field. It is also difficult to measure the magnitude of student engagement, when relevant content is often spread across the curriculum, while individual courses "live" in a wide array of academic departments and do not carry a title or program designation that would easily identify them as LGBTQ studies. In the end, the number of LGBTQ-related courses is difficult to determine since the content of college catalogs is not web-indexed. So, how can we support the claim that there is precedence for an introductory course at the community college level and that the course will transfer?

Community colleges in the United States have offered LGBTQ-focused courses since 1972, when City College of San Francisco enrolled students in a gay literature course for the first time ("LGBTQQI Studies"). Since then, the subject matter and methods related to LGBTQ Studies have infused college curriculum throughout the country. According to the list compiled by John G. Younger, *University LGBTQ/Queer Programs: Lesbian, Gay, Bisexual, Transgender, Transsexual Queer Studies in the USA and Canada Plus Sibling Societies & Study-Abroad Programs*, as of August 2016, 6 colleges and universities offer majors toward the bachelor's in LGBTQ studies, 54 offer minors, and 11 offer certificates or concentrations. The Associate of Arts in LGBTQ studies is offered at Sierra College and City College of San Francisco, both in California. He records individual LGBTQ courses offered at only four other community colleges: Santa Monica College, in California; Bunker Hill Community College, in Massachusetts; Salt Lake Community College, in Utah; and South Puget Sound Community College, in Washington. However, other sources suggest Younger's list presents an incomplete picture. For example, the Campus Pride Index, a national listing of LGBTQ-friendly colleges and universities, identifies eight other community colleges that offer LGBTQ-related courses: Tacoma Community College and South Seattle College in Washington; Fashion Institute of Technology, in New York; Red Rocks Community College, in Colorado, Pellissippi State Community College, in Tennessee, Santa Rosa Junior College and Napa Valley College in California; and Grand Rapids Community College, in Michigan. Furthermore, when we conduct a simple web search we see that most major colleges and universities offer certificates, majors, or degrees in LGBTQ studies, and at least two other community colleges offer LGBTQ studies courses: Glendale Community College, in California, and Highline College, in Washington. We should note, however, that the results of our search under-represent the actual number of courses and programs available in LGBTQ studies. Younger and the Campus Pride Index rely on colleges to self-report their course offerings, and search engines do not access content within college catalogs or schedules of courses. We know, for instance, that Anne Arundel Community College and Montgomery College are two institutions in Maryland that do offer LGBTQ curriculum. It stands to reason that other community colleges do as well, though an accurate listing is not as yet available.

The claim that LGBTQ studies are prevalent at the undergraduate/introductory level is further supported by the number of colleges who order LGBTQ studies textbooks, and the demand for new editions. For example, SAGE Publications' *Finding Out: An Introduction to LGBT Studies*, launched a third edition in 2017. This textbook has been on order as desk copy or student textbook for current course enrollment at nearly 100 colleges, and seems to serve as the standard textbook in Introduction to LGBTQ courses.

Knowing the history and current standing of LGBTQ studies at other institutions will help you to argue for the need of an Introduction to LGBTQ Studies course at your school. Keep in mind, however, when you are asked to document the transferability of your course, it will be best to contact individual institutions to discover whether they accept the course you are designing and how it will meet requirements for specific degree requirements.

Tranferability will likely be determined by your decision to offer your course within one academic department or to cross-list it. Department designation will also affect how students will populate the course. Conversely, the place of the course within specific academic disciplines will affect its design. For instance, a course listed in women's studies would be informed by its methodolgy. Content and method would be in line with a feminist pedagogy and a critical awareness of the sociocultural and political systems that structure power differentials and oppression as well as critical interventions and advocacy that seek to affect change in the world. A course offered in psychology, history, or cultural studies would use a different approach.

There is also the question of titling your course. Will it be a course in human sexuality, gender studies, gay and lesbian studies, or LGBT studies? Will you incorporate the "Q" to signify queer? Will you aim for full inclusion with an acronym such as LGBTQQIA? The title you select indicates the focus and scope of the course. Your title and catalog description may specify that your course covers American LGBTQ culture and current events rather than global perspectives and a wider historical range. Will the title be too lengthy? Will the old guard of the faculty balk at having the words "gay, lesbian, bisexual, transgender, and queer" in the course catalog? Will they insist on an acronym like LGBTQ for brevity's sake and to avoid more explicit language from appearing on the college transcripts? In any case, your title should accurately reflect the content of the course and satisfy curricular needs.

Also consider whether you want your Introduction to LGBTQ Studies to stimulate the development of more courses in this subject area. Is yours a first in a sequence that would qualify a student for an undergraduate certificate, minor, or major? Do you need to align learning outcomes for this purpose?

Though the decisions you make about the content of your introductory course should be influenced by all of the elements discussed so far, and each institution, indeed each instructor, may design this course differently, most Introduction to LGBTQ Studies courses include much of the following content:

1. Introducing LGBT studies

   1.1. Central concepts of LGBT studies: questioning definitions

      1.1.1. Vocabulary: words, phrases, and acronyms, including sex, sexuality, gender, and LGBT (lesbian, gay, bisexual, queer, transgender, transsexual, intersex, etc.)

      1.1.2. Concepts of sexual and gender identity including those based on sex, gender, desires, behaviors, orientations, identities, communities, stereotypes, "closet," and "coming out"

1.1.3. Essentialist/constructivist debates (genetic/scientific/bio-logical arguments/approaches like those of Dean Hamer, Simon LeVay, Anne Fausto-Sterling); cultural contextualiza-tion and variability of sexualities and genders across lines of race, ethnicity, generation, religion, ability, class, culture, etc.

1.1.4. Systems of privilege, power, and empowerment; internal and institutionalized phobias and oppression; heteronormativity

1.2. Genealogy of LGBT studies as an academic/scholarly discipline

1.2.1. Influences of the civil rights movement, the minority studies model, women's studies, feminism, gender studies, the mod-ern gay rights movements with Stonewall as a mythic origin, AIDS epidemic, and trans movement, with special emphasis on the United States

1.2.2. Institutionalization of gay and lesbian studies and the emer-gence of queer studies and queer theory

2. Cultural studies

2.1. Cultural images of LGBT people that perpetuate stereotypes, op-pression fear, ridicule, and hate (such as film images from *The Cel-luloid Closet*)

2.2. LGBT culture and communities with discussion of popular culture such as symbols, flags, film, TV shows (such as *The L Word* or *Will & Grace*), marches and other events (such as Pride, National Coming Out Day, National Trans Day of Remembrance, National AIDS Awareness Day), advertisements, cartoons and comics (such as *Dykes to Watch Out For*), and music/video (such as k.d. lang, George Michael, Michigan Womyn's Music Festival), drag performance (such as queens and kings), sports icons, and publications (such as *Out*, *Advocate*, *Washington Blade*), etc.

    2.3.    LGBT contributions to the arts including literature (such as poems from the Harlem Renaissance, coming out stories, AIDS literature, children's literature, memoirs), musical theater, dance, painting, photography, sculpture, fashion, design, etc.

3.    Psychology, health, and wellness

    3.1.    Early psychological theories of the origins and causes of homosexuality

    3.2.    Categories, hierarchies, and continuums in psychological and sexological paradigms

    3.3.    DSM (changing criteria, depathologizing homosexuality and the continuity of "gender identity disorder" for medical treatments, sex change, etc.)

    3.4.    Transgender/sexual medical interventions; hormones to surgery

    3.5.    Intersex conditions

    3.6.    Conversion treatments and ex-gay ministries

    3.7.    HIV/AIDS and other STIs

    3.8.    Sex education, safer sex, and health risk prevention

    3.9.    Rape and domestic violence

4. Socio-anthropology

   4.1. Cross-cultural perspectives: Native America, China, Japan, India, etc.

   4.2. Religious, theological, and spiritual perspectives

   4.3. Dis/ability and aging

   4.4. Socio-economic class

   4.5. Race differences

   4.6. Regional differences

5. History

   5.1. Antiquity (to 5th century); topics such as Greco-Roman and biblical precedents; China and Japan

   5.2. Middle Ages (5th to 15th century); topics such as Judeo-Christian theological perspectives, monastic lives

   5.3. Early modernism (15th to 18th century); topics such as the invention of gender and sexual identity

   5.4. Modernism (18th to mid-20th century); topics such as Magnus Hircshfeld and modern sexology

   5.5. Contemporary history (mid-20th century to the present with special emphasis on LGBT history in the United States) including key historical moments and movements such as Shoah/Holocaust and Paragraph 175, the Mattachine Society, the Harlem Renaissance, the impact of wars, McCarthyism, Daughters of Bilitis, the Stonewall rebellion and the Gay Liberation Front, Lesbian separatism, HIV/AIDS epidemic and ACT UP, and Queer Nation

6.   Laws, policies, legislation, and rulings in the United States

   6.1.   Civil rights issues such as marriage, civil union, and domestic partnership, inheritance legislation, family rights legislation, adoption policies and legislation, immigration legislation, anti-obscenity legislation, sodomy legislation, etc.

   6.2.   Safety issues such as shelters and housing, hate crime legislation

   6.3.   Work issues such as anti-discrimination policies, military policies, sex work legislation, etc.

   6.4.   Health issues such as insurance rights, healthcare proxy rights, mandatory HIV testing, etc.

7.   Current issues in the United States

   7.1.   Overview of current advocacy organizations such as the Human Rights Campaign; the Gender Public Advocacy Coalition; National Center for Transgender Equality; Parents, Families and Friends of Lesbian and Gay people; and the National Gay and Lesbian Task Force, etc.

   7.2   In-depth discussion of current issues in the LGBT community such as hate crimes legislation, ENDA: Employment Non-Discrimination Act, transgender civil rights, marriage, civil unions, partnership recognition, elections and politics

Keep in mind in designing your course that you will need to meet the needs of the undergraduate student at the introductory level, and the community college student more specifically. Your college may have an open-enrollment or open-admission policy, a significant portion of your student population may be remedial or developmental, and some may be seeking continuing education or professional development credit rather than a full degree. "Nontraditional students," adult learners, military veterans, international students, students with unique needs—students enrolled at community colleges may possess diverse skills, knowledge, experiences, and concerns. Keep this in mind as you design your course. What prerequisites or corequisites in reading and writing are best suited? Will a face-to-face or online format be preferable? Some of your choices will be determined by your college or the program within which your course will be offered, but you may be able to make certain decisions that will lower barriers and increase accessibility to your Introduction to LGBTQ Studies course.

To support your learning objectives, choose readings and texts carefully. A textbook such as *Finding Out: An Introduction to LGBT Studies* by Michelle A. Gibson, Jonathan Alexander, and Deborah T. Meem is very useful, and seems to meet the needs of a student with basic reading competency. Alternatively, you might use an anthology of more advanced texts that have in some ways established the canon in LGBTQ studies—Butler, Foucault, etc. A third option is to assemble a packet of readings in which you juxtapose complex theoretical essays with news articles, political speeches, cartoons, or advertisements, and activity sheets. In any case, take into account the reading level of your students. At the introductory level, they may find the theoretical concepts and jargon in the field of LGBTQ studies a bit daunting.

A word about the community college student perspective: Consider why students might take this course. What may motivate them to enroll? What do they hope to gain? How do they themselves measure their own success? It is possible that their goals are not purely academic. While they may need to complete diversity or other general education requirements, some students will have a more personal motivation for enrolling in the course. For instance, some may be in the process of coming out or have a personal stake in talking through specific issues that concern them. They may want to understand the experiences of family, friends, co-workers, etc. They may be concerned about the current political and social climate in the United States. Or they may be interested in advocacy and political activism.

Set the course in context as well. Consult local law enforcement agencies to determine the prevalence of hate crimes against LGBTQ people in your community. Determine the population of LGBTQ individuals living in your community. Take note of the federal, state, and local laws that affect the way they can and do live their lives. Know your campus climate from the point of view of LGBTQ people. Conduct a climate survey if one has not been conducted in the past. Have there been recent incidents of prejudice, harassment, bullying, hate speech, micro-aggression? Does campus security respond to such incidents satisfactorily? Do students feel LGBTQ perspectives are lacking in other classes? Given that community college students are commuter students, do they report concerns within the local community, where they live, where they work? Do national trends in federal elections and appointments show a worrisome trend away from equal civil rights and protections under the law? When asked why an Introduction to LGBTQ Studies course is timely and necessary for your own community, this information will be useful.

How will you design a course that will meet the needs of these students and the needs of the community your college serves while maintaining the academic rigor of the course? Activities and assessment tools can be useful in this regard.

For example, the capstone assignment in my Introduction to LGBTQ Studies course asks each student to write a manifesto. Students must conduct research to establish a strong foundation in facts regarding a set of issue they select for themselves. They must formulate a coherent position statement on each issue. And they must articulate a personal resolution to engage in deliberate action that will create the change they desire. Such a project reasonably requires research of outside sources to establish the foundation and context of the manifesto, to reference other voices the manifesto aligns with or against, and to understand the range of possibilities for action in personal, local, state, national, and global contexts. You can design activities and projects such as this one to give each student room for private investigation into the issues of the course. You might also connect activities and assignments directly to needs that present themselves within your local community. Will you forge partnerships with local organizations, non-profits, businesses, and agencies in your community so that students can address local concerns linked to the course content? Will you create formal internships that earn credit for your course and encourage professional development for your students? If the community college serves the local community, how will your course meet local needs and address local issues?

This may go without saying, but I also encourage you to be mindful of your own role in the course. Reflect on the position you hold in relation to the students, the extent to which you are willing to disclose information about yourself, and the importance of confidentiality and ground rules that foster a safe space not only for your students but also for yourself. Reflect on the larger implications of how you deliver your class. Focusing on LGBTQ people as "victims of oppression" or celebrating the virtues and accomplishments of this "minority" group are both problematic approaches. Rather, employ intersectional analysis and emphasize how power and oppression function in complex ways. Deliver accurate, current, and thorough coverage of the course content, provide a range of perspectives, and help students to think critically, even if this means interrogating their own assumptions.

Also, reflect on the relative benefits of face-to-face and online delivery. Working online allows student a certain degree of anonymity, and while this can open a space for uncritical and perhaps at times abusive dialogue, it can also create a safe zone within which students are keenly aware that they are accountable for what they say and how they behave. They are the text they produce, and everything they write or post online is saved to the learning management platform. They seem to be more self-conscious and more deliberate online, but often in the best of ways. Face-to-face students, on the other hand, may be motivated by social interactions within the classroom. They may be somewhat impulsive and reactive during discussions, and they may prefer demonstrating their learning not by writing, but by giving oral presentations, presenting visual or performance art, engaging in problem-based group work, etc. They may need the instructor to assert limits and enforce ground rules at each class meeting, but their energy can be harnessed in productive ways.

Search for resources within your institution that will support student learning and engagement in your course. At the end of this essay, I have included a list of resources you may want to recommend for purchase to your library's collection. Consider DVDs, periodicals, and database subscriptions as well. And don't overlook the value of grant funding and technological support. My home institution provided a grant and release time from teaching so that several faculty members could create a Virtual Resource Center for the

Study of Sexuality and Gender to support students enrolled in our Introduction to LGBTQ Studies course.

And lastly, time your proposal to college administration wisely and take into account other initiatives or policies that impact the success of your proposal. You may need to manage college politics in some unexpected ways. For instance, in 2007, my own proposal was put on hold because senior faculty advised me that it was not the right time to put it before the Educational Policy Committee of the college. They anticipated that it would interfere with a very different sort of proposal: a motion that had been put before the college's board of trustees to implement domestic partnership benefits. I waited. But, when I realized one year later that the board was continuing to table that motion, I decided to propose my course, and it was approved. If I had waited for the board to approve domestic partnership benefits, my course never would have been added to the college curriculum.

Designing an introductory course in LGBTQ studies for community college students may be a daunting prospect, but when your proposal is accepted, students will greatly benefit from the opportunity to explore important issues pressing on us during a time of great political upheaval, and they will develop the skills they need to be informed and engaged. This course raises student awareness of issues that affect LGBTQ people in diverse historical and cultural contexts, the material conditions that define their experiences, and their agency in responding to those conditions to effect change. Students become aware of the great range of diverse identities and experiences under the rubric "LGBTQ" and develop a sensitivity to variables of race, ethnicity, class, ability, religion, culture, region, ability, sexuality, etc., that influence the way LGBTQ people can and do live their lives and how they are understood and valued. Students gain historical perspective on LGBTQ issues and learn about LGBTQ contributions to world history and understand the long timeline of events that lead to and justify the modern gay and lesbian movement, the transgender rights movement, the intersex rights movement, etc. Students examine how attitudes about LGBTQ people are shaped and consider the consequences of such things as the concept of normativity, internalized and institutionalized oppression, and structured inequality. They gain a greater awareness of LGBTQ culture and the current LGBTQ political and social climate in the United States and around the world. Students examine how sexual orientation and gender identity are concepts that rely on a complex system of power, privilege, and oppression and that these concepts are not static or universal; they can and do change. Students have the opportunity to develop, refine, and articulate their own positions on these issues. They are better prepared to participate in their communities with greater sensitivity, awareness, and informed perspectives and, if they choose, to address the issues that affect the lives of LGBTQ people in their local communities. Introduction to LGBTQ Studies has a place in the curriculum of the community college because it prepares students to be informed and active participants in their global, national, and local communities. For these reasons, it is arguably an essential part of the curriculum at any community college.

# Works Cited

*Campus Pride Index: National Listing of LGBTQ-Friendly Colleges and Universities.* 2016. www.campusprideindex.org. Accessed 16. November 2016.

Gibson, Michelle, et al. *Finding Out: An Introduction to LGBT Studies.* 2nd ed., Sage, 2014.

"LGBTQQI Studies." *City College of San Francisco.* http://www.ccsf.edu/en/educational-programs/school-and-departments/school-of-behavioral-and-social-sciences/LGBT.html. Accessed 16 November 2016.

Middle States Commission on Higher Education. "Characteristics of Excellence in Higher Education: Requirements for Affiliation and Standards for Accreditation." Middle States Commission on Higher Education. Philadelphia, PA. 2006.

"Virtual Resource Center for the Study of Sexuality and Gender." Anne Arundel Community College. http://ola4.aacc.edu/vrc/sexuality_and_gender_studies/. Accessed 16 November 2016.

Younger, John G. *University LGBTQ/Queer Programs: Lesbian, Gay, Bisexual, Transgender, Transsexual Queer Studies in the USA and Canada Plus Sibling Societies & Study-Abroad Programs.* U of Kansas. 2016. http://people.ku.edu/~jyounger/lgbtqprogs.html. Accessed 16 November 2016.

# Resources

Abelove, Henry, Michele Aina Barale, and David M. Halperin, eds. *The Lesbian and Gay Studies Reader*. Routledge, 1993.

Beemyn, Brett and Michey Eliason. *Queer Studies: A Lesbian, Gay, Bisexual, and Transgender Anthology*. New York UP, 1996.

Bornstein, Kate. *My Gender Workbook*. Routledge, 1998.

Butler, Judith. *Gender Trouble: Feminism and the Subversion of Identity*. Routledge, 1990.

Castle, Terry, ed. *The Literature of Lesbianism: A Historical Anthology from Ariosto to Stonewall*. Columbia UP, 2003.

Corber, Robert J. and Stephen Valocchi, eds. *Queer Studies: An Interdisciplinary Reader*. Blackwell, 2003.

Crompton, Louis. *Homosexuality and Civilization*. Harvard UP, 2003.

Duberman, Martin, ed. *A Queer World: The Center for Lesbian and Gay Studies Reader*. New York UP, 1997.

Eng, David L, et al., eds. *Social Text: What's Queer about Queer Studies Now?* 23(3-4; 84-85) Fall-Winter 2005. <http://socialtext.dukejournals.org/content/vol23/issue3-4_84 85/#ARTICLES>

Foucault, Michel. *The History of Sexuality: Volume I, An Introduction*. Trans. Robert Hurley. Vintage, 1978.

Fox, Ronald C. *Current Research on Bisexuality*. Haworth, 2004.

Jagose, Annamarie. *Queer Theory: An Introduction*. New York UP, 1996.

Jennings, Kevin, ed. *Becoming Visible: A Reader in Gay and Lesbian History for High School and College Students*. Allyson, 1994.

Johnson, Patrick E. and Mae G. Henderson, eds. *Black Queer Studies: A Critical Anthology*. Duke UP, 2005.

Lancaster, Roger N. and Micaela di Leonardo, eds. *The Gender/Sexuality Reader: Culture, History, Political Economy*. Routledge, 1997.

Lovaas, Karen E., et al., eds. *LGBTQ Studies and Queer Theory: New Conflicts, Collaborations, and Contested Terrain*. Haworth, 2006.

Medhurst, Andy and Sally R. Munt, eds. *Lesbian and Gay Studies: A Critical Introduction*. Cassell, 1997.

Minton, Henry L., ed. *Gay and Lesbian Studies*. Haworth, 1992.

Morton, Donald, ed. *The Material Queer: A LesBiGay Cultural Studies Reader*. Westview, 1996.

Nardi, Peter S. and Beth E. Schneider, eds. *Social Perspectives in Lesbian and Gay Studies: A Reader*. Routledge, 1998.

Piontek, Thomas. *Queering Gay and Lesbian Studies*. U of Illinois P, 2006.

Sandfort, Theo, et al. *Lesbian and Gay Studies: An Introductory, Interdisciplinary Approach*. Sage, 2000.

Sedgwick, Eve Kosofsky. *Epistemology of the Closet*. U of California P, 1990.

Storr, Merl, ed. *Bisexuality: A Critical Reader*. Routledge, 1999.

Stryker, Susan and Stephen Whittle, eds. *The Transgender Studies Reader*. Routledge, 2006.

Sullivan, Nikki. *A Critical Introduction to Queer Theory*. New York UP, 2003.

Weinberg, Martin S., Colin J. Williams, and Douglas W. Pryor. *Dual Attraction: Understanding Bisexuality*. Oxford UP, 1994.

Wilton, Tamsin. *Lesbian Studies: Setting an Agenda*. Routledge, 1995.

# A Community College President of NWSA: A Personal Narrative

Judith M. Roy

I served as president of the National Women's Studies Association (NWSA) in 2006, and in leadership positions from 2005 as president-elect and in 2007 as immediate past president. I'd like to discuss how this happened, since no one from a two-year college held this position before or since. The structure of NWSA at the time made this possible, although it came as a total surprise for me. Then, I will discuss why I believe it could be difficult to elect another community college president for the current NWSA.

I attended my first NWSA conference in 1996. The Community College Caucus welcomed me and became my "home" in the organization. We supported one another and shared ideas to take back to our own programs. The conference was much smaller then, taking place on a college or university campus so attendees could choose a lower cost dorm room or a hotel. The conference was in June, a time convenient for many community college faculty or program directors. Given our heavy teaching loads during the regular academic year, more community college faculty found it easier to be away from campus in the summer. A peak of sorts was the 2001 conference at the University of Minnesota, where the large number of participants from the community college sector brought increased attention to the Community College Caucus from NWSA leadership. Overall, the reactions were very positive. However, a few made elitist negative comments, revealing their ignorance about what community colleges are and the important role they play in higher education.

As I became active in the Community College Caucus, another caucus had a direct impact on my path to the NWSA presidency, the Program Administration and Development group, known as PAD. PAD was formed in the late

1990s by university department chairs who felt NWSA did not give them all the resources they needed. The PAD sessions provided invaluable discussions of strategies and ideas to bring back to our campuses and our administrations to help support the existence and development of our programs. This group was a vital resource for NWSA, and a number of presidents came from its ranks. In addition to two co-chairs, PAD had an elected advisory group with a member from each category of institution, including two-year colleges offering a degree or certificate in women's studies. When I joined PAD, the Community College Caucus already had a strong presence there, under the leadership of Barbara Horn, from Nassau Community College in New York, and Shirley Parry, from Anne Arundel Community College in Maryland. I served in this group for several years, helping to plan the PAD preconference and working closely with PAD leadership. I got to know several PAD leaders personally, and this path led to my being nominated in 2005 to serve as president in 2006.

I had to hit the ground running as president-elect in 2005 while NWSA went through a major change. Under the leadership of 2004 president Colette Morrow and 2005 president Jacquelyn Zita, NWSA hired its first executive director: Allison Kimmich. Even though the organization had grown during the previous decade, it had lacked funds to hire an executive director and still operated with just the elected officers and Governing Council, plus a very small staff at the office in Baltimore, Maryland. Morrow and Zita launched the search and Kimmich came with great credentials, including a PhD in women's studies from Emory. However, the transition was not easy.

The NWSA Governing Council had at least 25 members at various times, each representing various groups in the organization, often with their own agenda. Some pushed back at the changes the executive director wanted to make. Some officers also expressed disagreement with proposed policy. It meant a very "hands on" presidency with multiple communications almost every day. For me, it was a second full-time job without any additional release time from my college. This was true for many prior presidents too since few received the release time or recognition they deserved. Individuals had to be persuaded and cajoled to accept a nomination for president. In fact, many presidents left office burned out and a few did not return to the organization. Given the heavy teaching load at community colleges, the burden of the presidency was even greater for me.

My term in office was hectic to say the least. I felt I had the support of the other officers, the executive director, and many on the Governing Council. Change is always hard, but I successfully mediated multiple disputes. One skill I brought to the table from my experience at a community college was the ability to work with faculty members from many different departments. Women's studies did not have stand-alone departments at community colleges then and had to draw faculty "on loan" from other departments. While some members from elite institutions might have looked down on me privately, no one addressed opposition to me or to the Governing Council. At the end of the 2006 conference, a long-time NWSA member congratulated me by saying, "Judith, you finished your term, and no one hates you!"

I made a lasting contribution to the national conference by introducing Presidential Sessions, an idea borrowed from (and credited to) the American Historical Society (AHA). These sessions allowed us to invite scholars who were not NWSA members to present their work in special lectures and were part of the move to raise the scholarly level of the conference. I am most proud of personally inviting scholar Susan Stryker to present at the conference for the publication of her book, *Transgender History*. Stryker, a transgender woman and historian, spoke during an early Presidential Session. At the same time, both Allison Kimmich and myself had to deal with at least one demand that a session should be closed to all but "women born women." We upheld the non-discrimination policy of NWSA and that has held to this day. It is wonderful to see the inclusion of trans women and men and their scholarship in the conference today.

Throughout my years in leadership, I said the NWSA presidency should be an honor and held by a senior person in the field, just as in other national discipline organizations. That hope became a reality with one signal event: a Ford Foundation grant. The grant raised the image of NWSA, and Executive Director Kimmich established closer relationships with institutions granting PhDs in women's and gender studies. The conference moved from June to November, allowing time and space for colleges and universities to interview job applicants at the conference, and reinforced the commitment to excellence and diversity. However, this shift in focus diminished attention to community colleges and their mission.

Beverly Guy-Sheftall became the new NWSA president in the new era. From her presidency onwards, all presidents have been women of color and all have been from four-year colleges and universities. Admirably, they have increased the commitment to diversity in NWSA. One of those presidents, Yi-Chun Tricia Lin, spent 10 years teaching at a community college, but moved to Southern Connecticut State University as chair of women's studies before her NWSA presidency. Because of her experience at a two-year school, she is the closest past-president to the Community College Caucus and could be a resource to help us raise our image.

While I had respect and support as a president from a two-year college, unfortunately, I think it's unlikely NWSA will choose another president from a community college. Because of the ways in which the organization has changed, it would be difficult for person from a two-year school to get the position. The path to leadership in NWSA is different now. The organization is much larger and NWSA's Governing Council is much smaller; only two caucuses, the Women of Color and Lesbian Caucuses, have seats. The rest of the members are the elected officers plus two members-at-large. PAD no longer has a seat in the Council and has a diminished role in the organization. Still, PAD continues as a vital resource to all of us. While NWSA has changed, and even though it is difficult to imagine another NWSA president from a two-year school, community colleges should still have a seat at the table. It's important for the field to understand and support the important work going on at community colleges around the country. To increase the visibility of community colleges at NWSA, I urge all community college chairs and directors to attend and present at the PAD preconference. We should also nominate community college faculty to the Women of Color Leadership Project and encourage them to join the Women of Color Caucus. Additionally, we need to reach out to talk to NWSA leadership in one-to-one conversations. We need to promote our students for transfer and our colleges as potential job opportunities for graduate students in women's and gender studies programs. We also need to work to increase diversity in the Community College Caucus leadership and work to ensure that we are attracting students of color to our programs. Although NWSA might not have a president from a community college again, our colleges can be a key focus for the organization. I'm confident that our current community college leadership and our caucus can continue to be loud and proud.

# Student Voices: Hannah Bairo, Jefferson Community and Technical College

Louisville, Kentucky

Hannah Bairo completed an AA and a Certificate in women's and gender studies from Jefferson Community and Technical College. She is currently finishing her BA in women's and gender studies at the University of Louisville. In fall 2019 she will begin law school at the University of Louisville's Louis D. Brandeis School of Law. From there, she hopes to work as an attorney fighting for social justice, human and civil rights, and focusing her energy trying to put a dent in the discrimination and prejudice faced by minorities in the United States and maybe the world.

*What skills did you learn in your WGS course(s)?*

"I learned how to have constructive conversations about uncomfortable topics. I learned about intersectionality, which I think was probably the most important concept with which I gained an understanding. I learned how to channel my passion for social justice—when it was my turn to stand up and fight and when it was my turn to shut up and listen to those to whose oppression I couldn't relate."

*How did the course contribute to your career goals? How did the course prepare you for the workforce?*

"My first women's and gender studies class, WGS 200, helped me realize my passion for social justice and for helping people. I knew I wanted to make an impact in the world, I just didn't know what that would look like. That class changed my life. I switched my major from social work to women's and gender studies and made the decision to go to law school. I would not have found my passion without that first women's and gender studies class."

*How did the course help you in your private life (interpersonal relationships, parenting, self-esteem, self-love, etc.)?*

"WGS 200 made an impact in my life that I couldn't have seen coming. It transformed my perception of the world. It opened my eyes to both things that were heart-wrenching and worthy of outrage and ways in which I could put my mark on the fight against injustices. Not only did it transform my perception, but it has altered my relationships, the way I parent, and the way I interact with family and friends. I learned how to love myself, how to be gentle with myself, and how to care for myself in ways I'd never considered. In addition, I learned to love others, be gentle with others, and care for others in ways I'd never considered."

*Why do you think it's important for college students to take women's and gender studies courses?*

"I think it's important for everyone to take women's and gender studies courses, but especially college students. I don't believe I would have an accurate picture of oppression or privilege if it weren't for these classes. And I believe that the understanding of those things is crucial to being empathetic and aware of injustice."

# Keep "Doing Good": Women's and Gender Studies Programs and VAWA Education Initiatives against the Tide

Esther Schwartz-McKinzie

Five years ago, community colleges across the United States were scrambling to meet updated requirements of the Violence Against Women Act (VAWA). In addition to establishing new standards around reporting and student conduct, VAWA's 2013 reauthorization stipulated specific education objectives: schools were now obligated to train faculty and staff, as well as to educate students about specific topics, including the definition of consent, the signs of abusive behavior in relationships, and safe and positive options for bystander intervention.[63] From the start, working to meet this mandate has required creativity and collaboration. In particular, it has required the engagement and commitment of faculty and staff who care about this work, often pushing back against the "check-the-box" mentality that tends to accompany unfunded initiatives at community colleges grappling with tight budgets and rafts of compliance directives.

Through its "Not Alone" campaign, the Obama White House placed new emphasis on Title IX's protections against discrimination on the basis of sex in education programs receiving federal financial assistance. The impacts of

---

63    The Violence Against Women Reauthorization Act of 2013 (S.47) can be seen in full here: www.congress.gov/bill/113th-congress/senate-bill/47. Subsequent guidance provided by the American Council on Education, "New Requirements Imposed by the Violence Against Women Reauthorization Act," stressed the significance of this new guidance and advised colleges and universities that, "The interplay of VAWA and other pronouncements ... warrants legal risk management judgment by institutional counsel and compliance officers, and implicates a range of management steps." The document and guidance can be seen here: www.acenet.edu/newsroom/Documents/VAWA-Summary.pdf.

this increased attention were profound, both from a violence-prevention and victims' advocate perspective. Belatedly joining the discussion dominated by four-year schools with residence halls and Greek life, many community colleges appointed Title IX coordinators, revised codes of conduct, and generated new dialogues about tough issues like trauma-informed response. The coordinated community approach advocated by the Justice Department under Obama emphasized collaboration between administration, faculty, and local organizations. For many of America's *1,462 community colleges*, VAWA's reauthorization prompted first-ever efforts to develop partnerships with police and rape crisis centers, formalized through memorandums of understanding.[64]

Women's and gender studies curriculums, as a matter of course, address topics like sexual violence, domestic violence, and consent, and faculty who teach these topics often bring advocacy backgrounds of some sort to their teaching: as a group, our engagement with these subjects is both personal and political. We were always already poised to support VAWA education initiatives, and many picked up the charge, supporting (or even designing) campus violence-prevention programs and activities.[65]

In short, after VAWA's reauthorization, women's and gender studies programs found themselves suddenly—and somewhat surprisingly—aligned with their institutions' compliance goals. Colleges, required to provide to all students content that has long been a part of our teaching and learning objectives, were on notice, and administrators were eager to avoid lapses that could

---

64   "NOT ALONE, The First Report of the White House Task Force to Protect Students From Sexual Assault, April 2014" makes very clear demands on colleges and universities: In addition to "providing a checklist for schools to use in drafting (or reevaluating) their own sexual misconduct policies," the document instructs schools to bring "key stakeholders ... to the table" (3): "While some schools may be able to provide comprehensive trauma-informed services on campus, others may need to partner with community-based organizations. Regardless of where they are provided, certain key elements should be part of a comprehensive victim-services plan" (13-14). Additionally, "Not Alone" promised to "collect and disseminate a list of Title IX coordinators by next year. Every school must designate at least one employee to coordinate its efforts to carry out its Title IX responsibilities" (18). This document can be seen here: www.justice.gov/archives/ovw/page/file/905942/download.

65   At Montgomery College for example, faculty serve on the Title IX Advisory Committee, and women's and gender studies faculty trained in and helped to design the College's implementation of the University of New Hampshire's *Bringing in the Bystander Program*.

become apparent (and that could potentially impact an institution's reputation) in the face of a Title IX investigation.[66]

On the front line, women's and gender studies programs seized opportunities to participate in revising institutional policy, help build relationships with support organizations, and participate in designing and increasing educational offerings around consent, healthy relationships, and bystander intervention. The threat of fines and highly public Office of Civil Rights investigations created a momentum (and sometimes influenced funding) that enabled these programs to do more than they had before.

One of the most striking developments has been the implementation of climate surveys. Although still not federally mandated, some states, like Maryland, New York, Washington State and Louisiana, require biennial surveys, and many schools conduct voluntary surveys. Montgomery College (MC), a community college in Maryland, implemented the SpeakUpMC survey in spring 2016, and repeated it in 2018.[67] With 1,953 (2016) and 1,142 (2018) participants, the surveys represent only a fraction of our typically 30,000 enrolled students, but their results underscore the reality that community colleges must not dismiss sexual violence as a problem only for four-year colleges with residence halls and fraternities.

Maryland House Bill 571 requires that all state colleges and universities conduct climate surveys; however, it provides limited guidance about the form or content of surveys. This makes asking difficult questions about student

---

66    The trial of Penn State football coach Jerry Sandusky, who was found guilty of 48 charges of sexual abuse in 2012, was one of several highly publicized scandals that first highlighted the responsibility of colleges and universities to prevent sexual assault, as well as their liability in such cases. "Pending Cases Currently Under Investigation at Elementary-Secondary and Post-Secondary Schools," generated by the US Department of Education, and "Tracking Sexual Assault Investigations," generated by the *Chronicle of Higher Education*, continue to be discussed in education journals, and watched by university and college administrators and even parents. See: www2.ed.gov/about/offices/list/ocr/docs/investigations/open-investigations/tix.html?perPage=1000, and projects.chronicle.com/titleix/investigations/?search_term=st+mary%27s+college+of+maryland.

67    Though the surveys are not published in their entirety, fairly comprehensive reports of their results can be seen at Montgomery College's SpeakUpMC web page, which includes a statement by the College President, as well as links to the College's Sexual Misconduct Policy and the Title IX Office: cms.montgomerycollege.edu/SpeakUpMC/. This level of access to such resources was rare at community colleges only a few years ago, and some are still catching up.

knowledge and attitudes a choice. Through SpeakUPMC, Montgomery College expressed a genuine desire to understand our students' educational needs where it chose to include such queries. In both 2016 and 2018, participants revealed troubling views about sexual violence, and many reported a significant lack of prior learning: 37.6% and 26.8%, respectively, told us that they had not received any prior education about sexual misconduct. This perhaps explains the prevalence of students' belief in damaging myths, demonstrated in both surveys. Most notably, students agreed or strongly agreed at a consistent rate, 28.9% in 2016 and 26.8% in 2018, that "dressing provocatively or engaging in promiscuous activity is inviting sexual assault." When responses of "don't know" are included, these statistics inflate to 36.6% and 32.2%. Similarly, many students expressed a belief that sexual violence is inevitable or "natural." Despite increased educational efforts after 2016, the percentage of students who agreed or strongly agreed with the statement, "Sexual assault and rape happen because men naturally get carried away in sexual situations," rose from 23.2% in 2016 to 31.3% in 2018. These figures inflate to 33.4% and a stunning 42.9% when including "don't know" responses. At the same time, students expressed considerable uncertainty responding to the prompt, "Many women who claim they were raped had sex and regretted it afterwards." Again, the statistics were consistent over both surveys: 23.6% and 21.0% indicated "don't know," while another 17.5% and 19.7% indicated that they agreed or strongly agreed with this statement.[68]

Some changes in the question format make students' reported experiences of sexual violence over the two surveys more difficult to compare. In 2016, every survey participant was asked to indicate whether they had ever experienced specific types of sexual violence, including eight categories of violence. Most strikingly, 23.7% indicated that they had experienced sexual harassment, and 18% indicated that they had been stalked. Another 30.4% of students told us that "someone I care about" had experienced sexual violence.

In 2018, the revised question asked, "Since coming to the college, have you experienced any unwanted sexual violence or unwanted sexual contact (which

---

68  Readers may assume that these misogynistic attitudes are primarily held by men; however, SpeakUPMC participants self-identified as just over 60% female both years; 36% identified as male both years, with the remainder indicating other designations or that they "prefer not to say."

can include kissing, touching, harassment, stalking)?" Of the 9.5% of students who answered this question affirmatively, 51.2% indicated that they had experienced sexual harassment, and 36.9% indicated that they had experienced stalking. In 2016, 15.9% of students surveyed indicated that they had experienced assault or rape, and in 2018, 17.9% of students who experienced "unwanted sexual violence or unwanted sexual contact" since coming to college indicated that they had experienced assault or rape (SpeakUPMC 2016; 2018).

Though these statistics may seem surprising, they are generally consistent with the national average (Climate Survey Results 2018 1). The most compelling data here may not be that students experience sexual violence (we knew that), but what they told us about how experiences of sexual violence influence their ability to be successful in college, regardless of where this experience happened. Those who confided that they had experienced some form of sexual violence overwhelmingly reported feeling depressed: they described having difficulty focusing on their schoolwork, missing class meetings or assignment deadlines, or arriving late to class. Some told us that they dropped, failed, or even delayed taking classes because of these experiences. "This data highlights the negative academic outcomes that often result from experiencing sexual misconduct" (Climate Survey Results 2018 2). Until recently, the absence of residence halls on campus has allowed community colleges to stay on the sidelines with regard to the larger discussion about sexual violence. However, many administrators and faculty have begun to recognize that sexual violence impacts the success and retention missions our institutions hold dear.[69] Survey results pose a rousing challenge: what are we willing to do about that?

---

69   A January 2016 Justice Department report, released by the Bureau of Justice Statistics and funded by the Office on Violence Against Women, includes the results of a Campus Climate Survey Validation Study surveying thousands of students across nine schools. The report concludes: "Victims of sexual assault often suffer physical and emotional trauma that can linger for years and stretch into nearly every area of their lives ... we found that 19 percent of female rape victims dropped or considered dropping classes, 7 percent changed where they lived, 31 percent said their academic performance suffered and 22 percent considered taking time off or dropping out of school. Other studies draw similar conclusions, but given that most incidents of sexual violence are never reported (only 13% in this study), the impacts of sexual violence are difficult to quantify. The report summary can be viewed at https://www.justice.gov/archives/opa/blog/understanding-threat-sexual-violence-college-campuses.

While the basic format of climate surveys is necessarily multiple-choice, a best practice is to capture student comments. Some comments made by MC students underscore the need for education: where some complained about women dressing too provocatively, others more directly blamed victims: "In my experience, the people who are abused are the ones who asked for it." One student even commented that if they were to witness a rape, they "would probably watch if it's entertaining" (SpeakUpMC 2016).

However, a particularly gratifying outcome of SpeakUpMC has been how some students interpret the survey as a message of concern, expressing gratitude and making comments like, "Thank you so much for allowing us to take this survey," and "You're doing good." Others urged us forward: "People should be given more education about sexual violence," and "I would love for the college to make a big deal about [sexual violence] and I myself would love to be an advocate" (SpeakUpMC 2016). The more recent survey demonstrates the College's improved success in educating students about sexual violence, both in the classroom and through campus events. Notably, students acknowledged this work: "I appreciate the College's commitment to a safe environment for all students, and I applaud efforts to make students aware of the resources available to them" (SpeakUpMC 2018). These few quotes can't convey the totality of student remarks, but they do represent the enthusiasm among survey-takers for educational efforts to address sexual violence. Overall, SpeakUPMC affirms that sexual violence is an issue of immediate concern in the lives of community college students, and that they are receptive to efforts to develop more rigorous awareness and education programs.

In January 2017, millions of us in the United States and across the world participated in an historic Women's March, compelled to assert our belief in basic human rights and to express our desire for a safer world.[70] Protestors donned pink "pussy hats" and carried signs in direct reference to the "pussy grabbing" braggadocio of then newly elected President Donald Trump, a horrific contrast to the goals of justice and protection for victims of sexual vio-

---

70   An estimated 2.6 million people participated in the Women's March on January 21, 2017, and roughly three million people around the world participated in simultaneous marches, a stunning show of resistance to the values of the incoming presidential administration. For an overview of the march and its impact, see: www.history.com/this-day-in-history/womens-march.

lence prioritized by the previous administration.[71] The handwriting was on the wall, and many advocates of women's rights correctly predicted the de-prioritization and defunding of programs to protect women and decrease violence.[72] A farewell letter sent by the US Department of Justice from Bea Hanson, director of the Office on Violence Against Women, reminded us that, "All of us are in this together ... we have not put an end to sexual assault and domestic violence. The work continues, and the work remains critical" (Hanson). By 2018, Trump's Education Secretary, Betsy DeVos, had designed and proposed new regulations substantially changing the implementation of Title IX. After a brief comment period ending in February 2019, enactment of these regulations, which narrow the definition of harassment, heighten the burden of proof for victims, and dictate a more onerous process for responding to reports, is now considered imminent. Victims' rights advocates universally predict that as a result of these changes, fewer victims will report—or receive support.[73]

In other words, the tide has turned, and those of us who anticipated making great strides toward helping to reduce violence in our communities are taken aback. With at least two more years before a new administration is likely to again prioritize VAWA educational requirements, the impulse now, more than ever, for cash-strapped institutions sensitive to the political winds

---

71    On October 7, 2016, a video of then-candidate Donald Trump, as he prepared for a 2005 *Access Hollywood* appearance, was leaked to the press and dominated news cycles for many weeks. The shocking video featured Trump bragging about how his power and status enable him to "grab" women "by the pussy" with impunity. For a complete transcript of the video, see: "Transcript: Donald Trump's Taped Comments About Women," *New York Times*, Late Edition (East Coast); New York, N.Y. 08 Oct 2016.

72    President Trump's 2019 budget request confirms this prediction. For an overview, see "National Coalition Against Domestic Violence Denounces President Trump's FY'19 Budget Request," located at https://ncadv.org/blog/posts/ncadv-denounces-president-trumps-fy19-budget-request.

73    For a sampling of anticipated consequences of pending changes to Title IX, see: "Five Ways Trump and DeVos Are Failing Students on Civil Rights," educationvotes.nea.org/2017/08/01/5-ways-trump-devos-failing-students-civil-rights/; "DeVos Proposals for Campus Sex Misconduct Rules Are 'Worse Than We Thought,' Victims' Advocates Say," www.nbcnews.com/news/us-news/devos-proposal-campus-sex-misconduct-rules-are-worse-we-thought-n937316; "New U.S. Sexual Misconduct Rules Bolster Rights of Accused and Protect Colleges," www.nytimes.com/2018/08/29/us/politics/devos-campus-sexual-assault.html; "What Does Higher Ed Have To Say About the Proposed Title IX Rules?" www-chronicle-com.montgomerycollege.idm.oclc.org/article/What-Does-Higher-Ed-Have-to/245581.

will be to "check the box" when it comes to fulfilling VAWA educational requirements. One-size-fits-all online training programs, ranging from outright poor and misguided to thoughtful and nobly intended but difficult to access for many students (especially ESL or developmental learners who comprise significant populations at community colleges), allow institutions to achieve superficial compliance. This is not the answer.

This anthology is being published at a crucial moment: we are answerable to the many young people who marched in January of 2017 and again in 2018 and 2019, and who watched the "Me Too" movement evolve and expose the reality of sexual violence in our culture and around the world. We are answerable to the students who, over the past three years, have taken our surveys, attended workshops on consent and bystander intervention, and who have expectations of us. Still on this front line, it is up to women's and gender studies programs to maintain momentum, defend footholds, keep dialogues going, and continue to assert the importance of educating students about sexual violence.

Climate surveys will continue to be important. Maintaining a seat at the table to ensure that survey tools are substantive should be a primary goal, along with using survey data to make the case for prevention, education, and response. Asking the right questions is important: survey results that demonstrate a connection between sexual violence and student retention and success will make the strongest case for colleges to invest in prevention and education.

At community colleges, survey data must be used to remind administrators that our institutions are not islands, and that our students' experiences outside of school influence their ability to succeed in school. Survey data suggests new ways to honor institutional missions, implicit to the community college ethos, that include helping our communities to deal with the crucial challenges they face.

Most significantly, women's and gender studies faculty will continue what they have always done: teach. As educators, we will take the lead in the delivery of initiatives that get students thinking; we will help them to question their assumptions and to grow in their sense of their own power to reduce violence. Over the past several years at Montgomery College, we have, for example, partnered with our Title IX program to implement colloquia focused on topics like "Gender-Based Violence, Sexual Assault and the Community College Experience," and "Gender/Identity-Based Violence," and on how "Radical Inclusion" requires, as its prerequisite, safety and respect. Faculty and staff on all three Montgomery College campuses deliver bystander intervention training throughout the academic year as trained volunteers. Many of us who teach in a range of disciplines have also integrated violence-prevention education into our non-women's studies courses. In the coming years, such efforts may receive less formal support at community colleges; where institutional motivations generated by the previous White House administration fade, it will be up to us to remind each other of the difference this work makes and to keep "doing good."

# Works Cited

Hanson, Bea. "Farewell Message from Bea Hanson." The United States Department of Justice Archives. Office on Violence Against Women, 19 Jan. 2017, www.justice.gov/archives/ovw/blog/farewell-message-bea-hanson. Accessed 3 Feb. 2018.

Montgomery College, "Climate Survey Results 2016." SpeakUpMC Voices Against Sexual Violence. Montgomery College, 2016. cms.montgomerycollege.edu/SpeakUpMC. Accessed 3 Feb. 2019.

Montgomery College, "Climate Survey Results 2018." SpeakUpMC Voices Against Sexual Violence. Montgomery College, 2018. cms.montgomerycollege.edu/SpeakUpMC. Accessed 3 Feb. 2019.

Montgomery College. "SpeakUpMC Climate Survey on Sexual Violence and Misconduct." Survey. 8-26 Feb. 2016.

Montgomery College. "SpeakUpMC Climate Survey on Sexual Violence and Misconduct." Survey. 1-28 Feb. 2018.

# Student Voices: Kayla Miskell, Anne Arundel Community College

Arnold, Maryland

Kayla Miskell is a gender and sexuality studies major at Anne Arundel Community College. Majoring in gender and sexuality studies has awakened Kayla's passion for activism and made her realize the importance of civic engagement. She volunteered at the 2019 Women's March—it was her first time attending—and she plans to continue her involvement in gender-related activist work. She also advocates for the LGBTQPAI+ community.

*What skills did you learn in your WGS course(s)?*

"The skills I learned throughout this class are many—one particularly is confidence. Having a better understanding of WGS topics has equipped and prepared me to provide a strong and valid argument, and evidence to support my claim. I have been able to correct people when a term or phrase has been misused as well as handle uncomfortable situations in regards to gender and pronouns…. This class challenged me to think outside of the stereotypical woman and mother roles as well as to understand gender and sexuality on a spectrum. [My professor] provided me multiple opportunities to flourish within the community as an activist and hopefully one day, a leader. Even though it has only been one semester, I feel like I have achieved so much more these past six months then I have in my lifetime. I cannot wait to see what next semester holds as I continue to push myself further academically, emotionally and physically!"

*How did the course contribute to your career goals? How did the course prepare you for the workforce?*

"This course helped contribute to my career goals by providing me with the assurance that at the age of 26 it is okay to be working on myself and focusing on my career. Women sometimes feel pressure in their mid-20's to start planning to have a family, when that has never been ideal for me."

*How did the course help you in your private life (interpersonal relationships, parenting, self-esteem, self-love, etc.)?*

"My private life benefitted from this course in the aspects of being more open and understanding of when femininity is displayed by males…. It has also helped me understand the myths and lies that are put onto women to appear, dress, and act a certain way. I learned that it is okay to fight those ideal beauty standards, which has increased my self-love and strengthened me emotionally and mentally."

# Endangered Studies, Women's, Gender, and Sexuality Studies and Community Colleges in #MeToo Times: A Case Study of Kingsborough Community College as a Microcosm of Neoliberal Education

Red Washburn

At this political juncture of #MeToo, #TimesUp, #BlackLivesMatter, #TransLivesMatter, and Sanctuary Campus Movements, among others, women's, gender, and sexuality studies (WGS) is arguably more relevant than ever, especially at the community college level where at-risk and marginalized populations reside, for the field challenges dominant narratives of power relations and social inequalities, explores different angles of vision, repositions marginalized groups across location, and links critical examination and practical intervention in students' lives and in the world through civic engagement. Approximately 50 years ago, WGS emerged out of social movements; its present life is focused on involvement in them, but its future is in jeopardy, specifically because of its politicization. The field is not neutral; it's very intellectual nature questions sexism, racism, classism, ethnocentrism, cisgenderism, heterosexism, abelism, etc. Therefore, it is no surprise that the recent trend to defund and eliminate WGS serves a political purpose to uphold privilege and power as connected to structural conservatism and neoliberalism under academic capitalism. The American Association of University Professors, based in DC with chapters across the nation and committed to higher education standards, procedures, freedom, and governance for faculty, completed a 2016 report entitled "The History, Uses, and Abuses of Title IX":

We urged universities and colleges to foster and fund gender studies and other allied departments and disciplines—including African American studies, queer and trans studies, and ethnic studies—as essential sites for research into how differences are used to legitimize structures of power. These studies inquire into the sources of sex discrimination and potential means of addressing the structures of institutional misogyny and racism.... The 2016 report condemned the gutting and diminishment of these programs that had occurred while the bureaucratic apparatus of Title IX continued to garner funding and expand. We now reiterate the necessity of robust gender studies (its research and curriculum) as essential to addressing the goals of Title IX: the elimination of discrimination in education. Attempts to fix the meaning of gender are not simply moves against the "special interests" of certain individuals, although trans, intersex, nonbinary, and gender nonconforming people—and especially poor people and people of color—will disproportionately suffer for it.

Their argument emphasizes that undermining Title IX and defunding and eliminating WGS creates a space in which blocking access to social justice education and social services is acceptable, setting the stage for undoing gains in education and allowing inequality.

This year marks the 50th anniversary of Stonewall in New York and the 25th anniversary of women's and gender studies at Kingsborough Community College (KCC). According to the WGS and College Council files, Kingsborough was one of the earliest community colleges in the nation to offer WGS courses and the first community college in the City University of New York (CUNY) to offer a WGS Concentration, after which many CUNY community colleges modeled their own programs, including most recently Hostos Community College, LaGuardia Community College, and the Borough of Manhattan Community College, the latter of which now offers the first WGS major at the community college level within CUNY. For these reasons, the story of Kingsborough is an important case study of the attack on WGS at this historical moment.

In 1994, Dr. Inez Martinez (English) and Dr. Fran Kraljic (history and liberal arts) created women's and gender studies under liberal arts (LA). Dr. Martinez and Dr. Kraljic assembled faculty across the disciplines, devised an advisory board, and College Council voted to establish WGS. Since its inception under President Leon Goldstein, WGS has received institutional support from every president and provost. Besides the cofounders and me as the current director, Kingsborough's WGS program has had many directors, including Dr. Susan Farrell, Dr. Caterina Pierre, and Dr. Alison Better, all of whom received reassigned time releasing them from some of their teaching obligations to complete administrative duties. Institutional support included not just reassigned time (three credits for each director in the fall and spring), but also administrative staff (Ms. Josephine Crowley was the first), and an interdisciplinary office. In 2005, President Regina Peruggi celebrated WGS as the "concentration model" of the Liberal Arts Task Force. The English Department, chaired by Dr. Steve Wiedenborner, even voted to gift its adjunct office to WGS, honoring Dr. Martinez's germinal work. WGS has much support at other CUNY colleges, with classes articulating at City College, Hunter College, John Jay College of Criminal Justice, Lehman College, Medgar Evers College, New York City College of Technology, Queens College, College of Staten Island, York College, and Adelphi University, perhaps with new possibilities for smooth transfer to City Tech, Brooklyn College, Vassar College, and Columbia University in the future. Faculty and students want the program to grow, as it has with more than 550 students in WGS classes per semester and 20 core and 40 affiliated faculty since I have been director, the highest the program has known. Despite the record enrollment, the long history of institutional support, and Kingsborough's status as a leader in the field of WGS both within CUNY, but also within community colleges across the country, there has been a marked shift in our relationship with the college's current administration.

This year the administration deviated from its unwavering history of WGS support, strategically using the turbulent climate of rampant local and global dissent in society and in university settings to support its own agenda. In late May 2018, just before finals, we were told that WGS directors would no longer receive reassigned time. Reassigned time is essential for the work necessary to maintain and grow the program: organizing faculty meetings, making revisions to the concentration and proposed major, creating a stable interdisciplinary home, generating a schedule of classes, negotiating offerings with chairs, mentoring students, creating new classes, revising transfer options for existing courses, creating new articulation agreements, organizing panels, and working on faculty development for grants and conferences. In addition, the administration told WGS it needed a departmental home, and that it was now under behavioral sciences and human services, whose administration has not approved curricular growth for WGS, its drafted major. The follow-up notes to the meeting included that we were losing our administrative assistant, Ms. Nettie Wiener, who worked for WGS for much of its history.

Perhaps the most hurtful action against WGS occurred in early September 2018, just days into the fall semester, when administration notified WGS it was losing its office, its home for almost 25 years. When I became director of WGS, I turned the WGS office into a community space for students and faculty. It offers a library of files, books, journals, and student art projects, which have been carefully cultivated over the past two decades. It has technology for faculty and students, including a computer, scanner, copier, and office supplies. It is a space for faculty and students to create community: it contains faculty mailboxes, many core faculty members have keys to the office, it is where WGS faculty meetings are held, and it is where the WGS student club meets. It offers free materials (e.g., writing instruments, sanitary products, safe sex supplies, and caffeinated beverages) to students and faculty. Undoubtedly, it is the hub of academic life for WGS on campus. WGS, like many programs, needs an institutional frame and central location and visibility to put it on the campus' intellectual map. Taking away a space makes WGS invisible and leaves it without a home base. Many conversations about collaborative intellectual work have materialized from this space, so much so that WGS even requested a campus email and listserv, which it also has not received. The most concerning issue is whether WGS will lose all of its files, books, art, and student projects. The administration has not provided good options for rehoming these materials.

The administration has offered a myriad of explanations to justify defunding WGS, and I think it is useful to unpack these defenses. Undoubtedly, the defunding of WGS on the campus is linked to larger issues in our world— inadequate national support for higher education and the local budget cuts in

CUNY, particularly at the community colleges and Kingsborough. However, recently, the administration has hired two deans, a special projects manager, approved new hires in traditional disciplines, and increased the public safety budget. Austerity has been used to rationalize administrative control rather than faculty governance to further top-down ideologies and priorities, and cost-cutting strategies are not being applied across all disciplines. Traditional programs and departments are not losing resources in the same way.

The arguments made by the administration at Kingsborough are similar to ones being made at community colleges across the country: that lower enrollment and less state and county funding requires that the school be streamlined. It is true that while Kingsborough has the highest graduation rate among the CUNY community colleges and is the pipeline to the senior colleges, enrollment is down, and the effect of lower enrollment on the budget does necessitate a look at how we use our resources. However, these enrollment numbers are being used only selectively to justify the defunding of particular programs and without acknowledging institutional roadblocks such as administrative and technological problems (e.g., forms, selections, and online options) that may be hindering enrollment in these fields. Humanities and liberal arts programs and departments across the nation, both historically and presently, have lower enrollment than other fields, but we are not seeing the same targeting of disciplines like English, history, and math.

While WGS has experienced many negative issues with the current administration, there have been some positive results. The best outcome of the WGS restructuring and defunding at Kingsborough has been the unrelenting solidarity WGS has received. Tenured WGS faculty, approximately 20 of us, wrote a collective letter to the administration for a meeting to discuss reinstating resources (to no avail). Since I have been at Kingsborough, it was the first time I have witnessed faculty coming together to support WGS in such a bold way. It gives me great pride to work with this community of scholars, professors, and social justice advocates. Hundreds of KCC faculty, students, and alumni have written letters and petitions in support of maintaining WGS resources. JC Amorini, a WGS alumnus completing the CUNY BA for interdisciplinary studies, said, "It is crucial to expose students to different worldviews, to different modes of being and relating, and—most importantly—to the value of difference itself." Jozette Belmont, a WGS alumnus studying WGS at The Graduate Center, affirms, "It was due to this concentration that I had the courage to transfer to a senior college and earn a dual degree in Psychology and WGS." Nehal Naser, a former WGS student now studying at City College said, "Now more than ever it is essential that students everywhere are taught to think critically about issues like identity, discrimination, privilege, and intersectionality, and WGS is instrumental at making that happen at KCC." Current students have also expressed their solidarity; they have become leaders in this campaign to re-fund WGS.

The support we have solicited from WGS scholars across the CUNYs and the nation has been very helpful and bolstering during this challenging time. Judith Butler, Joan Scott, and Mary Hawkesworth have voiced their solidarity for the continuing necessity of WGS resources. Butler, Maxine Elliot Professor in the Department of Comparative Literature and the Program of Critical Theory at the University of California, Berkeley, has advocated for WGS at Kingsborough on the gender international listserv. Scott, professor emerita at the Institute for Advanced Study at Princeton, has offered to speak and reach out to presses like *The Nation*.[74] In her letter of support, Hawkesworth, Distinguished Professor of Women's and Gender Studies at Rutgers University, has compared Kingsborough to Hungary, whose Prime Minister Viktor Orban closed all gender studies programs in the country (and while WGS has not been eliminated, it is on its way to elimination without resources to maintain and promote). In her letter of support, Premilla Nadasen started her term as the president of the National Women's Studies Association by supporting WGS, stating "it is imperative that the WGS program at Kingsborough has the resources and institutional support to continue its groundbreaking work." WGS directors at other CUNY campuses, such as Antonio (Jay) Pastrana, Dana-Ain Davis, Catherine Raissiguier, Jerilyn Fisher, Asale Angel-Ajani, JV Fuqua, Ria Banerjee, and Laura Westengard have sent in letters and petitions. Entire departments have signed letters in support of WGS academic resources at Kingsborough, including at City Tech, Hunter, and The Graduate Center, the latter of which had hundreds of signatures alone.[75] Columbia's

---

74   She communicated this to me via email correspondence.

75   All of the above mentioned letters were submitted to the Kingsborough administration during the 2017-18 school year.

Jack Halberstam visited Kingsborough, offering two talks, one with me and one with approximately a dozen WGS core and affiliated faculty, which were disseminated publically on YouTube and WGS listservs (WMST-L and Gender Studies NYU).[76] *AM New York* and News 12 are covering WGS here, too.[77] Students have done panels in support of the program and written articles in the campus newspaper, decorated the office door with their words of support on post-it notes, and created t-shirts to raise awareness. Directors, coordinators, and chairs will be participating in a panel called "Women's, Gender, and Sexuality Studies Across the CUNYs" in the spring for Women's History Month to promote collaboration and support across the CUNYs for the field of WGS, discuss our programs and departments and the importance of them in this current climate, and celebrate Kingsborough's 25th anniversary, the same year as the 50th anniversary of Stonewall.[78] Participants joining me include the following: Antonio (Jay) Pastrana, John Jay College; Jen Gaboury, Hunter College; Mobina Hashmi, Brooklyn College; JV Fuqua, Queens College; Laura Westengard, New York City College of Technology; Jerilyn Fisher, Hostos Community College; Brianne Waychoff, Borough of Manhattan Community College; Allia Abdullah-Matta, LaGuardia Community College; and Jacqueline Jones, LaGuardia Community College. Other guest speakers will come to give talks, including Robyn Spencer, Visiting Endowed Chair of Women and Gender Studies, Brooklyn College, and associate professor of history at Lehman College, as well as Flavia Rando, Brooklyn College, art historian and professor of women's and LGBTQ studies, member of Gay Liberation Front and Radicalesbians, and coordinator of the Lesbian Herstory Archives and its Lesbian Studies Institute. Our campaign will continue with other strategies. As TJ Boisseau, a WGS professor at Purdue University currently conducting a comprehensive study on the attack on gender and gender studies programs

---

76   To see videos go to https://www.youtube.com/watch?v=zV1FFQoZ6jA&t=2378s and https://www.youtube.com/watch?v=pUuOy2vxYKs&t=1s.

77   For news coverage see https://www.amny.com/news/kcc-women-gender-studies-1.23979823 and www.news12.com.

78   For more information on the ways in which WGS programs are working together across the CUNY system see: https://www.youtube.com/watch?v=IAtmvvgGPRM

nationwide, of which Kingsborough is now a part, stated in her letter of support, "The eyes of the nation are on Kingsborough at this time."

The future of the field depends on strategies of risk and defense connected to the politics of solidarity. Intellectual risk not only comes with challenging hegemonic knowledge projects, but also with offering support across feminist knowledge communities. Meetings, letters, petitions, roundtables, lectures, press, surveys, and articles are some strategies of dissent. Additional strategies we are considering include a CUNY-wide conference, meetings with college delegates and the board of trustees, a Professional Staff Congress (PSC) union action, and more off-campus press. Other college campuses have used call-ins, walk-outs, sit-ins, and other demonstrations for social protests, as well, and Kingsborough will continue exploring all strategies of resistance for its ongoing campaign, while soliciting support from colleagues within the field. Maintaining solidarity both within and outside of CUNY contributes to the hope of WGS, and thus, it is in the spirit of social change. Kingsborough is just one example, but it provides a critical case study for community colleges across the nation struggling with administrations restructuring and eliminating programs, as well as for understanding how the politics and practices of solidarity are essential to keeping women's, gender, and sexuality studies intellectually alive during this conservative turn and regressive time for gender in the world and for gender studies in academia.

# Works Cited

"The Assault on Gender and Gender Studies." On Freedom of Expression
and Campus Speech Codes | AAUP, Nov. 2018, www.aaup.org/assault-
gender-and-gender-studies.

Flaherty, Colleen. "'The Assault on Gender and Gender Studies'." *Inside
Higher Ed*, 16 Nov. 2018, https://www.insidehighered.com/
quicktakes/2018/11/16/%E2%80%98-assault-gender-and-gender-
studies%E2%80%99.

Redden, Elizabeth. "Global Attack on Gender Studies." *Inside Higher Ed*, 8
Dec. 2018, www.insidehighered.com/news/2018/12/05/gender-studies-
scholars-say-field-coming-under-attack-many-countries-around-globe.

Simas, Kayla. "KCC Students, Faculty Fight for Women's and Gender
Studies." Am New York, 28 Nov. 2018, www.amny.com/news/kcc-
women-gender-studies-1.23979823.

# Contributors[79]

*Jill M. Adams* is a professor of English and coordinator of women's and gender studies at Jefferson Community and Technical College in Louisville, Kentucky. She is finishing her doctoral work in gender and women's studies at the University of Kentucky and has a master's in multicultural literature from East Carolina University. Her research interests include campus-based activism; the impact of social class on/in education; intersectional, inclusive instruction; student leadership development; and campus-community connections. Jill's commitment to social justice has a welcome outlet working with students to create change on campus and in their communities.

*Genevieve Carminati* (co-editor) was educated at Vermont College of Norwich University and West Chester University of Pennsylvania. She is a professor of English and the college-wide women's and gender studies program coordinator, at Montgomery College. Under her direction, the program has won a Community College Award from the American Association for Women in Community Colleges and was chosen for recognition by Maryland NOW and the Maryland Women's Heritage Center. Genevieve teaches women's and gender studies, essay writing, creative writing, women and film, and literature. Her research and writing focus on social justice and issues of power related to class, gender, race, and health. She is a winner of the Grace Cochran Award for Research on Women and a NISOD Excellence Award. Genevieve is president of the Mid-Atlantic Women's Studies Association and of the HERS Foundation Board. She is also a poet and fiction writer.

*Paquita L. Garatea* earned a BA and an MA in history, in addition to a Black Studies Certificate from Portland State University. She is a retired residen-

---

79   The "Student Voices" pages contain the biographical entries for the students.

tial faculty member in history from Chandler-Gilbert Community College (CGCC) where she developed and taught courses in African American history, Mexican American history, American Indian history, history of women in America, world history, and US history. Throughout her career, Garatea served in a variety of leadership roles including president and vice president of the CGCC faculty senate. Her scholarly works include "Etxekoandreak: Basque Women and Their Boarding Houses" published in the *Journal of the Society of Basque Studies in America* (2007).

*Holly Hassel* is professor of English at North Dakota State University. Previously, she served as chair of the University of Wisconsin Colleges Gender, Sexuality, and Women's Studies Program from 2008 to 2014 and taught at the UW Marathon campus in Wausau from 2002 to 2016. She is the co-author of *Threshold Concepts in Women's and Gender Studies: Ways of Seeing, Thinking, and Knowing* (Routledge, 2018) an introductory textbook for WGS and is the current editor of *Teaching English in the Two-Year College*.

*Sara Hosey* is an associate professor of English and women and gender studies at Nassau Community College. Her scholarly work has appeared in publications including the *Journal of Literary & Cultural Disability Studies* and *Feminist Formations*. Her critical study *Home is Where the Hurt Is: Wives and Mothers in U.S. Television and Film* will be published by McFarland in 2020.

*Amanda Loos* is associate professor of humanities/fine arts/WGS at Harold Washington College in Chicago, where she also provides academic leadership of the Committee for the Study of Women, Gender, & Sexuality. She has an MA in humanities from the University of Chicago and a graduate certificate in WGS from DePaul University. When not busy advocating for community colleges as radical sites of resistance, she can be found in Rogers Park with her husband and two young kids.

*Ann Mattis* is an associate professor of gender, sexuality, and women's studies and English at the University of Wisconsin-Green Bay, Sheboygan Campus. Her book *Dirty Work: Domestic Service in Progressive-Era Women's Fiction* is forthcoming with University of Michigan Press. Recently, she wrote an article on teaching representations of working women in modernist literature and media, which is slated to appear in a special issue of the Modern Language Association's Options for Teaching series.

*Richard E. Otten* holds a PhD in cultural studies from George Mason University and teaches American studies and gender and sexuality studies courses at Anne Arundel Community College and the University of Maryland, Baltimore County. His research interests include popular culture and urban communication, in addition to masculinities.

*Amy Reddinger* is now the dean of arts and sciences at Bay de Noc Community College in Escanaba, Michigan. Previously she was associate professor of gender, sexuality, and women's studies and English at the University of Wisconsin Colleges. She co-authored "Surfacing the Structures of Patriarchy: Teaching and Learning Threshold Concepts in Women's Studies" with Jessica Van Slooten and Holly Hassel.

*Heather Rellihan* (co-editor) earned a PhD in women's studies from the University of Maryland, College Park. She is coordinator and professor of gender and sexuality studies at Anne Arundel Community College (AACC). She is assistant director of AACC's Curriculum Transformation Project, an organization that encourages attention to diversity and equity issues in curriculum and pedagogy. She was a 2014 recipient of the John & Suanne Roueche Excellence Award for her achievements in community college teaching. She is co-editor of *Introduction to Women's, Gender & Sexuality Studies: Interdisciplinary and Intersectional Approaches.*

*Judith M. Roy* was a founder of the Women's Studies (now Gender Studies) Certificate Program at Century College, the first academic certificate program in any discipline in the Minnesota two-year college system. She directed the program from 1996 to 2010. In addition, she had leadership roles in the History Department and later served as chair of the college curriculum committee for four years. She has an MA in women's history and completed PhD coursework at the University of Colorado, Boulder. She served as president-elect and president of the National Women's Studies Association from 2005 to 2007.

*Esther Schwartz-McKinzie* has taught women's studies, literature, and composition courses at Montgomery College as a full-time faculty member since 2001. She received her PhD in British and American 19th century literature from Temple University, and her scholarly research has focused on recovering "lost" women's voices—especially those who used popular media as a venue to speak out against inequality, sexual violence, and domestic violence. Since 2014, she has participated in the development and implementation of Violence Against Women Act and Title IX initiatives at Montgomery College, where she is the former coordinator of, and a lead trainer for, the Bringing in the Bystander program.

*Grace Sikorski* is professor of English at Anne Arundel Community College (AACC) in Arnold, Maryland. She also designs curriculum and teaches for the AACC Gender and Sexuality Studies Program and has designed and taught their Introduction to LGBT Studies course. Her research interests include American literature of the 20th century, narratives of human sexuality and desire, and theories of identity and gender.

*Alissa Stoehr* earned a PhD in higher education from Iowa State University. She is a lecturer in the Sociology Department and Women's and Gender Studies Program at Iowa State University in Ames, Iowa. Her research interests include women's and gender studies programs at community colleges, human trafficking, LGBTQ centers at community colleges, racism within college athletics, and work-life balance of female PhD students.

*Donna M. Thompson* is a native of Flint, Michigan. She holds a BA in English from Yale University, and an MA in English and a graduate certificate in women's studies from Duke University. She is a faculty member at Chandler-Gilbert Community College where she teaches courses in composition, film, literature, and women's studies. Thompson served on the governing board of the National Women's Studies Association and participated in the Women of Color: Theory and Activism Institute for Junior Faculty sponsored by the Ford

Foundation. Her published works include "Moving Images: LGBTQ Films for A New Millennium," (2017) and "We Denied Our Sisterhood" and "Prioritizing Race," both included in *Engaging Feminism: Students Speak Up & Speak Out* (1999). Thompson's other research interests include early modern women, Milton, film, and the history of science.

*Jessica Van Slooten* is associate professor of women's and gender studies and English at the University of Wisconsin-Green Bay, Manitowoc Campus. Previously, she was the gender equity coordinator, and chair of gender, sexuality, and women's studies at the University of Wisconsin Colleges. A former Wisconsin Teaching Fellow, she co-authored "Surfacing the Structures of Patriarchy: Teaching and Learning Threshold Concepts in Women's Studies" with Amy Reddinger and Holly Hassel.

*Red Washburn*, PhD, is associate professor of English and director of women's and gender studies at Kingsborough Community College (CUNY). They also are adjunct associate professor of women and gender studies at Hunter College (CUNY). Red's articles appear in *Journal for the Study of Radicalism*, *Women's Studies: An Interdisciplinary Journal*, and *Journal of Lesbian Studies*. Their poetry collection *Crestview Tree Woman* was published by Finishing Line Press. Their recent poems were published in *Sinister Wisdom: A Multicultural Lesbian Literary and Art Journal*, and they are the co-editor of three recent issues of the journal: *Celebrating the Michigan Womyn's Music Festival*, *Dump Trump: Legacies of Resistance*, and *The Lesbian Herstory Archives*. Red is a coordinator at the Lesbian Herstory Archives and of the Rainbow Book Fair, as well as on the board of directors of *Sinister Wisdom* and the Center for Lesbian and Gay Studies.

# Acknowledgements

This book began with the idea that the valuable work of women's and gender studies programs at community colleges should be recognized and lauded. To carry a germ of an idea through to the text that you hold in your hands today requires the support of many. The editors first would like to thank the Community College Caucus (CCC) of the National Women's Studies Association for providing a space of camaraderie and encouragement. It was at the annual CCC meetings that we began to realize that we owed this book to ourselves and others in community college WGS programs and that indeed it was necessary to the discipline for us to document our research and highlight our accomplishments and those of our students. To paraphrase the Combahee River Collective Statement, we recognize that we are the only people who care enough to work unfailingly for our own continuance and forward progress. Even our title, *Theory and Praxis*, emerged from a CCC discussion about the significance and mission of women's and gender studies at community colleges, spaces in higher education that focus on underserved and less privileged students and consistently address the needs of the very persons about whom our discipline theorizes. Our gratitude to the CCC is vast, and to its leaders and members we say, thank you.

Obviously, a book cannot exist without the dedication of its publisher. We are grateful to Gival Press and especially to Robert L. Giron, its editor-in-chief, for the patience and foresight that allowed this book to grow and transform into more than we could have initially envisioned. Robert came on board quickly and enthusiastically in the fall of 2015. Over the next three and a half years, he staunchly stood by us as we worked through the process of soliciting, selecting, editing, and revising essays, losing some writers along the way and adding more. Robert always reminded us that he understood that making a meaningful book "took time." We offer our immeasurable gratitude to Robert L. Giron and Gival Press.

The contributors to this edition come from community colleges across the United States. Some are our esteemed colleagues from the CCC, but some we know only from their skillful words on the page. All are scholars and teachers we admire and respect. We thank them for their tireless dedication to making this text strong. Their willingness to rethink and rework their essays many times deserves to be noted and applauded. Clearly, their final work shows their commitment and perseverance.

"But the students are great," is a mantra often repeated during discussions among community college women's and gender studies folks in response to the disregard we can experience in the discipline and even in our own institutions. It is a reminder of why we do what we do: it is because of our remarkable students. The student writers in this book certainly are great, and their writings show the importance of our programs in their lives, as students, as citizens, as people. The student writings in this book add a richness of thought and experience that would be missing without them. We thank them for their openness, their generosity, and their scholarship. We are comforted to know that they hold the future in their good, caring, competent, and activist hands.

A copy editor's job is exacting, and a text is far less without such precise attention to detail. We want to thank our copy editor, Michael Coffey, for his unrelenting focus on each and every word and mark in this book. He made us more aware of the importance of cohesion and consistency throughout a collection of writings as varied as this one. We recognize the importance of his diligence and expertise to the success of this book. Thank you, Michael, for your hard work.

We would be remiss if we did not express our unending gratitude to those who went before us in the discipline, who forged the way for our programs to exist today, who created the Community College Caucus, and determinably brought women's, gender, and sexuality studies to community colleges. We might never know the sacrifices they made nor the obstacles they confronted. What we do know is that they persisted—and succeeded, and for this we are indebted and thankful.

First and foremost, Genevieve would like to thank Heather Rellihan for her daring and willingness to join hands and jump into the abyss. Making a book is a daunting process, but Heather's wisdom, diligence, patience, and caring gave me comfort and certainty that it could be done well. Thank you,

Heather, for your commitment to the community college mission and to the students. I am grateful for my foremothers, spirit guides, and teachers in the discipline, the late Melanie Kaye/Kantrowitz and Elizabeth Larsen, and to Myrna Goldenberg and Shirley Parry for modeling how a woman leads with strength, flexibility, and courage. Many thanks to Deborah Stearns and Mickey Moran for helping me to keep my feminist chops in good shape through your intellectual challenges and high standards of discourse. I am appreciative that my students continue to teach me and thankful for all that I learn from them. I am grateful to Om Rusten for her loyalty and constancy, allowing me the freedom that comes when you know someone trustworthy is watching the shop. Unending gratitude to you, Lone; you know the many ways that I am indebted to you. And always, thank you, Bob, for standing by and believing in me.

Heather would also like to start by thanking her co-editor. In addition to producing a book, this project created a deep and lasting friendship. Thank you, Genevieve, for your care and camaraderie, and for your calming responses to my sometimes-frantic and usually late-at-night emails. I would also like to thank my friends, colleagues, and students at Anne Arundel Community College. Thank you to these individuals who bring dedication, love, generosity, humor, understanding, thoughtfulness, and curiosity to their teaching and learning: you inspire me to think more deeply, ask more questions, and always work to be a better teacher. Many thanks, too, to Michael, for giving me time for last-minute questions and long walks, and most of all, for your friendship. Finally, I am especially grateful to my parents whose love and support is a constant in my life. They believe I can accomplish anything, which always gives me the strength to try.

# More from Gival Press

*Barrow's Point* by Robert Schirmer
*The Best of Gival Press Short Stories* edited by Robert L. Giron
*Boys, Lost & Found* by Charles Casillo
*The Cannibal of Guadalajara* by David Winner
*A Change of Heart* by David Garrett Izzo
*The Day Rider and Other Stories* by J. E. Robinson
*Dead Time / Tiempo muerto* by Carlos Rubio
*Dream of Another America* by Tyler McMahon
*Dreams and Other Ailments / Sueños y otros achaques* by Teresa Bevin
*The Gay Herman Melville Reader* edited by Ken Schellenberg
*Guess and Check* by Thaddeus Rutkowski
*Ghost Horse* by Thomas H. McNeely
*Gone by Sundown* by Peter Leach
*An Interdisciplinary Introduction to Women's Studies* edited by Brianne Friel
    and Robert L. Giron
*Julia & Rodrigo* by Mark Brazaitis
*The Last Day of Paradise* by Kiki Denis
*Literatures of the African Diaspora* by Yemi D. Ogunyemi
*Lockjaw: Collected Appalachian Stories* by Holly Farris
*Mayhem: Three Lives of a Woman* by Elizabeth Harris
*Maximus in Catland* by David Garrett Izzo
*Middlebrow Annoyances: American Drama in the 21st Century* by Myles
    Weber
*The Pleasuring of Men* by Clifford H. Browder
*Riverton Noir* by Perry Glasser
*Second Acts* by Tim W. Brown
*Secret Memories / Recuerdos secretos* by Carlos Rubio
*Sexy Liberal! Of Me I Sing* by Stephanie Miller
*Show Up, Look Good* by Mark Wisniewski
*The Smoke Week: Sept. 11-21. 2001* by Ellis Avery
*That Demon Life* by Lowell Mick White

*Theory and Praxis: Women's and Gender Studies at Community Colleges*
    edited by Genevieve Carminati and Heather Rellihan
*Tina Springs into Summer / Tina se lanza al verano* by Teresa Bevin
*The Tomb on the Periphery* by John Domini
*Twelve Rivers of the Body* by Elizabeth Oness

For a complete list of Gival Press titles, visit: *www.givalpress.com*.

Books are available from Ingram, Follett, Brodart,
your favorite bookstore, the Internet, or from Gival Press.

Gival Press, LLC
PO Box 3812
Arlington, VA 22203
givalpress@yahoo.com
703.351.0079

www.ingramcontent.com/pod-product-compliance
Lightning Source LLC
Chambersburg PA
CBHW031415270326
41929CB00010BA/1461